GW01606548

The Heritage of Oman

a celebration in photographs

His Majesty
Sultan Qaboos bin Said

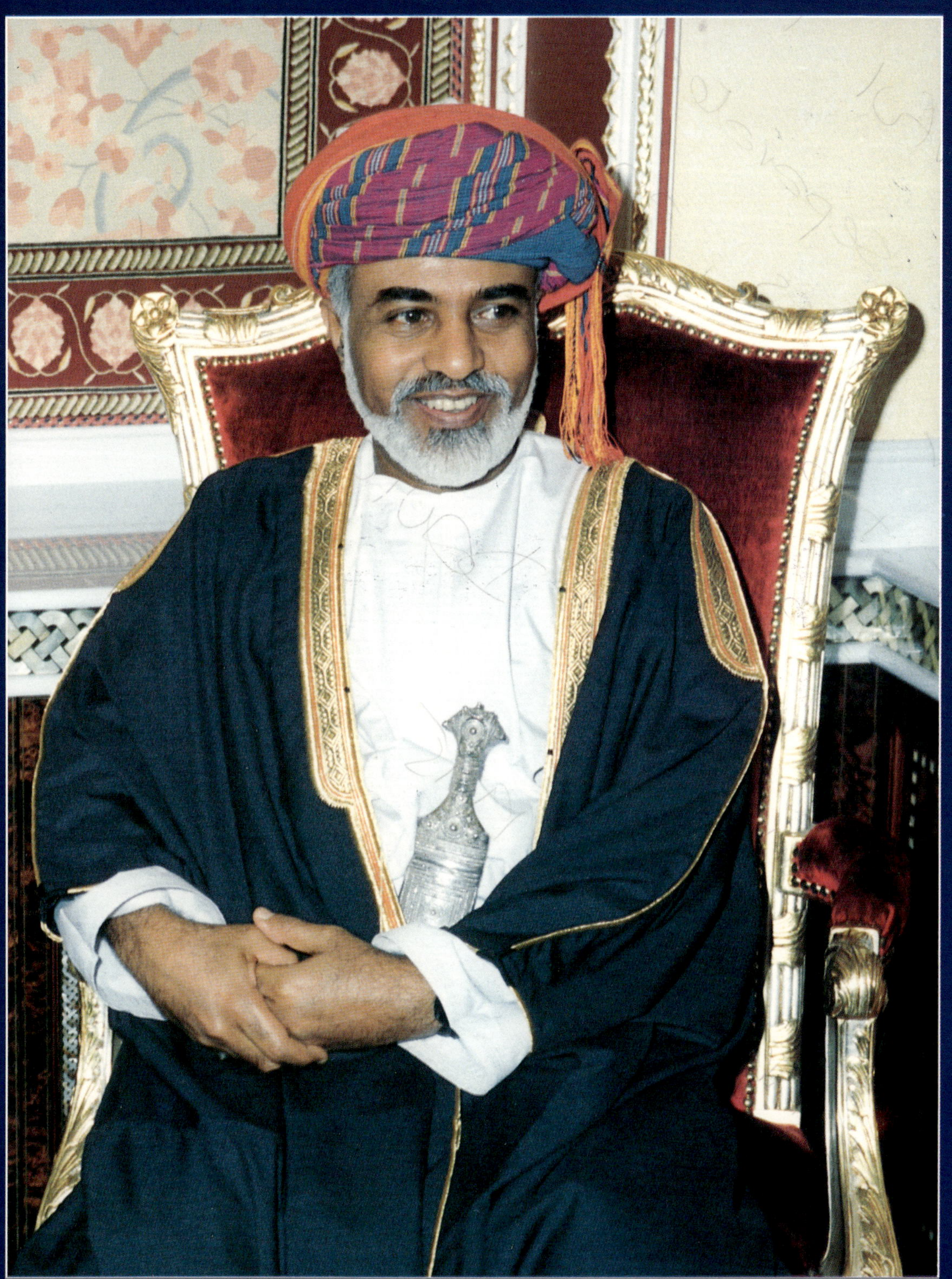

——x——

To my wonderful Mum
– though we're separated by
thousands of miles, and in
contact not too often, you can be
sure I think about you all the time!

All my love – David xxxx

Christmas 1995.

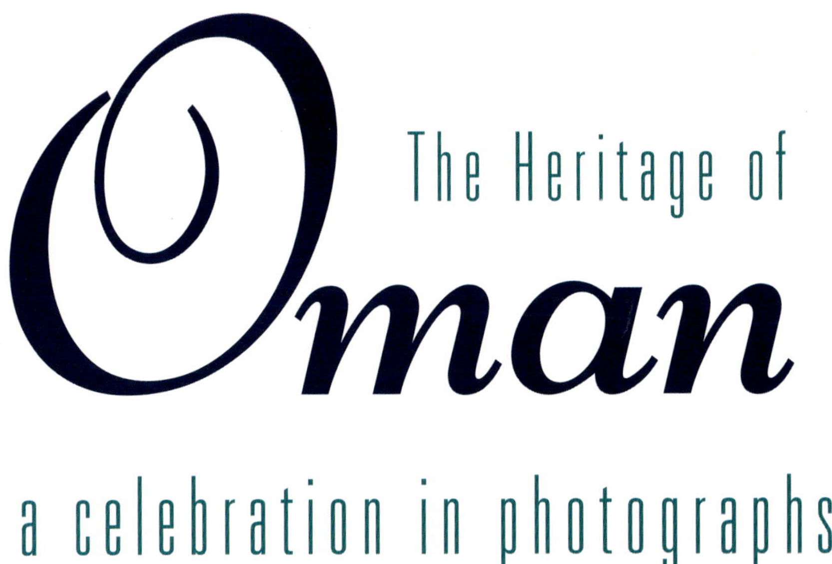

The Heritage of Oman

a celebration in photographs

photographs by Ozzie Newcombe

with an introduction by Pauline Shelton

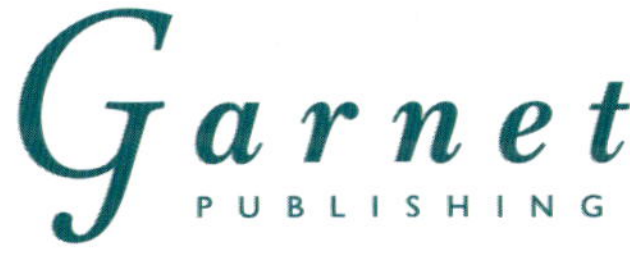

Garnet Publishing

The Heritage of Oman

Published by Garnet Publishing Limited
8 Southern Court
South Street
Reading
Berkshire RG1 4QS
UK

First Edition

ISBN 1 85964 068 0

British Library Cataloguing-in-Publication Data
A catalogue record for this book is available from the British Library.

The photograph of His Majesty Sultan Qaboos bin Said on *page 3* is reproduced courtesy of Mohamed Mustafa with grateful thanks.
The photographs on *pages 8, 17, 116* and *117* are reproduced courtesy of Hanne and Jens Eriksen with grateful thanks.
The photographs on *page 44* are reproduced courtesy of the Centre for Educational Technology, Sultan Qaboos University, with grateful thanks.
The photographs on *pages 92, 110* and *113* are reproduced courtesy of Teresita R. Loyola with grateful thanks.

The Publishers would like to thank Mr Tim Callan for his assistance and advice.

House editor: Anna Watson
Design: David Rose
Production: Sarah Golden
Colour by Riverline Reprographics Limited Oxford UK

Printed in the Lebanon

Contents

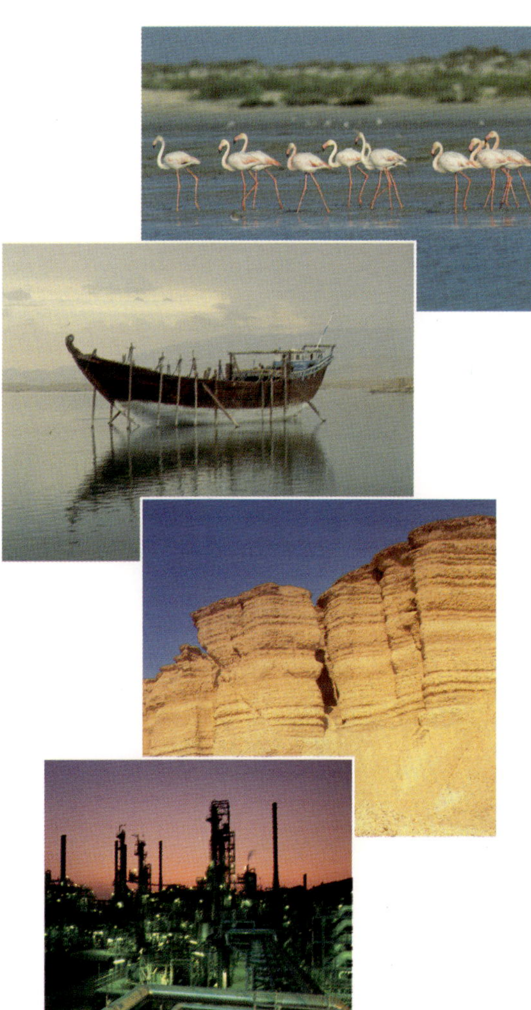

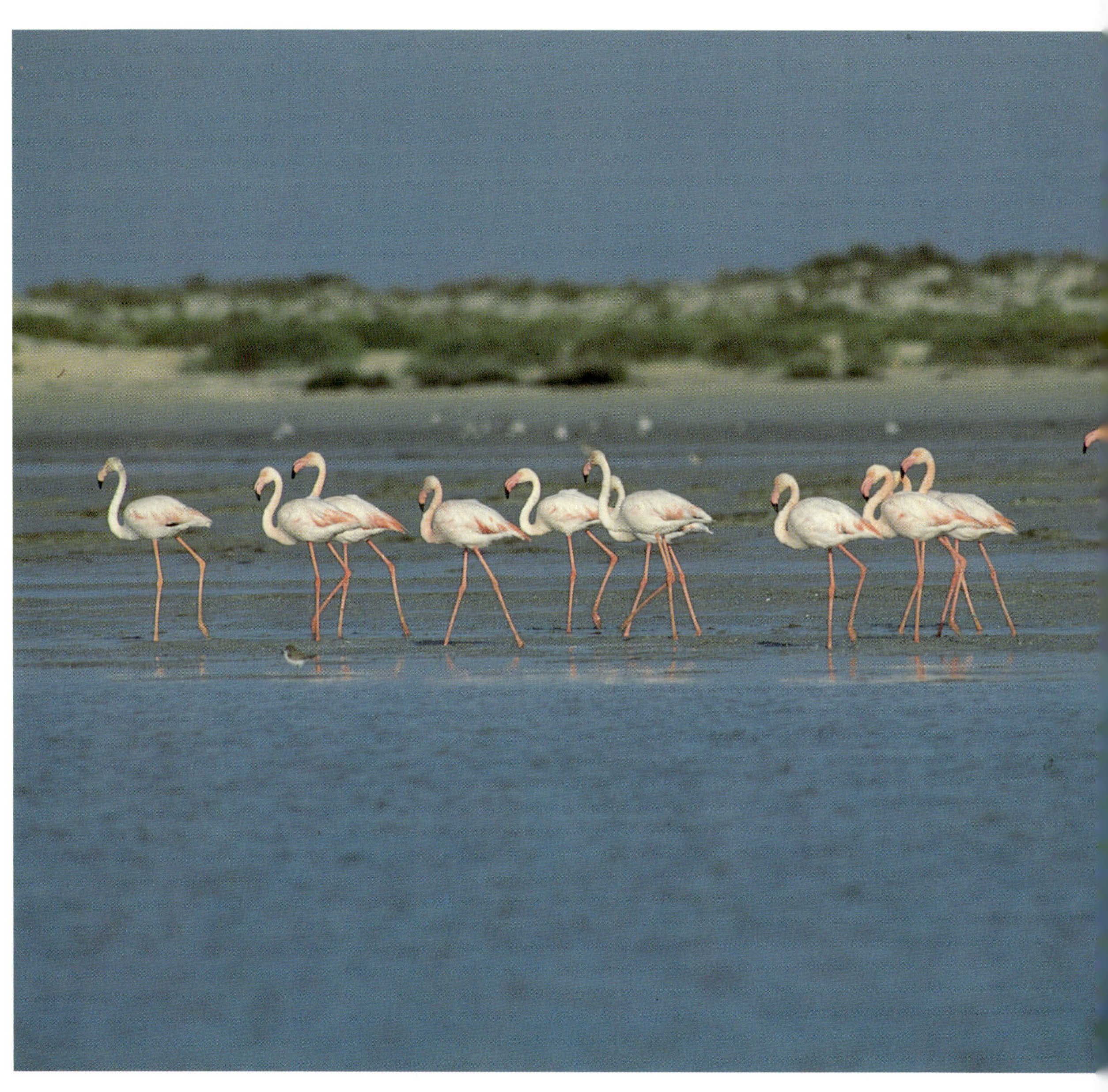

INTRODUCTION

A Celebration of Success

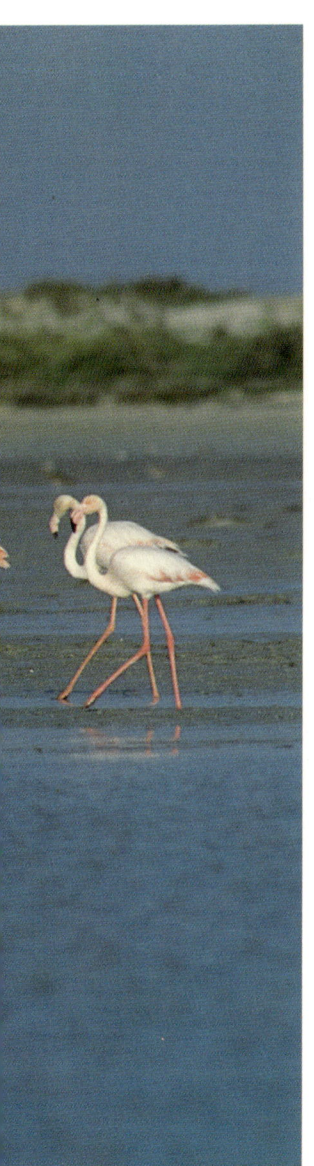

left
One of the most graceful sights is the flamingos along the shores of the Indian Ocean. These birds pass through Oman in autumn and winter. They can be found wading in the saline lagoons and mud flats, feeding on small shellfish which live there.

Oman is a land with much to celebrate. A land of variety and great natural beauty; a land with a rich history and bountiful heritage; a land which, in the twenty-five years since the accession of His Majesty Sultan Qaboos bin Said, has been transformed into a significant player on the contemporary world stage.

Indeed, the achievements of the Sultanate of Oman, since its renaissance twenty-five years ago, have been staggering. In 1970, Oman was insignificant and backward, seemingly devoid of opportunities for genuine change. Yet change did come. The combination of the newly crowned Sultan's pragmatic wisdom, and the prudent use of revenue from Oman's recently exploited oil-fields, resulted in the creation of a modern state, poised to enter the twenty-first century – a state that continues to fascinate and charm, a state that receives as much praise from economists and businessmen as it does from visitors enchanted by its natural beauties and living traditions.

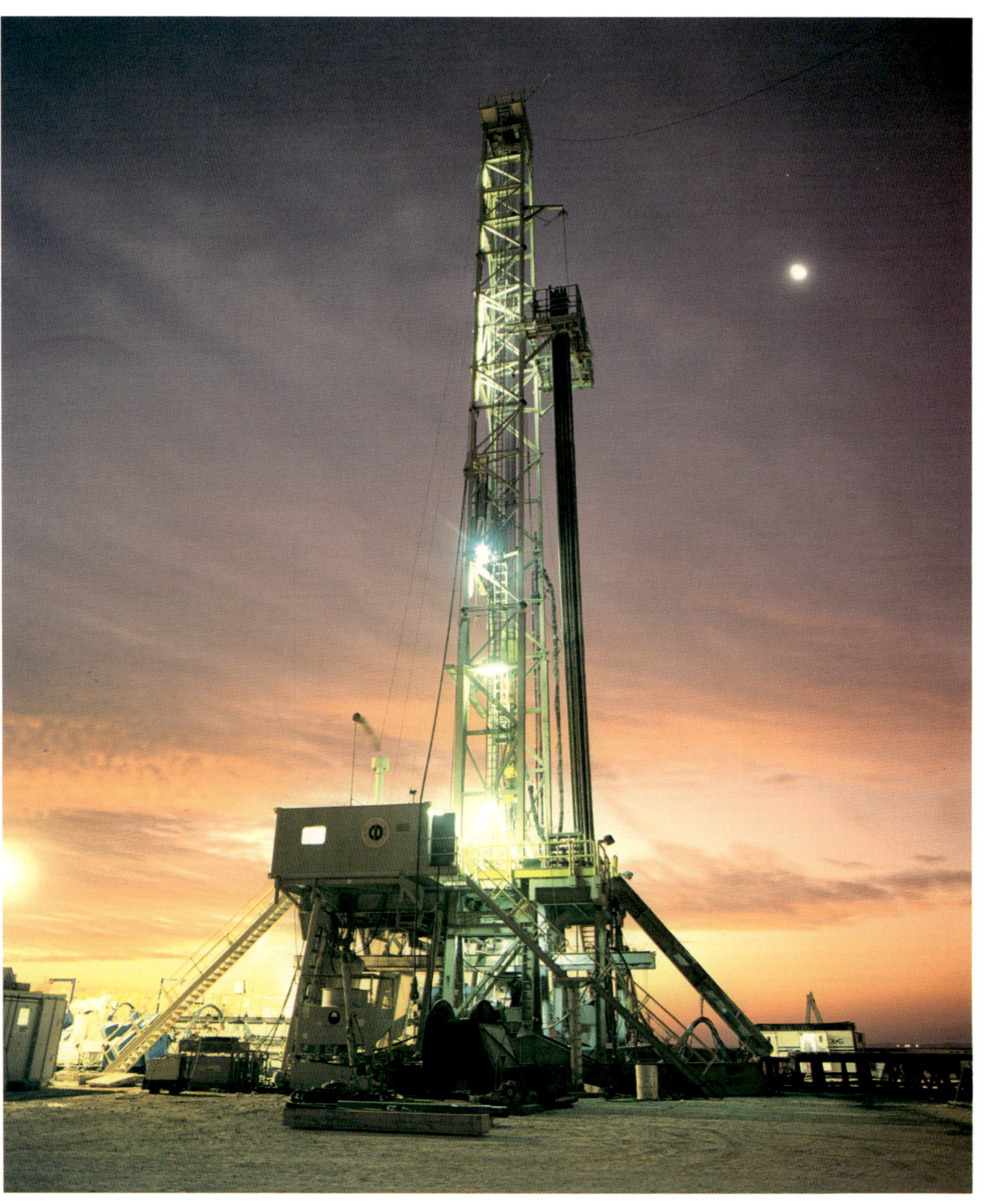

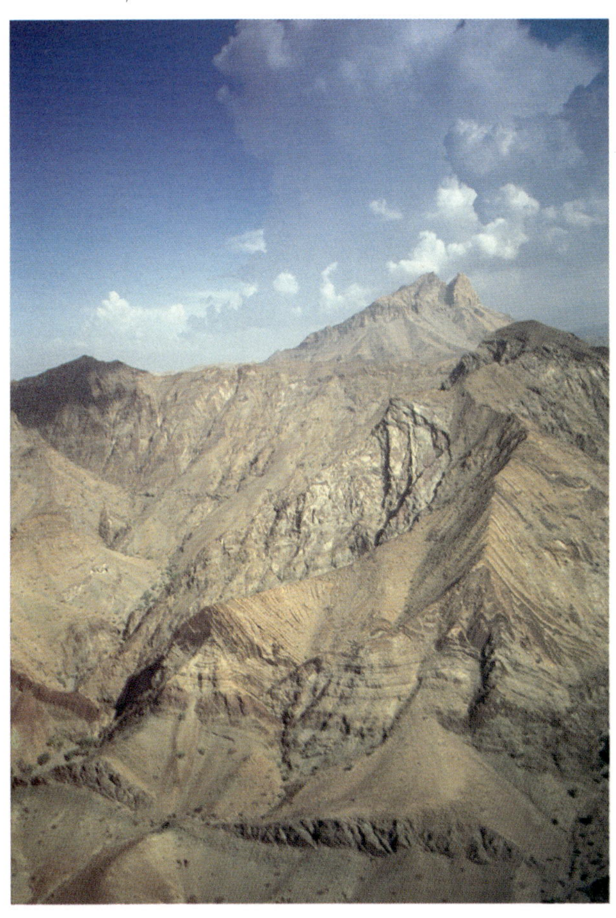

above
Oman's mountain peaks reach into the skies up to a height of over 3,000 metres. This part of the range known as Jebel Akhdar, or green mountain, is Jebel Sadat, seen here cloaked with clouds.

left
Working 24 hours a day, an oil prospecting rig is wreathed in early morning light. Oil reserves have been the source of funds used to develop the Sultanate's infrastructure, leaving it poised to enter the 21st century.

The Land

Oman's geological history stretches back more than 800 million years, during which time the land has been buckled and folded to form mountains, then eroded by the elements. Through the geological ages the land has moved from icy sub-polar latitudes to steamy tropical jungles and harsh, near-lifeless conditions. Fossil evidence indicates that dinosaurs once roamed where today's Sultan Qaboos University stands – a gleaming symbol of educational progress, and home to experts of different nationalities, many of whom are pioneering the study of Oman past and present.

Oman's land is of immense importance. It is the source, not only of academic study, but also of oil and gas riches, most of which are extracted and refined by Petroleum Development Oman (PDO). Oil remains the mainstay of the Sultanate's economy, contributing 42% of the 1993 Gross Domestic Product and accounting for nearly 80% of export receipts. Oman's oil and gas pipelines cross some of the world's most harsh and inhospitable terrain to bring these precious commodities to PDO's refineries on the coast.

It is not only in modern times that Oman's mineral wealth has provided an economic basis for prosperity. The earliest mention of Oman is thought to be in a cuneiform tablet of about 2,300 BC, which refers to the copper-producing land of Magan. Ancient copper-workings near Sohar, on Oman's northern coast, reveal that there was a flourishing copper-mining and smelting industry there some 4,500 years

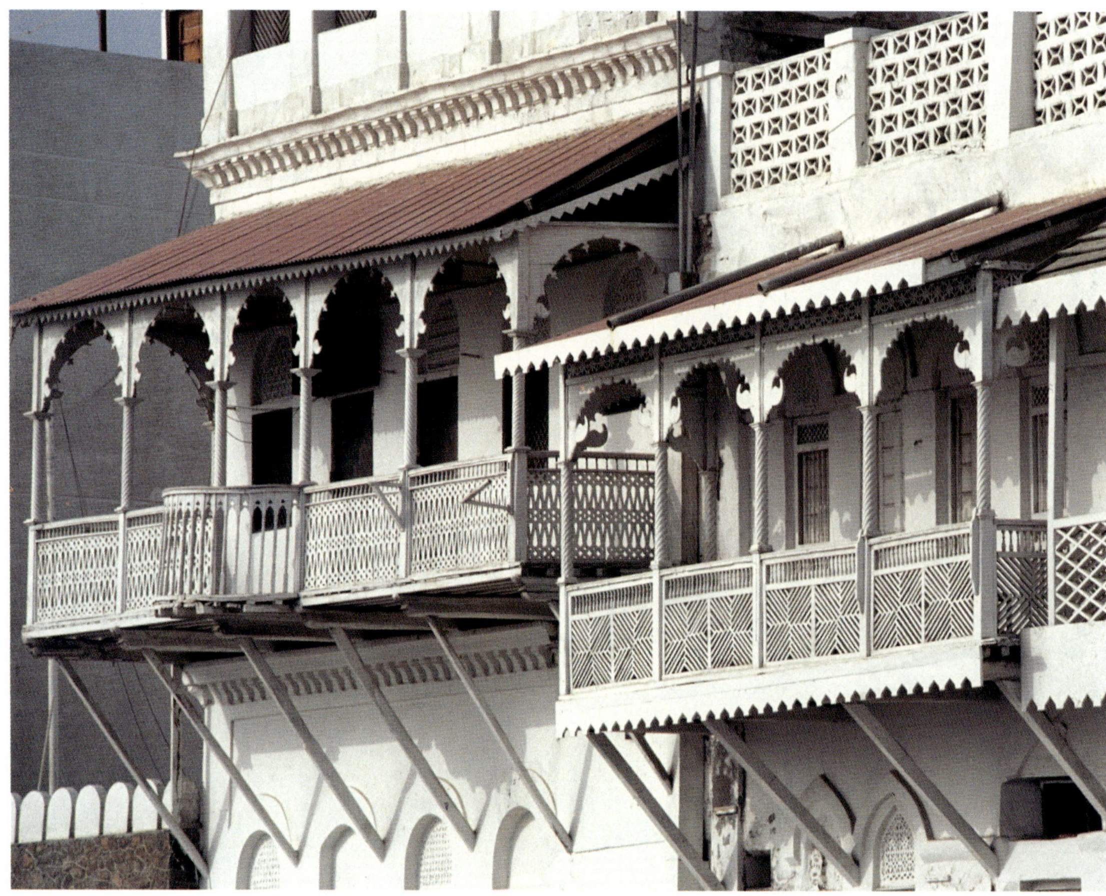

above
Oman has blended historic architectural styles with the demands of modern living conditions. Motifs, arches and windows have been inspired by architectural designs that are centuries old. The intricate trellis work on these old balconies and windows can be seen on the Corniche at Mutrah.

ago, making it very likely that Oman was ancient Magan. This trade brought Oman into contact with the great Mesopotamian civilisations, opening the country to new ideas and inventions, such as writing and banking, as well as sophisticated artefacts.

Throughout Oman's history the geomorphology has played a significant role. The northern coastal areas, where people traditionally lived by fishing, date-growing, boat-building and trading, are virtually cut off from the Interior by the craggy spine of the Al Hajar mountains, which rise to 3,000 metres and which were only traversable in three places

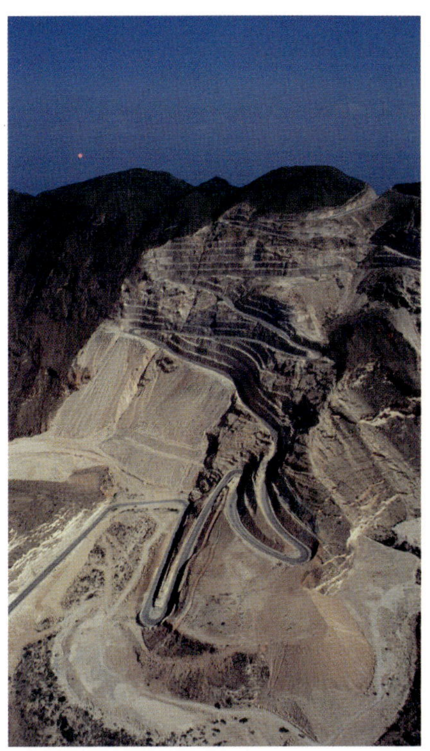

above
In the Dhofar region, this road is an engineering marvel. A series of astonishing hairpin bends spiral down the sheer face of a 1,100-metre mountain into a wadi, and then climb back up the other side.

along their 500-kilometre length. The peoples of the Interior either lived in oasis villages, making a living by farming, or were nomadic pastoralists – desert-dwellers who led their flocks of goats to find sparse pasture in the sandy deserts of the Wahiba Sands and the Rub al Khali (the Empty Quarter), or on the vast limestone plain of the Jiddat al Harasis.

These desert areas, until recent times, were a formidable land barrier between northern Oman and the country's Southern Region (popularly known as Dhofar). The fastest means of travelling from the northern capital Muscat to the southern capital Salalah was by a sea-journey which could take several days. Nowadays, the two cities are linked by a trans-desert highway of over 1,000 kilometres.

Oman's geomorphology contributes to its unique character, even today. The Capital Area, for example, (consisting of Muscat, Mutrah, Ruwi, Qurm, Medinat Sultan Qaboos and a number of other townships) is built around great fingers of ophiolitic rock – hard, craggy, and greenish-brown – which dictate the extent of building development in any area. The fine sweep of the Corniche – a road of breathtaking beauty linking Mutrah with Muscat along the sea-front – is a relatively new link, constructed in the early 1970s. Before that, these two towns – close together as the crow flies – were separated by virtually impenetrable mountains, across which a perilous donkey-track wound its way.

But perhaps Oman's greatest example of the triumph of modern technology over the landscape is in Dhofar, where the road linking Salalah to the coastal towns and villages of south-western Oman was cut into the previously solid limestone mountains of the Jebel al Qamar range. This road, completed in 1989 after a four-year building programme, has fourteen hairpin bends, which take the wide-eyed traveller down one side of a mountain to cross a wadi at sea-level, and up the other side to a height of 1,100 metres.

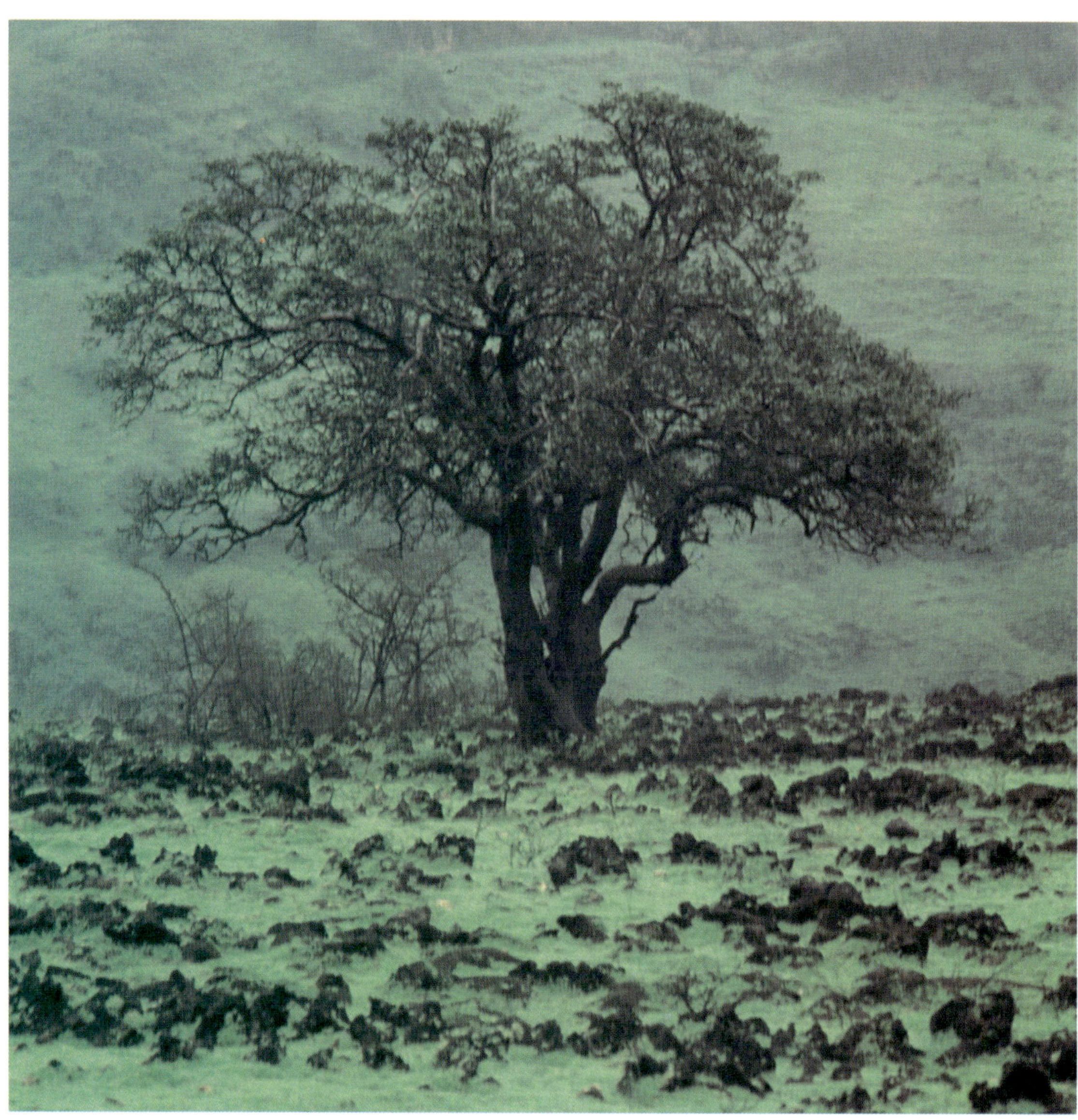

The Natural World

Oman's natural beauties and surprisingly abundant wildlife continue to delight and fascinate scientists, photographers and casual onlookers alike.

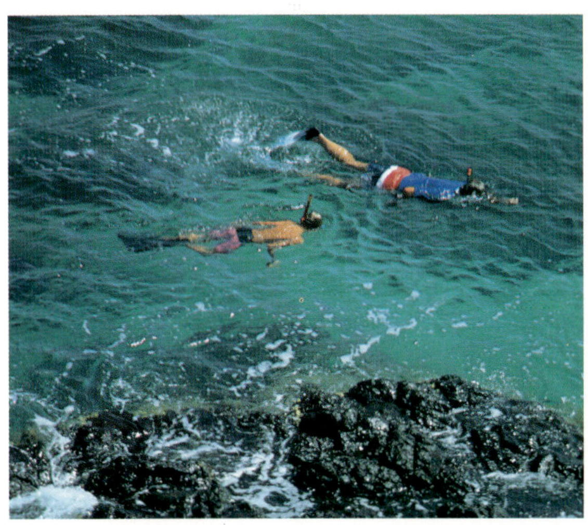

above
There's no end to the sporting opportunities which await visitors and residents in Oman. Underwater sports, in particular, have found enthusiastic support as the waters around Oman are rich in marine life. Snorkelling fans find the area around Al Bustan Palace Hotel particularly promising.

left
To the first-time visitor, Oman is a land full of surprises. Geological and climatic contrasts range from towering mountains, through desert wastes to the fertile uplands of the Dhofar region. Thanks to the moisture-laden winds of the south-west monsoon, scenes such as this tree on a verdant plain are typical during the wet season, from August to September. Oman is the only country of peninsular Arabia which experiences such a dramatic climatic shift.

The Dhofar monsoon

The southern region of Oman is unique in all Arabia, for its coastal mountains and plain catch the south-west monsoon, which enshrouds them in dense, moist fog each year, bringing life-giving water and transforming the arid hillsides and wadis (dry river-beds) into grassy, rolling down-land. Thanks to its unique climate, about fifty species of plants, as well as some insects, reptiles and small mammals, are endemic to the Dhofar area, occurring nowhere else in the world. Happily, the emphasis on conservation in Oman bodes well for this richness and diversity.

Dhofar also boasts a good variety of larger mammals, some of which (such as the leopard and hyena) show that, 25 million years ago, southern Arabia was joined to Africa. The African connection is confirmed by many other species, including a remarkable clump of baobab trees – 15-metre-high giants, with grey trunks up to two metres in diameter, which grow in Dhofar's Wadi Hinna (on the seaward side of the Jebel al Qara range) and nowhere else in the whole of Arabia.

No less unique is Dhofar's coastal and marine life, which combines two environments which rarely, if ever, co-exist elsewhere: kelp beds and coral reefs. Kelp, a species of seaweed, requires cool, nutrient-rich surroundings which occur during Dhofar's monsoon season; in the kelp beds live the shellfish abalone, much sought-after both for the delicacy of their meat and the lustrous beauty of their shells.

Coral, on the other hand, requires even, tropical sea-temperatures and relatively low levels of nutrient. It flourishes not only in Dhofar, but also around Oman's northern coasts, giving a glorious richness and diversity to the marine life which subsists on coral reefs – and a source of fascination to today's snorkelling and scuba-diving enthusiasts.

Conservation projects

Northern Oman's wildlife is also remarkable – perhaps first and foremost for the oryx story, a triumph of enlightened vision and conservation. By 1972, the Arabian white oryx *(Oryx leucoryx)* was extinct in the wild. This beautiful creature, whose white coat and long curved horns have led some to believe it to be the origin of the unicorn legend, had lived on Oman's central desert plain, the Jiddat al Harasis. The White Oryx Project began in 1979, and the first two small herds were released from captivity into the wild in the early 1980s. The local Harasis Bedouin staff the project, using their local knowledge and skills, as well as their semi-nomadic lifestyle, to keep track of the oryx herds.

In the last fifteen years, the oryx have successfully re-adapted to their wild habitat, and are now breeding and well-established – the only example in the world of a successful reintroduction to the wild of a virtually extinct species held in captivity. The White Oryx Project has had spin-offs for other species too – great numbers of Arabian gazelle and Houbara bustard live in the Jiddat. Both of these species were hunted throughout Arabia for many centuries and Oman is now the only country to have viable populations of these creatures.

Oman's conservation programmes have been prepared by the International Union for the Conservation of Nature,

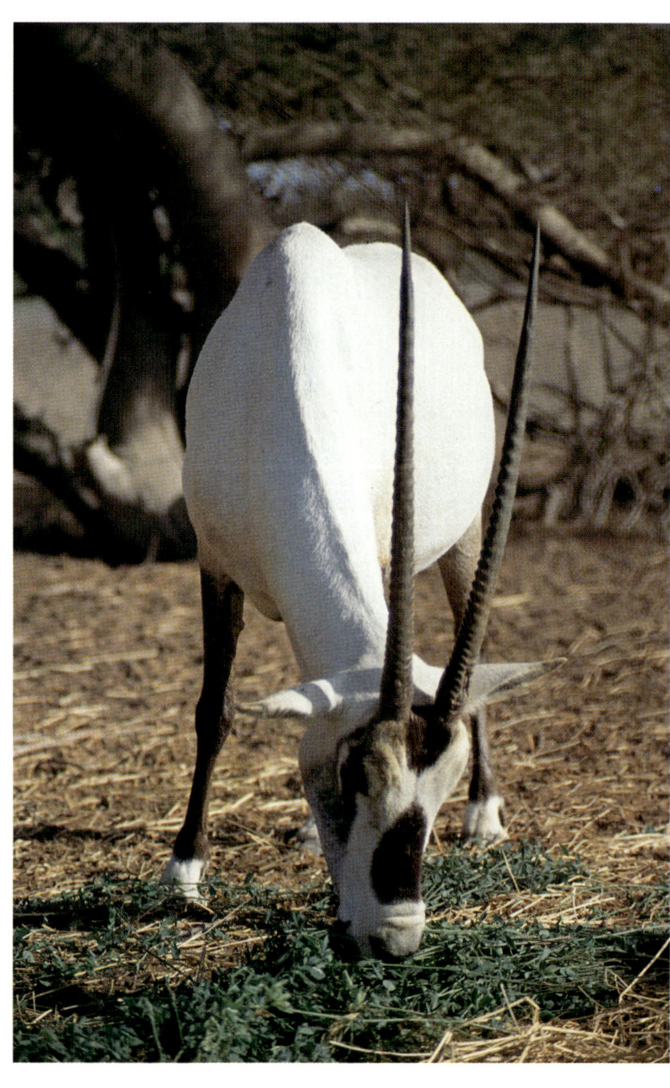

above
The white oryx is today identified as intrinsic to Oman. Not so long ago, the oryx was on the point of extinction but a timely and well-executed conservation programme by the government reintroduced it to the wild.

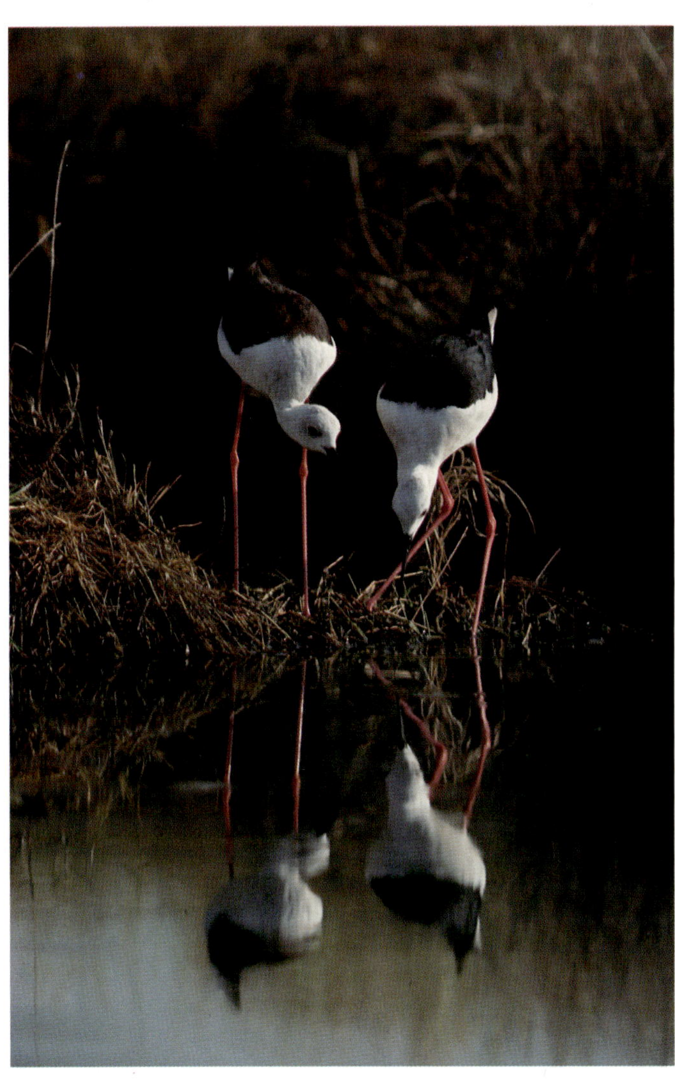

above
Oman's bird-life includes both migratory and local species. This pair of black-winged stilts, perched on long, very delicate red legs, hunt for food along the water's edge.

and also include projects to protect turtles, which breed along Oman's 1,800 kilometres of coastline – in particular the areas around Ras al Hadd and Ras al Junayz, where the Ministry of Regional Municipalities and Environment monitors and administers the sanctuaries. In the mountains of northern Oman there is also a special reserve for the "half-goat", the Arabian *tahr* (*Hemitragus jayakari*), which is now found only in Oman (though a few may also exist in the adjacent mountains of the United Arab Emirates).

Bird-life

Oman's geographical position makes its bird-life unusually varied, for the Sultanate lies at the junction of three of the six great bio-geographical realms of the world, and has many representatives from each. It also lies on the migratory path of many birds passing between Africa and Europe to Asia, so while the number of breeding species is not much more than a hundred (as far as is yet known), there are roughly three times as many passing migrants. Scientists and bird-watchers continue to discover more about Oman's bird-life: golden eagles are now known to breed in the deserts of the Interior – and bird sanctuaries have been established in various coastal areas to offer protected habitats to many species.

Frankincense

There is one species in Oman – a species which grows wild and is never sown or artificially planted by man, because its presence was considered to indicate God's bounty – which has played a major role in the country's history and economy. It is the frankincense tree (*Boswellia sacra*), from which fragrant resin is tapped. High-quality frankincense is produced only by trees in certain areas of Dhofar – and the product literally put ancient Dhofar on the map. Trade routes opened up, both by land and sea, to transport the precious resin which, when burned, gives off an exotic and delicious fragrance. Ancient Assyrians, Egyptians, Greeks and Romans all used frankincense in their religious observances – Roman senators took their oath of loyalty to the emperor in the light of a burning incense brazier. It was also widely used in the ancient world for embalming and burial practices. Many of Dhofar's ancient archaeological sites owe their existence to frankincense – Samhuram (modern-day Khawr Rawri) was the port by which it was exported, and sites at Shisur, Hanun, Andhur and Al Balid all owe their existence and prosperity to frankincense.

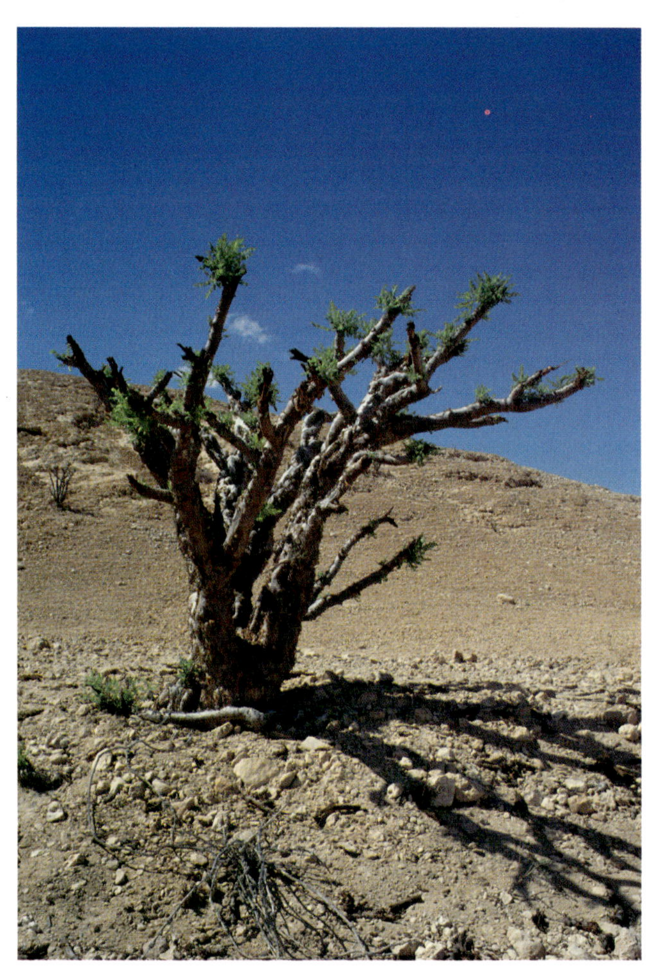

above
The Dhofar region in the south of Oman produces the finest frankincense in the world. For over 2,000 years merchants and traders from the ancient Greek, Roman and Indian civilisations have used Omani frankincense.

Even today, frankincense plays a part in the Omani way of life: it is used to perfume homes, linen and clothing, and is also used medicinally. The Public Authority for Marketing Agricultural Produce (PAMAP) now organises the collection, sorting and storage of frankincense, as well as its attractive packaging for the growing tourist market. PAMAP is also

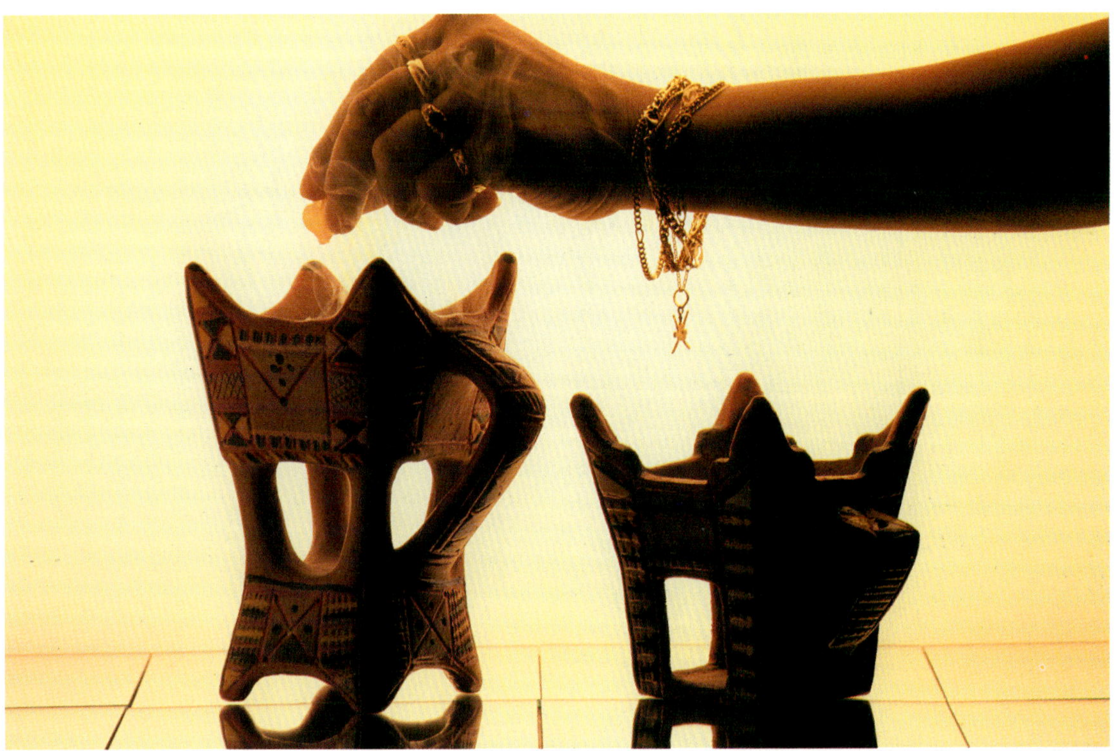

above
Frankincense is traditionally burned over glowing charcoal during the Eid festivities and during weddings. Its heady aroma was used by Omanis to impregnate their clothing and households with a strong perfume.

producing fine-quality kohl (traditional eye make-up) from carbonised frankincense. Because of its high oil-content, frankincense is used as a fixative in perfumes – notably in Oman's own *Amouage*, one of the world's most expensive perfumes.

Water

Without water, there is no life. In a largely desert land like Oman, where rainfall is scarce and sporadic, the discovery, transport and conservation of water has challenged people for many centuries. Bedouin tribes adapted their life-style to a search for water and grazing; villages grew up around oases – but to grow crops, irrigation was needed. The traditional solution to this is the *falaj* (plural *afalaj*) – an ingenious system whereby water from underground aquifers was channelled to emerge above ground by force of gravity, and to run in narrow open channels through a village and around its fields and agricultural areas. Legend has it that Prophet Suleiman Daoud (peace be upon him) visited Oman on a flying carpet, and ordered his servants, who were *jinn*, or spirits, to build 10,000 water channels in ten days. History suggests, though, that the technology came from ancient Persian inhabitants of the region.

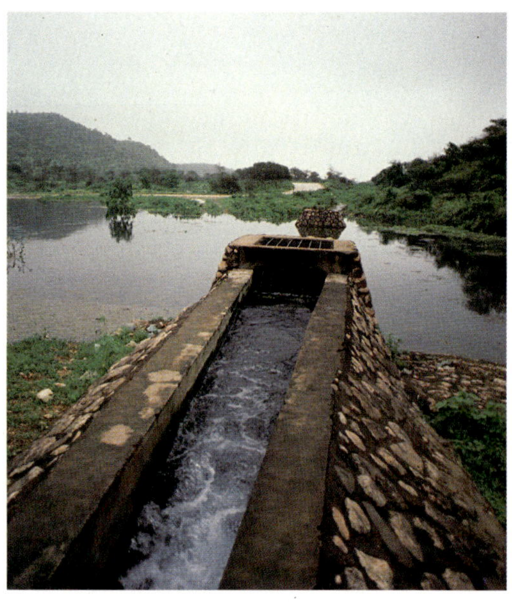

above
With so many years of development, some *afalaj* employ devices such as siphons. This system in Ayn Arzat, Salalah takes the clean *falaj* water across a main watercourse which flows after occasional rainfall.

The construction of *afalaj* was often a remarkable feat of engineering, the average depth of the main wells of a system being about 20 metres (though some are as deep as 60 metres). Between the main source of water and the final outlet, access shafts were dug every 50 or 60 metres, down which young lads were sent to do any necessary maintenance, such as clearing rocks or stones from the channel. At the outlet of each *falaj*, water is used for drinking – the first priority. Thereafter, the water is used for washing, before finally irrigating the fields. *Afalaj* are between 3 and 10 kilometres long, from source to village, and on average supply water at a rate of 40 litres per second. This is enough to supply continuous irrigation for quite large areas all the year round.

Within a village, each family's fields are watered by rota, with rocks and stones being used to divert the water into the required channels at different times of day. This egalitarian system has worked well in Oman for many centuries. Nowadays, with a rapidly increasing population and the benefits of twentieth-century technology, *falaj* systems are supplemented by other water systems. The underground aquifers themselves are replenished by means of recharge dams – structures which span wadis not far from their entry into the sea. These dams retain the rushing torrents of water which pour down the wadis after infrequent rain storms – and which

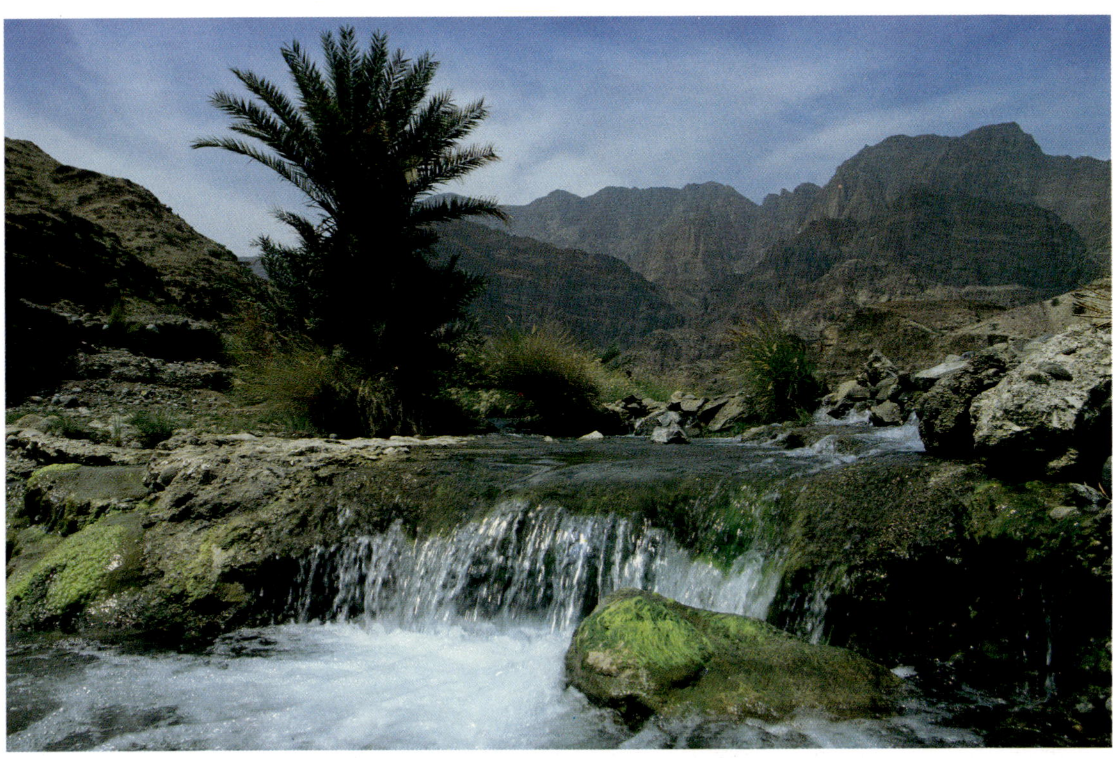

above
After sporadic spring rains the usually dry river beds, or wadis, become a sight to behold. Water brings forth life and is valued as a most precious resource, to be protected and used with great care.

used to be lost to the sea. By holding the water back, the dam allows more of it to seep into the earth, and thus recharge the underground supplies.

Muscat's desalination and power plant, built by the company of Suhail and Saud Bahwan, is another means of providing the Capital Area with water, at a rate of over a hundred million litres a day. Research is in hand to bring desalination costs down to an even more economic level. And the Sultanate also bottles its own high-quality mineral water from Wadi Tanuf, which is marketed throughout the country.

The importance of water is shown in the Sultanate's historic staging of multilateral water talks, as part of the 1991 Middle East peace conference – talks which underlined the importance of regional cooperation on the key subject of water conservation and management.

Ways of life

Farming

With a regular water supply, crops can be grown – and Oman's most traditional and best-loved crop is dates. The date-palm is a remarkable tree, flourishing in hot, dry conditions and not only producing sweet nutritious food, but also providing building materials, ropes and household items such as brushes, mats and baskets.

Records show that Oman was exporting dates about 2,000 years ago – so Omani dates are evidently not just a recently acquired taste. They are famous for their flavour and sweetness, and, at the height of Oman's seafaring glory (ninth and tenth centuries AD), they were the main item of cargo, as well as an essential food-source for the sailors (and, incidentally, the reason why Omani sailors didn't suffer from scurvy, or vitamin C deficiency, unlike their European counterparts). The date store was a strategically important feature of Oman's castles and forts – as a secure food-supply in case they were besieged. At Jabrin, the date stores have ridged floors, so that the juices from the fruits, which were stacked high in sacks made of woven palm-leaves, could drain away easily.

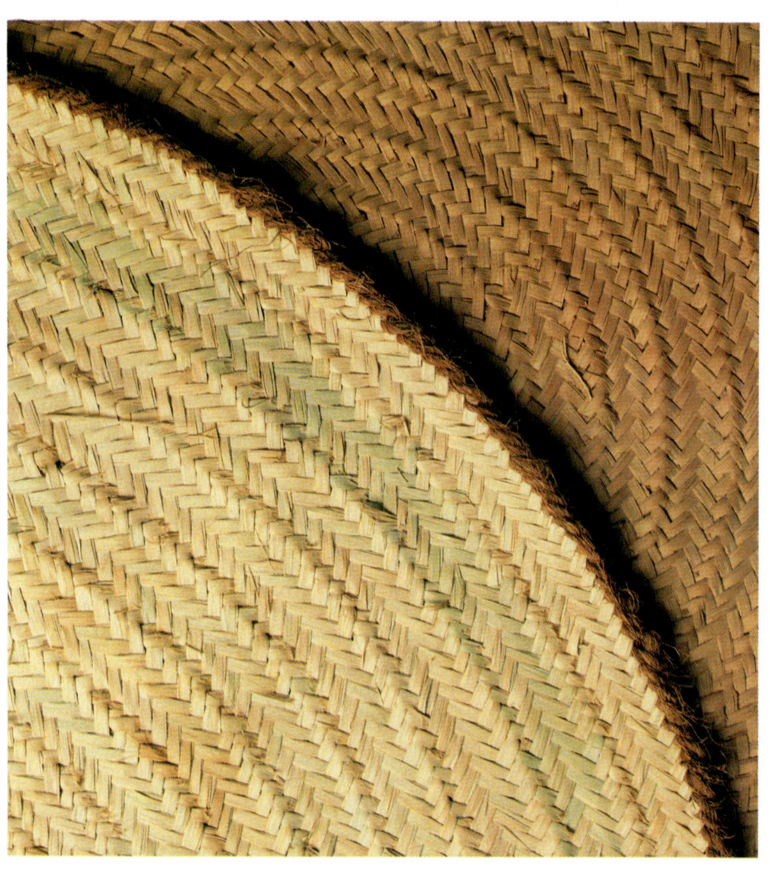

above
All parts of the versatile date-palm are put to different uses. Circular palm matting, as pictured here, is used for serving meals which are often eaten sitting on the floor.

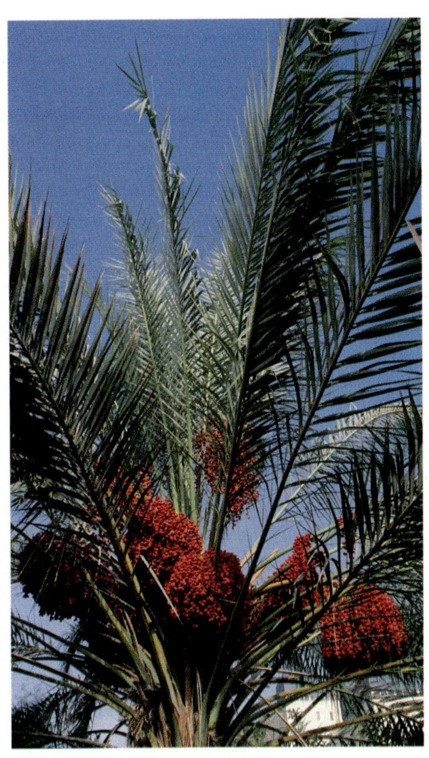

above
During the intense heat of the summer season, Oman's abundant date plantations seem to defy nature and bring forth their plentiful crop.

Date-palms require a good deal of tending. Trees are either male or female, and until recently were all pollinated by hand, by the farmer climbing the female trees, bearing, tucked into his belt, a flowering stem from a male tree. Nowadays, the Date Palm Improvement Project (DPIP) collects and freeze-dries the pollen from the male tree. Research has shown that optimum pollination occurs when the pollen is mixed with wheat flour in a ratio of about 7:1, and then sprayed on to the flowers of the female trees from a compact, hand-held sprayer devised by DPIP staff.

Oman has about 152 varieties of female date-palm – and just five male varieties. Some varieties are highly prized, some are used for drying and storing, some for cooking and animal-feed. Oman's date harvest is reckoned to be about 154,000 tonnes per year – about half the Sultanate's agricultural land is occupied by date-palms. Government-owned date factories in Nizwa and Rustaq wash, process and package the fruit ready for selling in a variety of markets. One of Oman's most successful dairy companies, Oman National Dairy Products (whose brand-name Zain is well-known throughout the Sultanate), has developed a truly Omani product in the form of date yogurt, energy-packed and nutritious.

Nowadays, with sophisticated irrigation systems, many crops are grown in Oman, especially along the Batinah coast in the north, and on the Salalah plain in the south. Everything from mushrooms to melons, from carrots to courgettes, is now grown, to place the country's self-sufficiency on a firm footing. In the mountains of Dhofar, a government experimental station grows a range of different crops and varieties, testing soil-types, and the watering needs, pest resistance and crop yields of vines, coffee plants, pineapples, and many other food products.

Livestock

Goats are the most commonly seen livestock throughout the Sultanate – it often falls to the youngsters or women in a family to herd and care for them. Dhofari goats are a different species from those kept in the North, being smaller, friskier and having very short coats. Sheep too are sometimes kept in northern Oman – but in the mountains of the South, cattle-herding was the traditional way of life, thanks to the monsoon, which produced the grass needed for fodder.

Cattle pastoralists with their own unique breeds of cows are still common in Dhofar – people who live much as they have done for the past thousand years or more. They speak Jibbali, one of at least five local languages, which linguistic scholars believe to be very ancient, and which may once have had an alphabetic, written script – though no longer. Such traditional ways of life might seem picturesque, but were often grindingly hard – herds had to be taken, often considerable distances, to find water and grazing, which became increasingly sparse and scarce as the lushness of the post-monsoon autumn was replaced by the droughts of winter, and the heat of spring and early summer.

Modern Dhofari cattle-herders tend to be more settled, less nomadic, due to government provision of round-the-year water-troughs, and the benefits of commercially produced cattle-feed (mainly manufactured by Dhofar Cattle Feed, one of Oman's biggest companies). And cattle are now farmed in Oman on a much larger scale, to meet the nation's dairy needs. Areas which previously could not have supported cattle are now able to do so. For example, Oman Sun Farms, based near Sohar on the northern coast, keeps its entire herd of eight hundred cattle under shade, in sprinkler- and fan-cooled yards.

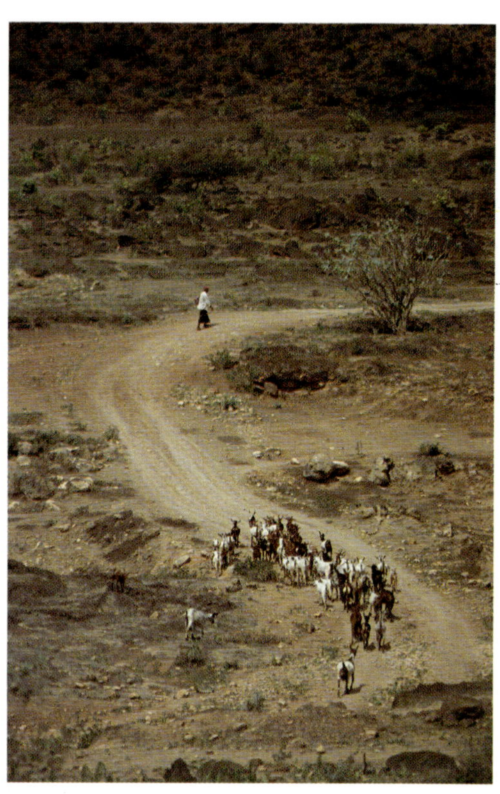

above
A goatherd in the valleys of the Dhofar region leads his livestock to their next feeding ground.

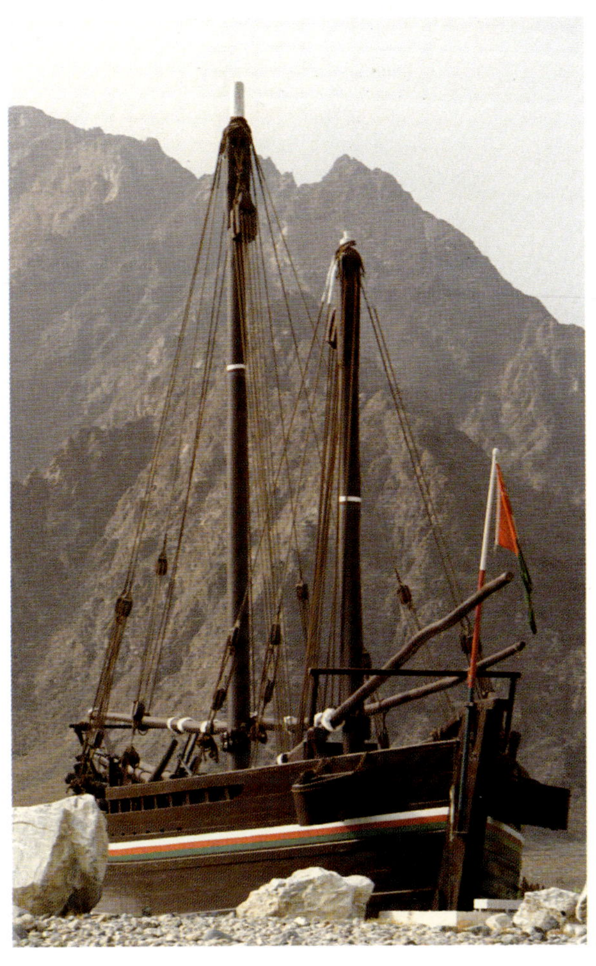

above
Legend has it that it was from Oman that Sindbad sallied forth on his adventures around the world. It was from here that the first ambassador from Arab lands journeyed to the then brand-new nation of the United States of America. This ship is the *Sohar*, a replica of those built centuries ago, with its planking held together with coconut fibre. In 1980 it was sailed on an epic journey to Canton, and now stands at Al Bustan in testimony to Oman's seafaring history.

The high seas

With 1,800 kilometres of coastline, and a harsh Interior, it was natural for Omanis to be proficient fishermen, seafarers, navigators and boat-builders from earliest times. In celebration of Oman's tenth National Day, explorer Tim Severin made a remarkable voyage from Muscat to China, in a wooden sailing vessel, with planks sewn together in the fashion described by ancient manuscripts – a replica of the vessels in which Omani sailors plied the high seas more than 1,000 years ago.

Oman is situated at what was one of the great trading crossroads of the medieval world, between Africa, South-East Asia and the head of the Gulf. Its ports prospered, as vessels of many nations touched land to replenish supplies and to trade. In the ninth-century Persian text *Hudud al-'Alam* Sohar was described as "the emporium of the world . . . There is no town in the world where the merchants are wealthier than here". About a hundred years on, Sohar continued to flourish as the great Islamic geographer Al Muqaddasi observed: "It is a populous and beautiful spot, where wealth and fruits are in abundance".

Marco Polo was impressed with Qalhat's magnificence in AD 1290: "It is a noble city . . . They grow no corn but get it from abroad, for every merchant vessel that comes brings some. The haven is very large and good, and is frequented by numerous ships with goods from India – and from this city the spices and other merchandise are distributed among the cities and towns of the Interior". Today, little remains of Qalhat, which was savagely devastated by Portuguese conqueror Alfonso de Albuquerque in the early sixteenth century. Only the haunting beauty of Bibi Maryam's mausoleum, built of fossilised coral and decorated with plaster-work, remains.

Omani sailors and merchant seamen plied their trade in exotic goods, regularly making the dangerous sea-voyage to Canton in China, which took about eighteen months (though only eight months of that was actual sailing time: the rest was spent waiting for favourable winds and currents).

Fishing too has been an Omani trade from time immemorial. In Dhofar, at certain seasons, the sardines were so plentiful that men stood on the shore and flung nets into the sea, only to drag them out full of shining fish. These were then spread out on the shore, above the tide-mark, to dry – after which they were used to supplement cattle-feed in the lean months before the monsoon rains, or to barter for other goods.

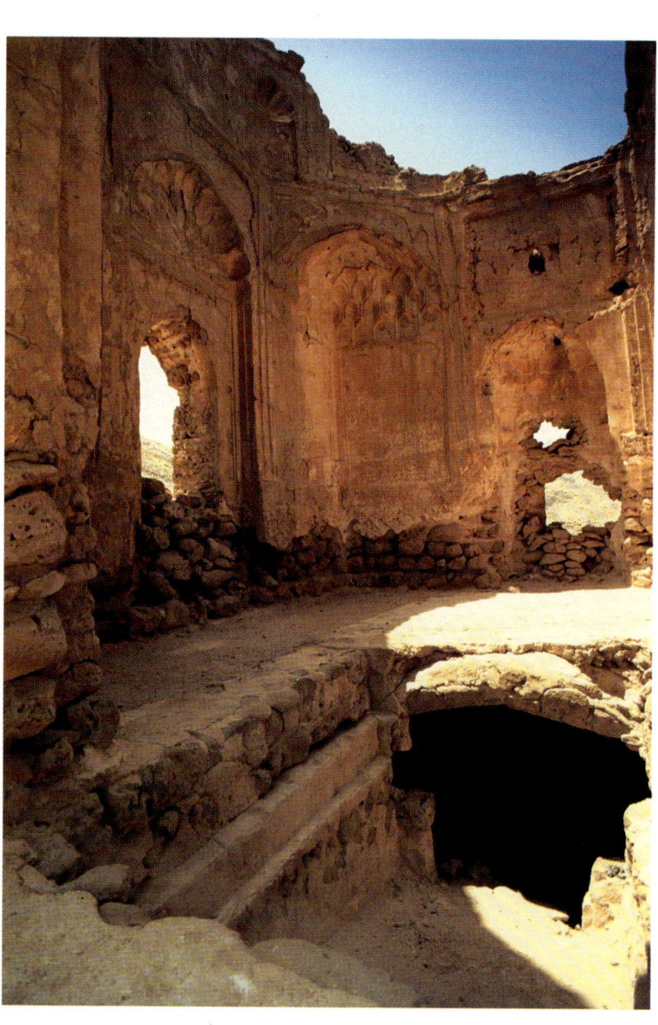

above
On the coast road from Quriyat to Sur, at Qalhat, lie the almost shattered ruins of Bibi Maryam's mausoleum.

Still today Oman's seafaring and trading past lives on – fishermen continue to harvest the marine riches around Oman's coast – though now most of them use boats of fibreglass not wood. Over the last twenty-five years, the Omani Government has built an infrastructure for fishing, including a network of harbours, workshops, cold-storages and marketing centres, meaning that fish can be preserved and transported (thanks to the road system) even to the most distant towns and villages. Top-quality fish – in particular, yellow-fin tuna,

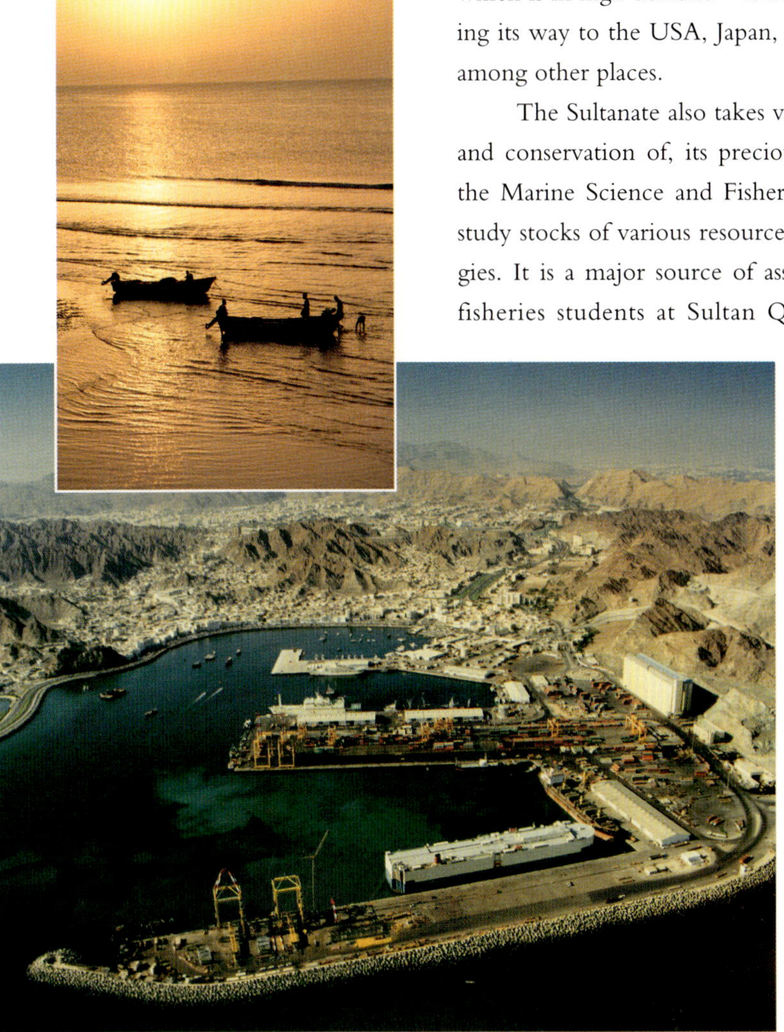

which is in high demand – is also exported from Oman, finding its way to the USA, Japan, the UK, Australia and France, among other places.

The Sultanate also takes very seriously the research into, and conservation of, its precious marine resources. In 1986, the Marine Science and Fisheries Center was established, to study stocks of various resources and plan management strategies. It is a major source of assistance to the agriculture and fisheries students at Sultan Qaboos University – the two organisations often work hand-in-hand.

Traditional boat-building also lives on at the ports of Sur and Al Ashkharah. In times past, many different styles of wooden vessel were built, from ocean-going ships to skiffs; now only one style is normally constructed – *the sambuq* – about one tenth of the size of the great merchant ships of the past. Even so, the construction looks impressive: boat-yards on the shore still ring to the traditional sounds of adze, plane and hammer. No electricity is used, no plans referred to – yet mysteriously and perfectly, the ships take shape.

Before 1970, there were no ports capable of handling modern ocean-going vessels: now, Mina Sultan Qaboos in the north and Mina Raysut in the south, handle the import, export and trans-shipment of containers and bulk freight.

top
In Oman, sunsets are a kaleidoscope of colour. Here fishing boats stand out in stark silhouette against an orange blaze.

above
In the years of its renaissance, sea trade through Oman has increased in quantum leaps. This is the port that has played the most vital role, Mina Sultan Qaboos.

Travel and transport

In 1970, there were just 10 kilometres of paved road in the whole country – and just 840 registered motor vehicles. People travelled by camel, donkey and on foot – and Mutrah had an open area near the souq which was used as a camel park, where visitors from the Interior could leave their transport. Nowadays, the Sultanate's road system is second-to-none, with over 4,000 kilometres of tarmac road, and 15,000 kilometres of graded roads. Major roads in the Capital Area are dual-carriageway – and an ambitious road-building project is under way, to make sections of the main Muscat to Nizwa road into a dual-carriageway.

Camels are still very much part of life in the Sultanate: in Dhofar, camel herds remain a status symbol. A man's wealth was, and still is to some extent, measured in the number of camels he owns, for the camel provided milk, hair for weaving into blankets and tents, and droppings for fuel – as well as being a means of transport. The prophet Job (Nabi Ayub, revered in Islam as in Judaism and Christianity), whose tomb is still a place of pilgrimage in Dhofar's Jebel al Qara mountains, was said to have owned 6,000 camels – and it was the camel, with its stamina in harsh terrain, which allowed the Bedouin way of life to develop. At certain times of year and of day, water troughs in Dhofar are besieged by great throngs of thirsty camels – and a really thirsty camel can drink up to 118 litres to rehydrate its tissues.

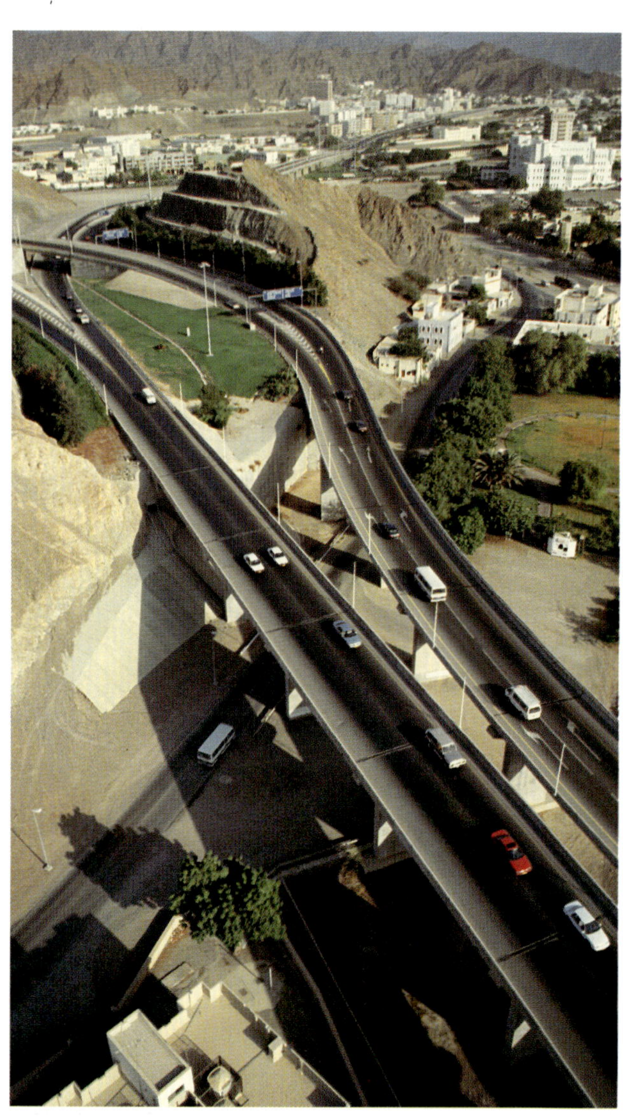

above

Some of the more obvious indicators of Oman's development have been the roads that link up the country. Nowhere are the benefits of modern road-building technology more impressive than the Darsait flyover, where dual-carriageways seem to hang effortlessly above the ground.

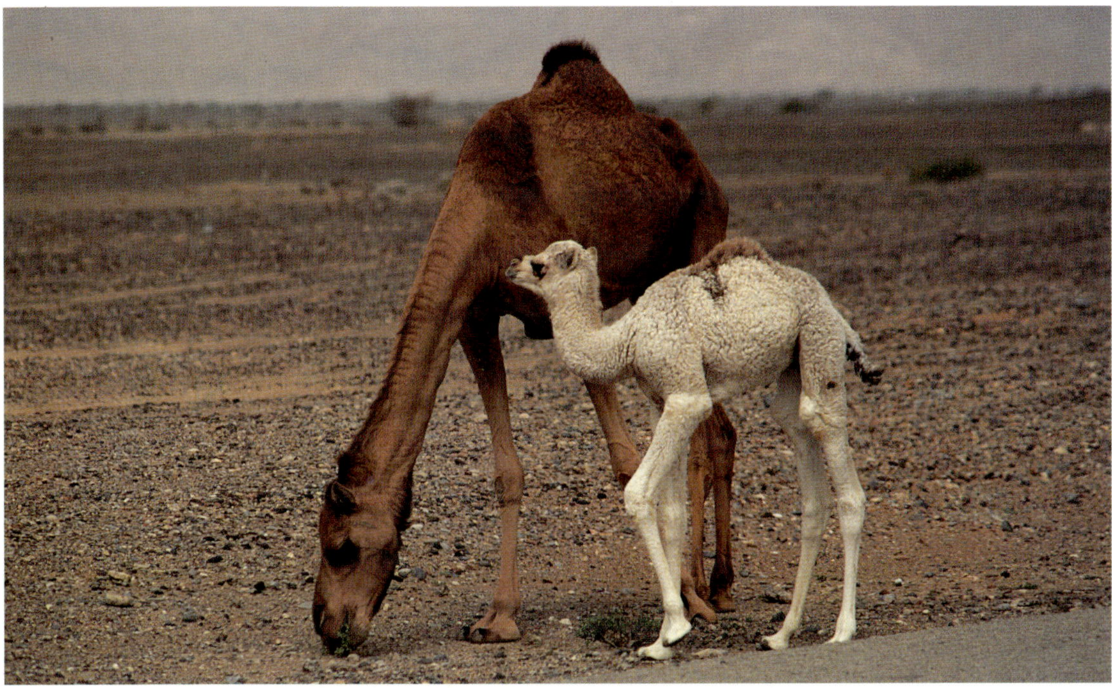

above
Today, Omanis travel in the very latest vehicles. However, this in no way detracts from the role the camel plays in Oman's life. These "ships of the desert" can be found deep into the Empty Quarter, the farthest reaches of Oman's desert.

Camel racing remains a popular and thrilling sport throughout the Sultanate, with successful racing camels fetching large sums of money, often from buyers in the neighbouring United Arab Emirates. The new ship of the desert, though, is the pick-up truck, which today's Bedouin steer up impossibly steep dunes with the maximum of skill and the minimum of fuss.

At the other extreme of the transport market, as it were, is air travel. In 1970, there was no airport capable of handling international traffic. One Omani, who had been born and brought up in the former Omani colony of Zanzibar, remembers her arrival in Oman in the early 1970s: "There was no airport in Oman then, just one narrow airstrip in what is now the centre of Ruwi. We came in a tiny light aircraft between huge mountains so close to us I felt sure that the wings of the plane would touch them!"

Since 1993, the Sultanate has had its own airline – Oman Air. Already it is flying to other Gulf countries and on a number of routes to Asia with its fleet of A320 airbuses – and it continues to expand rapidly. Its base is at Seeb International Airport, some 40 kilometres east of Muscat, which originally opened in 1973. Between 1988 and 1993, the number of passengers doubled, and the number of flights increased by 26%, prompting a recent major upgrade of facilities, at a cost of 8 million Omani rials (about £13 million).

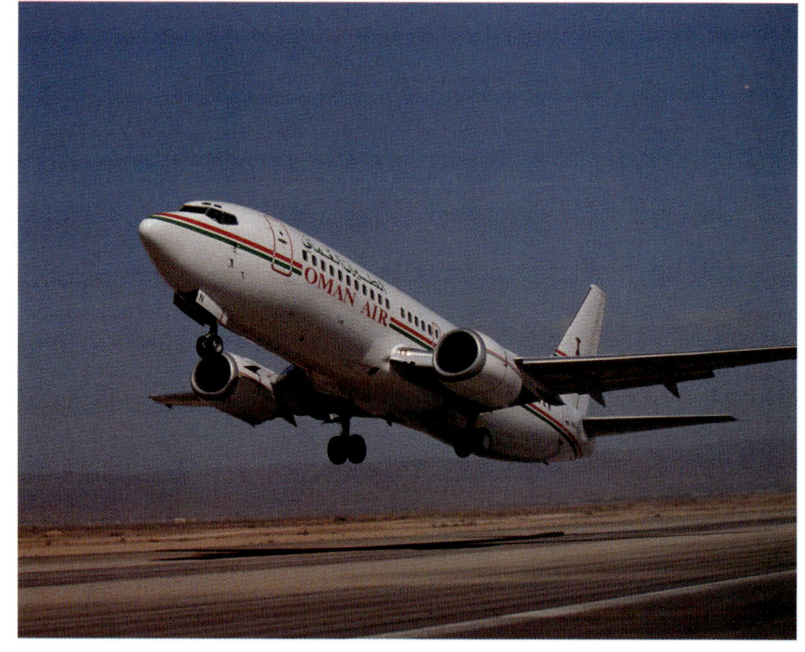

above
The flagship airline, Oman Air, is symbolic of the development of air traffic in Oman. Putting the Sultanate on the map, Oman Air currently flies to six countries, with more to come.

Oman also has a wide-ranging, efficient and profitable bus company, the Oman National Transport Company (ONTC), which began in 1975 with just four routes, served by 64 buses. Perhaps one of the most vivid anecdotes of the pace and quality of change in the Sultanate comes from ONTC who, in the mid-1970s, were asked by the government to send 20 buses from Muscat to Salalah, where National Day celebrations were being held that year. The tarmac roads did not yet cover much of the route – the rough ride took two-and-a-half days in each direction to cover the 1,000 or so kilometres between the two cities, with the buses travelling in convoy, wagon-train style – and setting camp at nightfall. Today, the same journey takes about twelve hours, in luxury air-conditioned coaches, with rest-stops at motels along the way.

Crafts ancient and modern

Oman is rightly proud of its many traditional crafts and industries – which, in times past, played an important part in the national economy. Changing employment and life-style patterns and the arrival of the modern world (in the form of plastics, for instance) have almost brought to an end some traditional crafts – such as silversmithing, copper-smithing and wood-carving, for example. However, the government is now actively encouraging many traditional craftsmen and women, helping them to market their goods and to adapt them to the tastes and life-styles of city-dwellers and tourists. This help and advice was indeed timely, for many Omanis were leaving their traditional village liveli-hoods, some of which had been handed down from generation to generation, perhaps even for thousands of years, as better-paid work became available in towns and cities – a process which has, in some cases, now been reversed. One partic-ularly good example of this is weaving.

below
Traditional Omani coffee pots made from hand-beaten copper and soldered brass are an intrinsic part of Omani life. Guests are still honoured in timeless fashion with a heady brew poured into tiny cups, to be sipped and appreciated.

Weaving

Traditionally, weaving has been a male occupation in Oman. In parts of the Sultanate, pit-loom weaving still thrives, whereby the weaver sits on the edge of a pit, with his feet at the bottom to operate the shafts, and so that the loom itself is at arm-level. The Interior village of Samad, for example, has a friendly workshop, where lengths of cotton are woven, often for making the *wuzar*, a loin-cloth worn by men under their formal white dishdashas – or by itself, with a shirt or T-shirt on top, for relaxing at home.

Many Omani weavers traditionally used ground looms, weaving goat or camel hair (more rarely, sheep's wool), which was readily available. It is still fairly common in some parts of Oman (for example, Wadi Sahtan or Wadi Ghul) to meet villagers, men and women, spinning yarn on a hand-held spindle as they walk about on their daily business. Goat and camel hair was used in its natural colours, whereas sheep's wool was dyed, often using the pounded roots of madder, mixed with water and dried limes, to produce a deep red. Nowadays, chemical dyes are usually used – though red remains a favourite colour.

Formerly, weavers mainly made rugs, saddle-bags, and trappings for donkeys or camels – and some of these are still made, a lot of them for sale to visitors. Nowadays, women in various parts of the Sultanate are being trained and encouraged to use traditional techniques for the creation of more varied products, mainly designed for sale in the Capital Area. The Harsusi women, Bedouin living on the Jiddat al Harasis – a desert plain of 40,000 square kilometres in central Oman – make brightly tasselled key-rings, using techniques traditionally developed for camel harnesses, by sitting cross-legged on the ground and looping the warp threads around their big toe.

In rural areas, the weaving is now often done by groups of women, who come together as part of a programme run

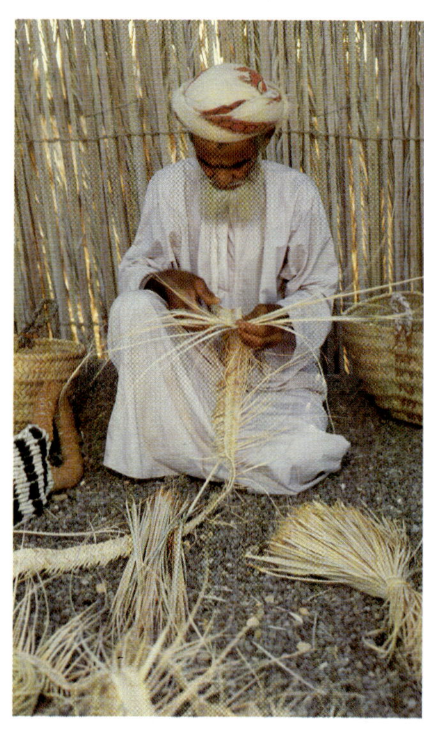

above
Weaving is an age-old handicraft in Oman. As a profession it has been followed for centuries and still contributes practical artefacts for use in daily life. This skilled weaver of baskets first braids together strips of palm leaves into strands and then joins them together to form the final shape.

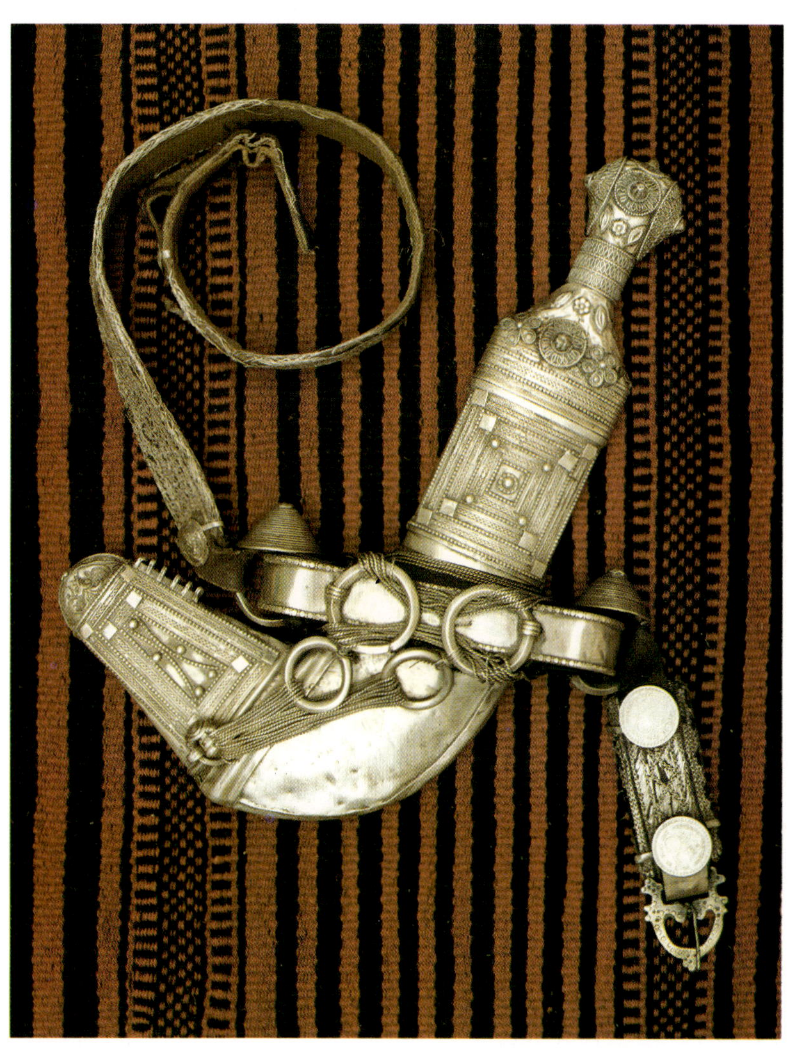

above
The curved Omani dagger, the *khanjar,* is still worn as a sign of manhood and at ceremonial occasions. This model, an antique "Saidi" is one of the many traditional and regional designs.

by the Directorate of Community Development at the Ministry of Social Affairs. The weavers use a rectangular wooden frame, to which the warp threads are attached and which is propped upright in front of the weaver. These are easily portable, and encourage the women to work in groups, making it a social occasion.

This programme first started in 1981, in the northern coastal town of Al Khabura. Training was given, and modern tools for spinning were distributed, making it a less time-consuming process and thereby increasing productivity – an experienced weaver now produces one or two exquisitely designed rugs or wall-hangings per month. Other similar centres have opened, both around Al Khabura and in the Rustaq area – a total of three hundred women have already been trained, most of whom can supplement their family income with their new-found skills. A formal curriculum has been developed to include everything from selecting raw materials to selling the produce – and the women are also learning which are the most marketable designs and items.

Pottery

Pottery is one of the oldest crafts in Oman – 4,000 years ago, Omani potters were making round-bottomed water-jars which, until recently, were in everyday use throughout the Sultanate – often hung from a tree-branch to keep the water in shade, and to take advantage of any cooling breezes. Bahla, an Interior town, has long been the traditional centre of pot-making: local clay deposits are particularly suitable for the craft. The kick-wheel is virtually the potter's only tool – that, along with the skills passed from father to son, enable him to make a variety of different style pots.

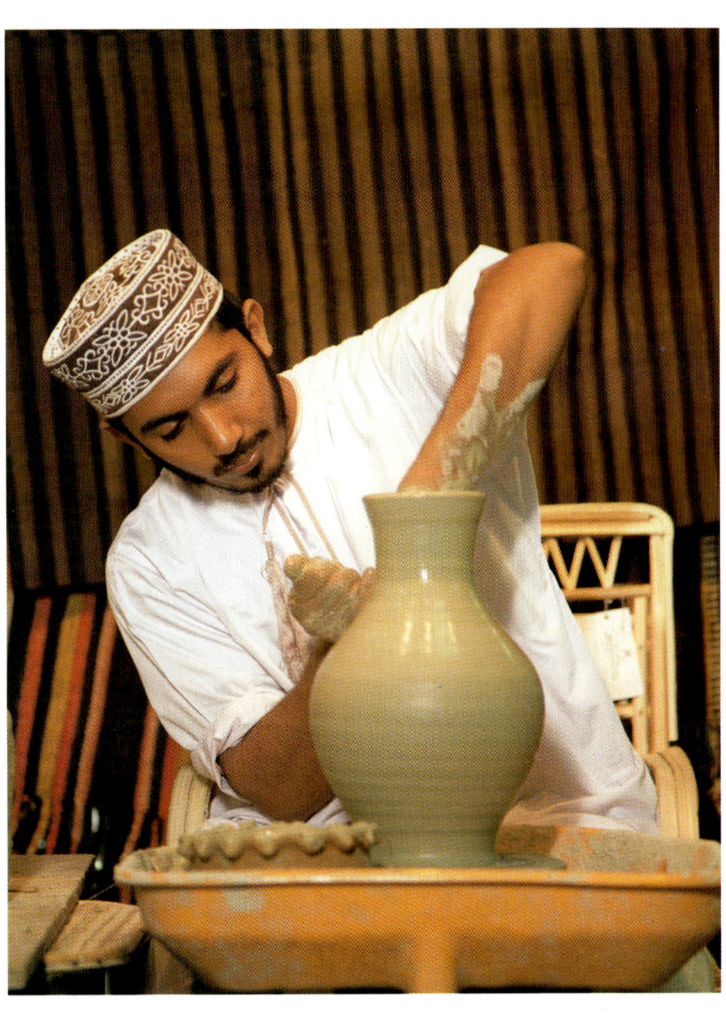

above
A young potter puts the final touches to the throwing of a delicately balanced pot.

Once a pot has been shaped, it is stacked outside in the shade to dry out slowly before firing. Omani pots are still fired in traditional kilns – large, dome-shaped structures which are sealed during the firing. Palm-wood is still used to fuel the kilns – substantial quantities are needed to ensure that a high and even heat is maintained throughout the kiln.

Recently, potters – just like the weavers – have been taught to develop their range of artefacts, and styles, to have a wider appeal. Different glazes are being used – most typically a rich brown or blue, decorated often with traditional Omani emblems in a yellow slip. Large jars, once used to store dates,

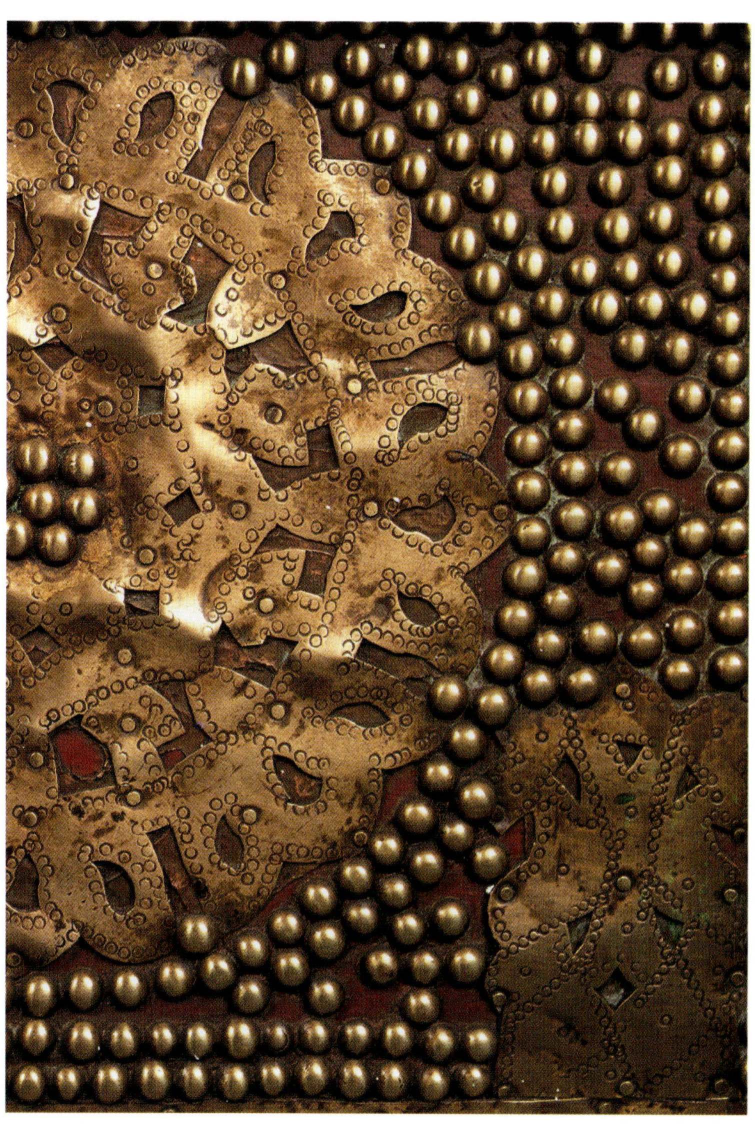

above
A highly decorated wedding chest shows the skill and care put into its manufacture many years ago. The industry still thrives with modern variations today.

are finding a place in the modern world as garden and household ornaments in the Capital Area – and even in export markets beyond. Furthermore, the government is encouraging youngsters to learn the traditional craft-skills, sponsoring secondary-school graduates to be trained at Bahla. A spokesman commented: "We will help them start their own workshops, and might even send them abroad for further training".

Southern Oman has also maintained and developed its pottery production, in a very specialised market: the making of clay burners for the frankincense produced locally. Traditionally these were made in all shapes and sizes, from a basic curved dish on a simple pedestal or four feet, to the huge, square-shaped pots which were carried on the head in processions – and were decorated with incised patterns and painted with plant dyes. Nowadays, the advent of paints has made the pots both brighter and easier to decorate. The burners are still made by women in their own homes – a cottage industry, especially in the Taqah area – and are sold throughout Oman as items both functional and decorative.

Industries of today

While many traditional Omani crafts are being re-established and developed for the modern world, most Omani manufacturing is on a larger and more mechanised scale. The Omani government is conscious of the vital importance of economic diversification, with limited oil supplies – and to this end, much planning and investment has been made in local industries. Industrial estates are taking shape throughout the country, led by the flagship at Rusail, some 50 kilometres east of Muscat. These estates offer advantageous incentives to businesses, to help them through the difficult early years, and in turn provide jobs, and a boost to the regional economies. The schemes are evidently working – the non-oil sector of the economy grew by 9% in 1993.

Remarkable progress has been made on the industrial front. In 1975, the Sultanate had just 10 factories, worth about 500,000 Omani rials; today, there are 3,700 industrial units with a total investment of more than 400 million rials. The companies are varied – from heavy industry providing machinery and components to oil and gas producers, or developing Oman's own natural resources (such as the quarrying and polishing of Omani marble), to Nabil's prize-winning biscuit factory or a sophisticated pharmaceuticals manufacturer.

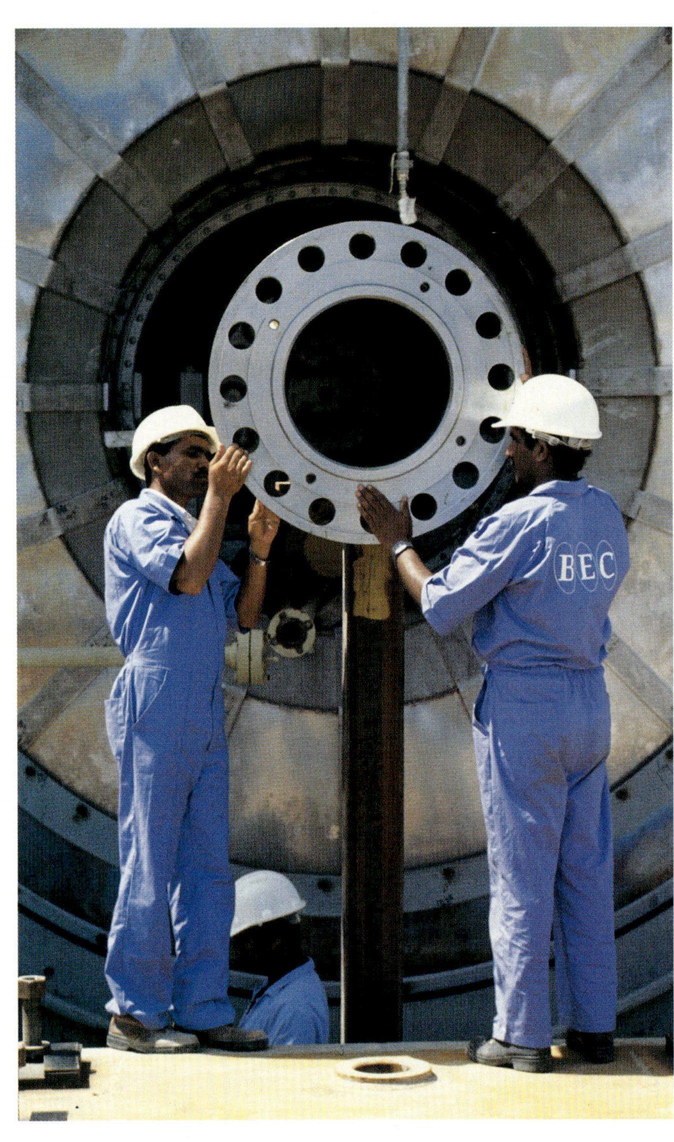

above

In a land where water is, probably, the scarcest resource, desalination of water has had to keep pace with the development needs of the nation. Here at the desalination plant at Ghubra, men are working at extending the desalination plant's capacity even further.

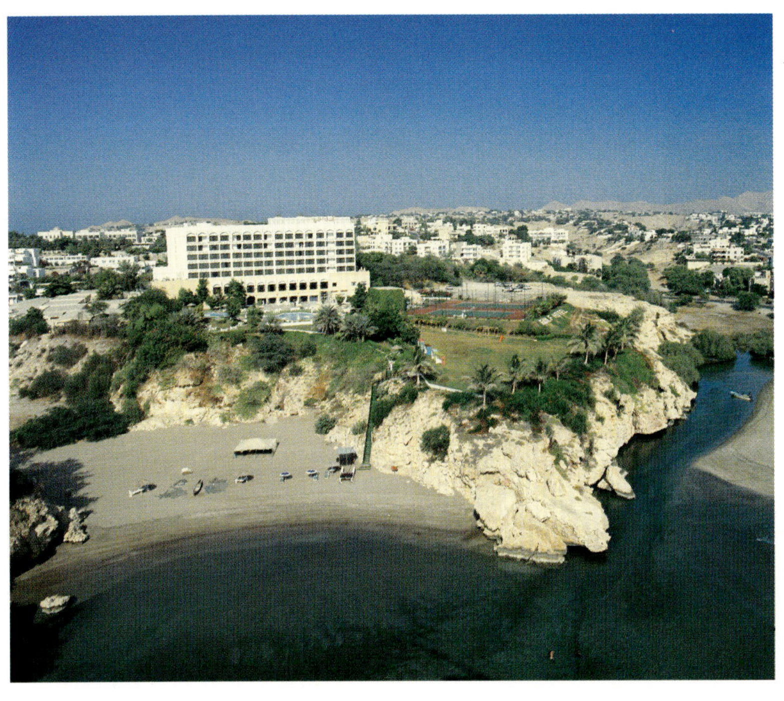

Oman is also abreast of the new service industries, in particular tourism. The country boasts the best hotel in the Middle East, in the form of the magnificent Al Bustan Palace Hotel, winner of many prestigious awards. The photographs throughout this book bear testimony to the delights that Oman has to offer to tourists – indeed, the government is hoping to increase the number of tourists three-fold within the next ten years.

above
Perched on a rocky outcrop over the crystal-clear water of the Gulf of Oman, the Gulf Hotel in Qurm has an enviable location. From here the view stretches north along glorious white sandy beaches.

Homes and buildings

Oman's forts are perhaps one of her most dramatic architectural features, dominating many of the towns and villages of the Interior and northern coast – whether restored to their pristine beauty or as craggy and mysterious ruins. The bay of Muscat is picturesquely flanked by the twin forts of Mirani and Jalali (built in 1587 and 1588 respectively) – while the forts of the Interior vary greatly in style – two extremes perhaps being represented by Nizwa and Jabrin.

The starkly massive bulk of Nizwa fort, with its huge tower, dominates the town, and is surrounded by old mud-brick houses and a warren of tiny streets and alleyways, set amid date plantations. The fort was reputedly built around 1660, with walls thick enough to withstand attack from cannon-fire. Its water supply (a crucial defensive feature in case of seige) was assured by means of a number of wells, and

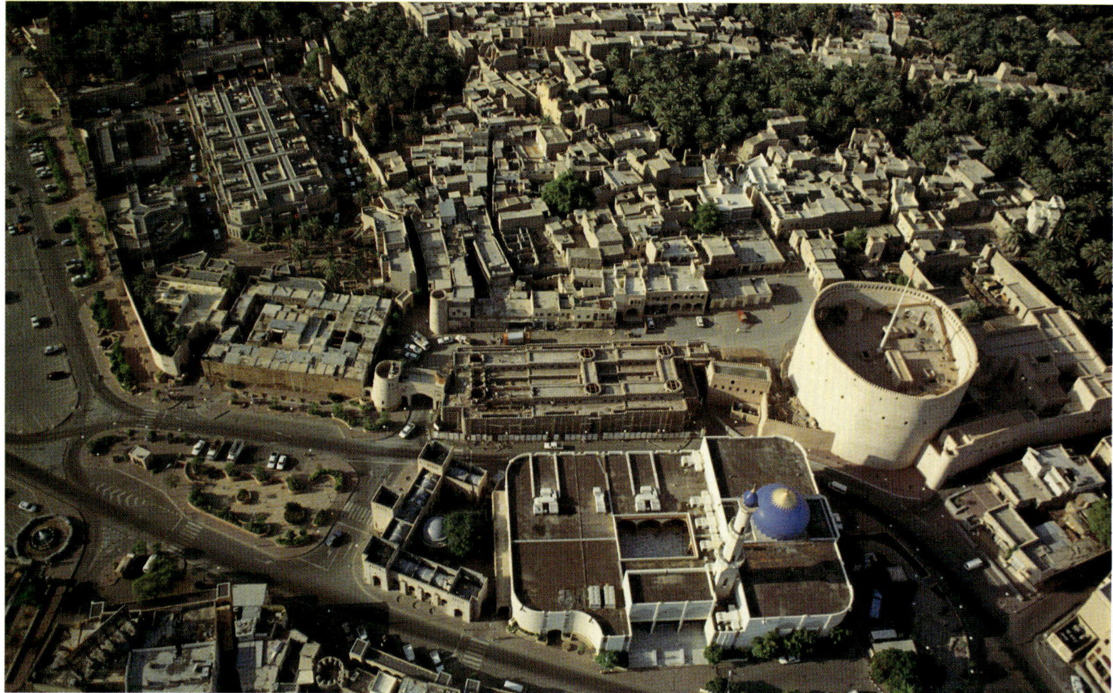

above
A mosaic of the old and the new. Age-old dwellings, some of them hundreds of years old, jostle cheek by jowl with more modern houses. Seen from the air, Nizwa seems to be dominated by its fort – and so it has been since the 17th century.

the presence of a *falaj* running beneath the castle. Nizwa tower consists mainly of a central core filled with earth and stones, and a long, curving stone staircase leading up to the defensive position at the top. The staircase has no fewer than seven doors, each several inches thick and beautifully carved, and each with a sinister slit inside the curved arch above the door, to enable the defenders to pour boiling honey or oil on to the attackers – altogether rendering Nizwa virtually impregnable.

By contrast, Jabrin fort, a mere 50 kilometres away and probably built a mere 25 years later, is by any standards a marvel of delicate and refined architecture. Its elaborate fluted arches over inward-looking windows and doors are reminiscent of Moghul design – and the ceilings are breathtakingly beautiful, whether in vaulted, finely-decorated plasterwork or in wooden beams, painted in glorious colours and intricate designs.

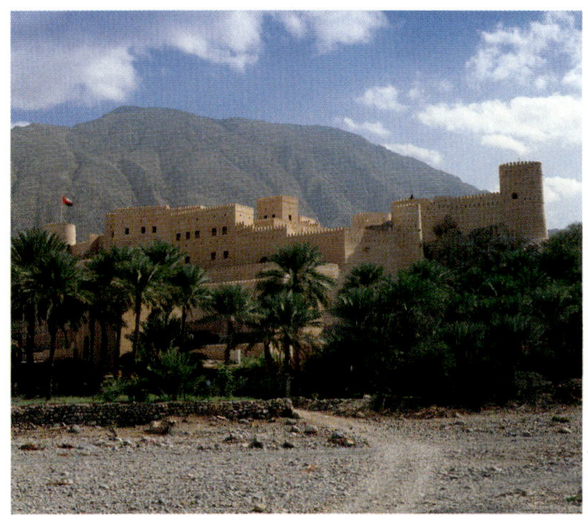

above
Many of Oman's historic forts, such as this example at Nakhl, have been restored by the Ministry of National Heritage and Culture, using natural materials and traditional construction methods. These historic buildings now welcome citizens and tourists within their walls.

Modern Omani architecture owes much to this fine heritage. The themes, shapes and colours of Oman's historic buildings are often reinterpreted in modern materials and functions. Buildings can be made both inexpensively and quickly: a simple structure is erected, made of reinforced concrete, which is then clad in custom-designed panels made in glass-reinforced concrete (GRC). Amiantit Oman is one of the companies specialising in this combination of art and technology, in which traditional designs are made in GRC – a substance which is made up of minute granules, and which can fit into the tiniest space in a mould, reproducing perfectly even the smallest design details. The product responds well to colouring, and a few brush-strokes in gold-leaf or whatever can add the finishing touches. Much the same technique, incidentally, is used by Amiantit to make the elegant and lifelike groups of animals which perch beside the main motorway into Muscat.

Traditional Omani homes were usually made of mud-bricks, with flat roofs for summer-sleeping, or for drying dates and limes. In areas where such basic building materials were unavailable (such as along the northern Batinah coast, or on the fringes of the great deserts), *barasti* houses were made, using the split trunks of the date-palm to construct a framework, and creating walls of palm fronds. Such buildings could be large and sophisticated in design, and were a perfect example of appropriate technology – not only were the building materials abundantly available, but the structures were cool, encouraging air-movement through the walls and thus taking full advantage of any breezes. Today, the craft of *barasti*-making has almost been lost, as cement-block houses with air-conditioning have replaced this traditional architecture. Crude *barastis* can still be seen in parts of Oman, where they continue to be used for animal byres.

Some of Oman's most distinctive architectural features are its carved wooden doors. These are found throughout the Sultanate, from the richest palace to the remotest village – though styles vary between north and south. Omani houses, both traditional and contemporary, are private family places, almost always set in a walled courtyard – access to which is through a wooden door (some modern houses have brightly painted and ornamented metal doors).

The most elaborate doors show superb craftsmanship, with verses from the Koran worked into finely chiselled geometric or floral patterns. A stroll around the old city of Muscat reveals an incredible variety of styles, ancient and modern. One famously beautiful door, in the Interior village of Mudayrib, bears an inscription saying that it was carved in Zanzibar, Oman's former East African colony. The massive door was brought by ship to Sur, then carried, in pieces, on donkey-back on a 150-kilometre journey inland – one elderly villager remembers his father describing the exhausting trip.

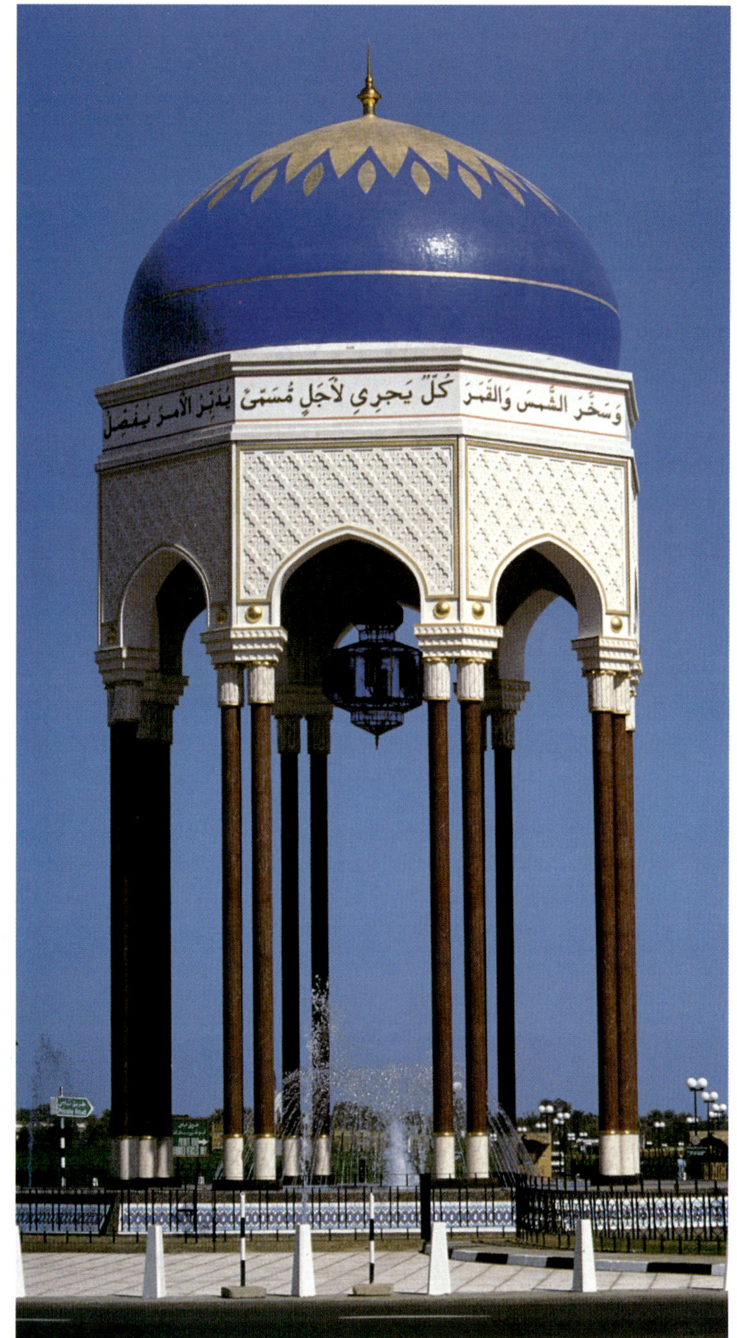

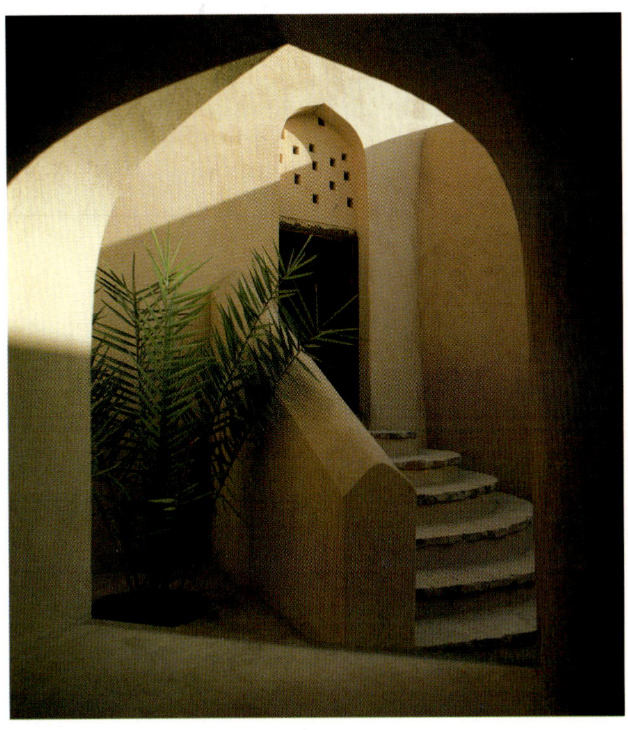

A few skilled Omani carpenters still ply their trade – though its future prospects look precarious. Nizwa, once a centre of wood-carving, has just one carpenter-craftsman left – a man following in the footsteps of his father and grandfather before him (though his own sons have chosen office jobs). It takes Mohammed about 24 days to carve a set of double doors – and he knows all the doors of old Nizwa like friends, describing the date of each, the wood of which it was made, and the carpenter who made it. Sur still has a thriving wood-carving business, with a number of workshops sending doors all over the Sultanate – and exporting a few to the United Arab Emirates.

above
Traditional architecture has been respected and restored faithfully within the walls of Nizwa fort, where light and shade play in the cool courtyards.

The People

Oman's people must be her greatest asset – and the changes in ways of life over the last twenty-five years have brought immeasurable benefits. For example, on the health front, where until recently fatal and crippling diseases were rife, there is now free health-care for all, with a network of hospitals and clinics, many equipped with state-of-the-art technology, throughout the land. The signs of this are everywhere – not least in the numbers of Omani children, for infant mortality, which in 1970 was running at a rate of 100 deaths per 1,000 births, has been reduced to fewer than 30. Furthermore, the medical school at Sultan Qaboos University is now training the cream of Omani students to become doctors – the first group, of 44 men and women students, graduated in 1993, after a six-year training.

left
Oman is a country in which expression of art is integrated into the very landscape and it boasts many monuments which are not only decorative, but symbolise the centuries past. This one, at Bait al Barakah, is a wonderful illustration of modern-day Islamic art.

Similarly, in the priority field of education, the Sultanate has leaped forward, offering free and compulsory education for all children – and again, with Omani teachers now replacing the expatriates who once staffed the schools. In 1970 there were just three schools in the whole country – the present-day school system has 478,000 students, with equal educational opportunities for both boys and girls.

New departments continue to open at Sultan Qaboos University – the College of Commerce has recently opened its doors to students, and there are soon to be degree courses in archaeology and environmental sciences. The University's 1994 intake was its highest ever, with 1,300 new students arriving to take up their courses. Vocational training is also a priority, with a strong national desire to train Omanis in all areas of work. Regional Vocational Training Centres have been established throughout the country, offering a wide range of courses.

Perhaps one of the greatest delights of Oman is that, despite such great progress, certain qualities are cherished and unchanging – the warmth and hospitality of her people, the friendliness to strangers, the animation and generosity.

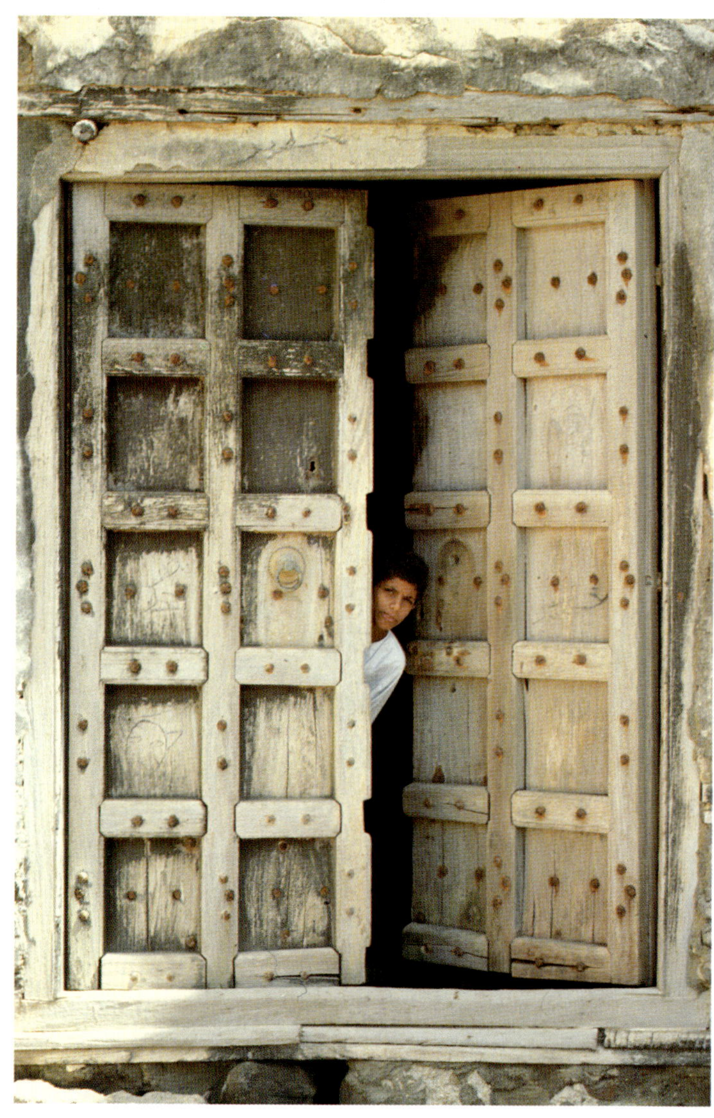

above
Doors have always held pride of place in dwellings, large and small, across the Sultanate. Being considered an art-form, the craft has been handed down the years from generation to generation. This door to an old merchant's house in Mirbat is in a style characteristic to the region of Dhofar.

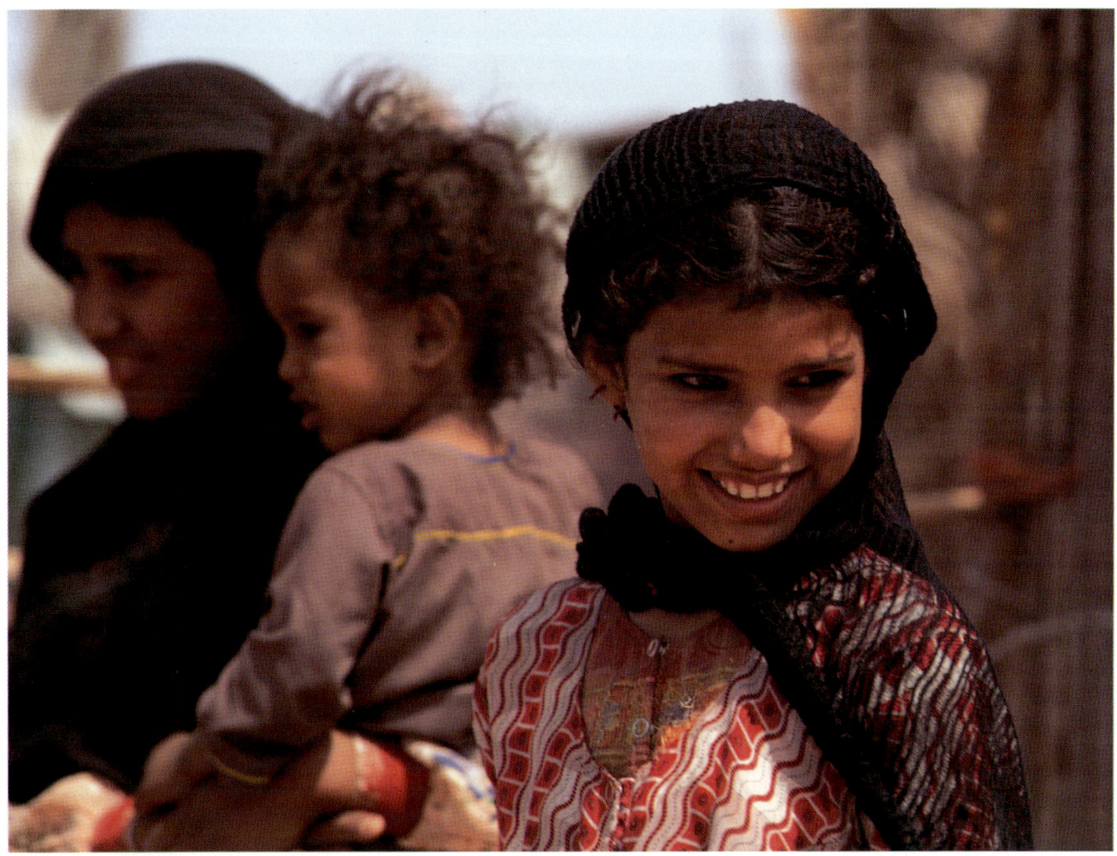

above
Today, the younger generation of Omanis is assured of a certain standard of living, education and employment opportunities.

In years to come, when an objective history of the Arab world in the late twentieth century is written, there will be no portrait more vivid than that of the Sultanate of Oman. In twenty-five short years Oman has emerged from virtual feudalism into one of the most enlightened and prosperous countries in the Middle East. International obscurity and economic insecurity have made way for a dynamic nation, with a proud reputation for international diplomacy, and for its vision, which has resulted in the best of the new combining with the best of the old ways of life. If so much has been achieved in the first twenty-five years, what will the next twenty-five bring?

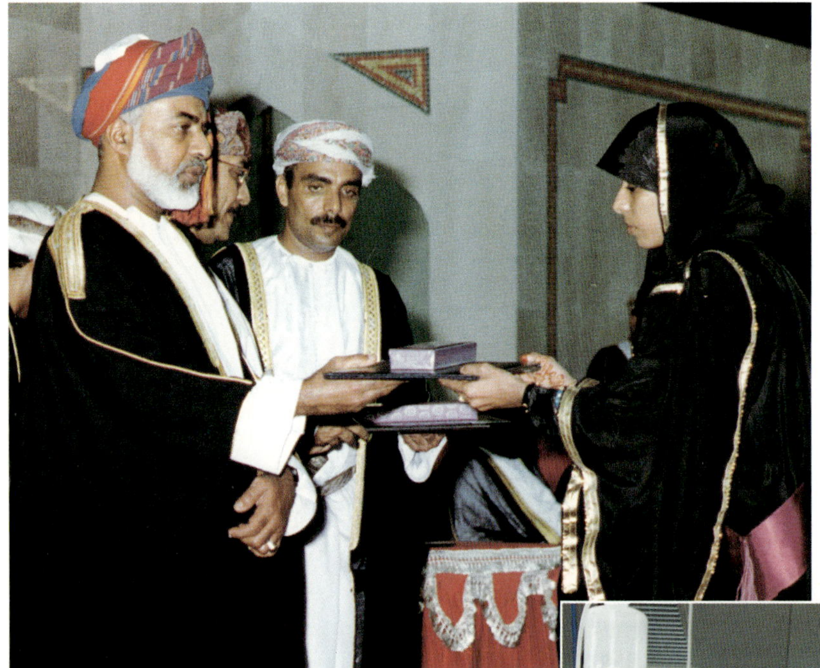

above

Since its inception, Sultan Qaboos University has been the proud Alma Mater of thousands of Omani graduates. Here, His Majesty Sultan Qaboos presides at the graduation ceremony of another graduate ready to step into the working world.

right

No expense and effort have been spared in providing the best facilities and teachers for the students at Sultan Qaboos University. Here, students are concentrating on making best use of the facilities available in the laboratory.

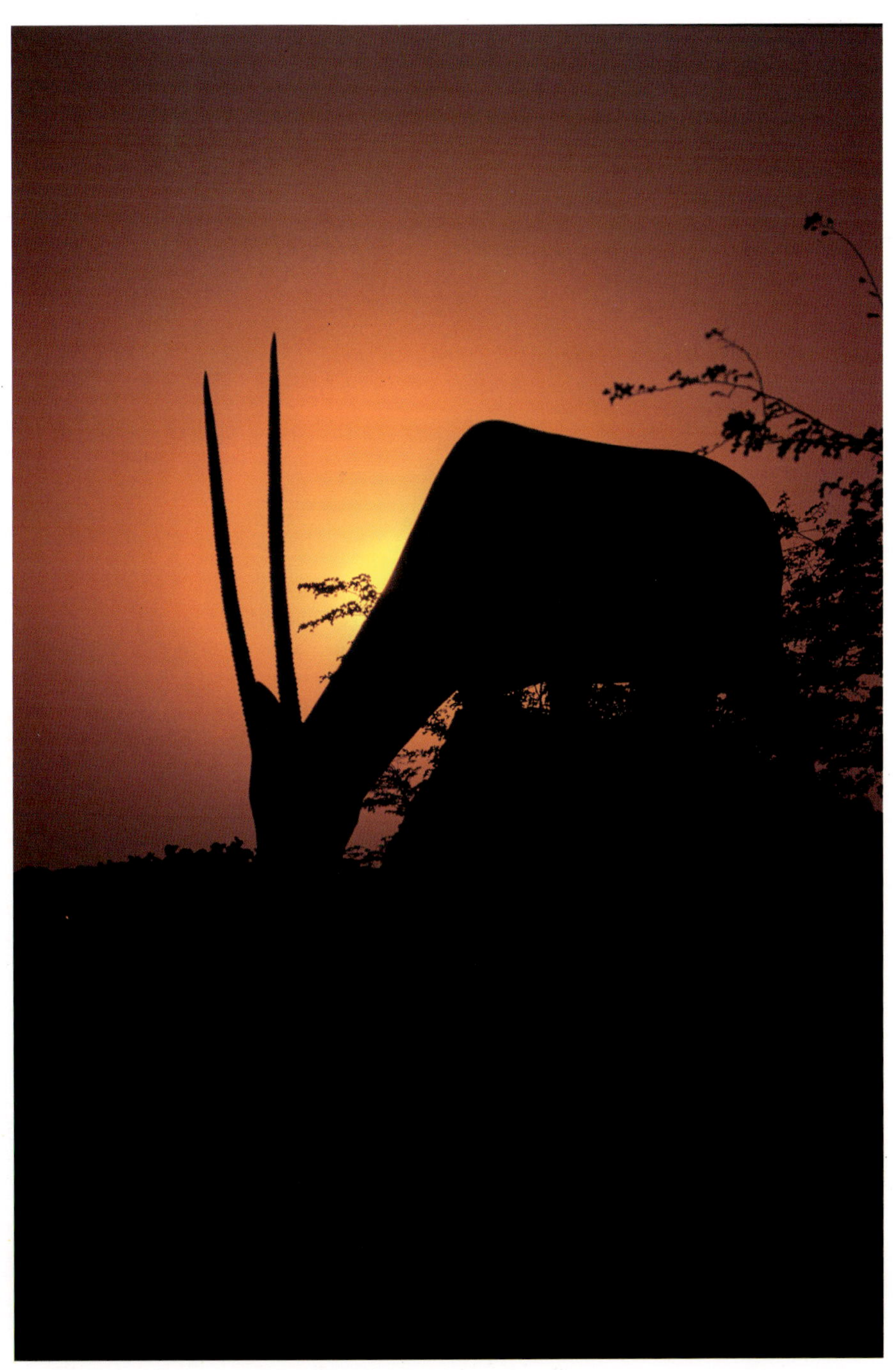

right
Every sunset in Oman is a panoramic picture in glorious Technicolour.

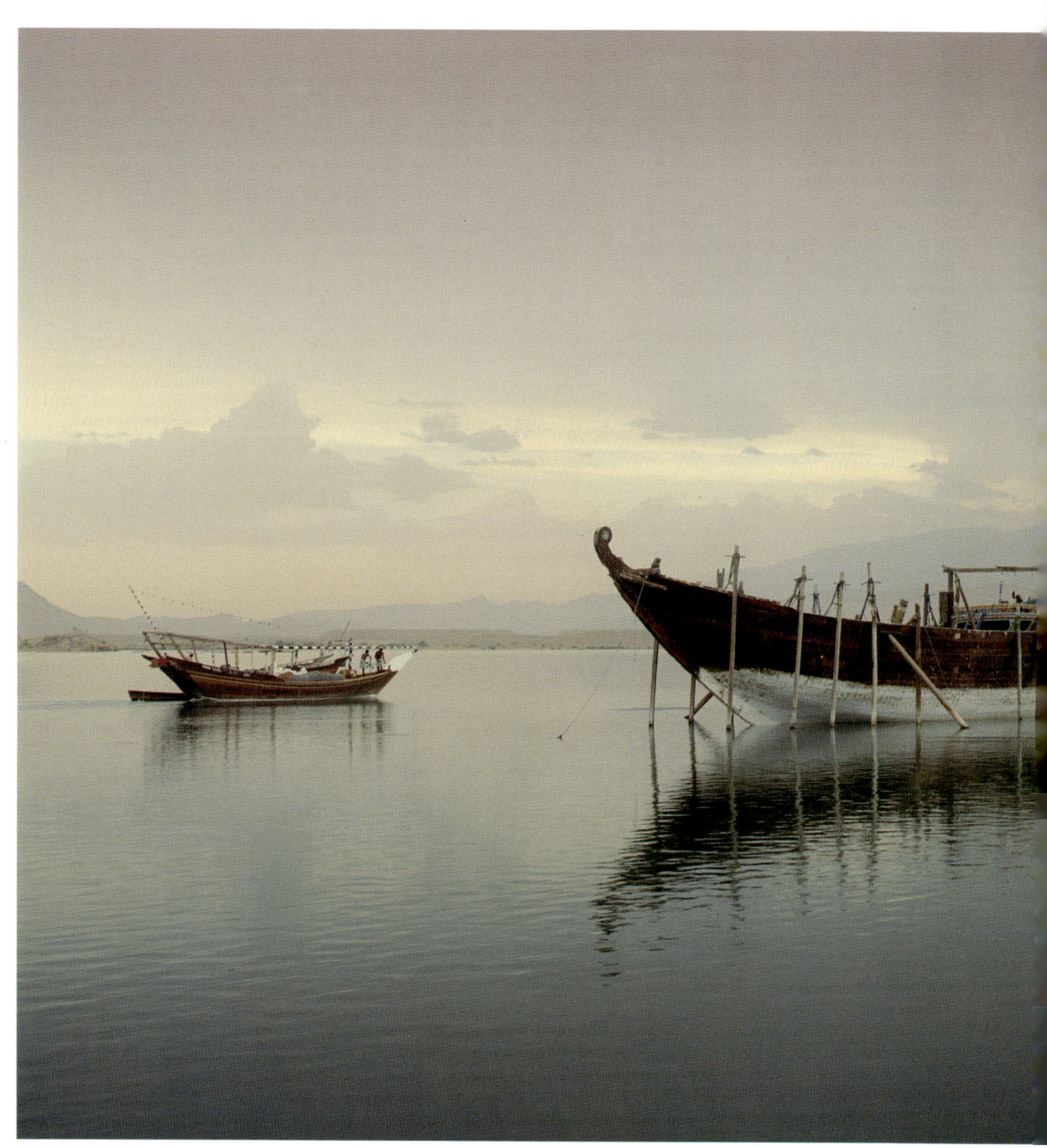

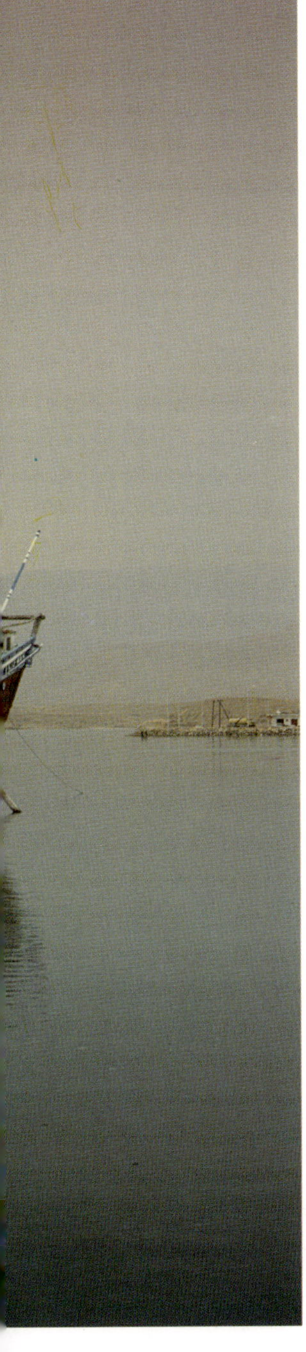

left
In a seafaring nation, the role played by traditional dhows cannot be overestimated. The dhow shown here belongs to Suhail and Saud Bahwan, one of Oman's oldest seafaring families.

Oman's Cultural Heritage

One fascination of Oman's rich cultural heritage lies in the juxtaposition of timelessness and modernity. Chic new shopping malls mushroom in the Capital Area – while traditional souqs continue to flourish. Coppersmiths and sandal-makers sit cross-legged, continuing the trade of their fathers and grandfathers before them, and traditional products are sold, from Omani *halwa* (a delicately flavoured sweet of jelly-like consistency) to silver *khanjars* (the curved silver dagger, still today a sign of manhood and status).

This very juxtaposition is not new, but arises from Oman's geography. Throughout history, there has been a contrast between the coastal areas, whose seafarers voyaged throughout the known world, and whose ports were in turn visited by foreigners from afar, bringing new ideas and ways of life, and the remote Interior regions, where life changed little from generation to generation. Here, goats are still herded, dates and limes still grown, irrigated, harvested, dried and stored much as they always have been. Women still carry home the family's water in pots, elegantly balanced on their heads – and sit together in a shady spot, grinding spices with a pestle and mortar, chatting, while small children play. Extended families often live under the same roof, with grandmothers playing a large part in bringing up the children.

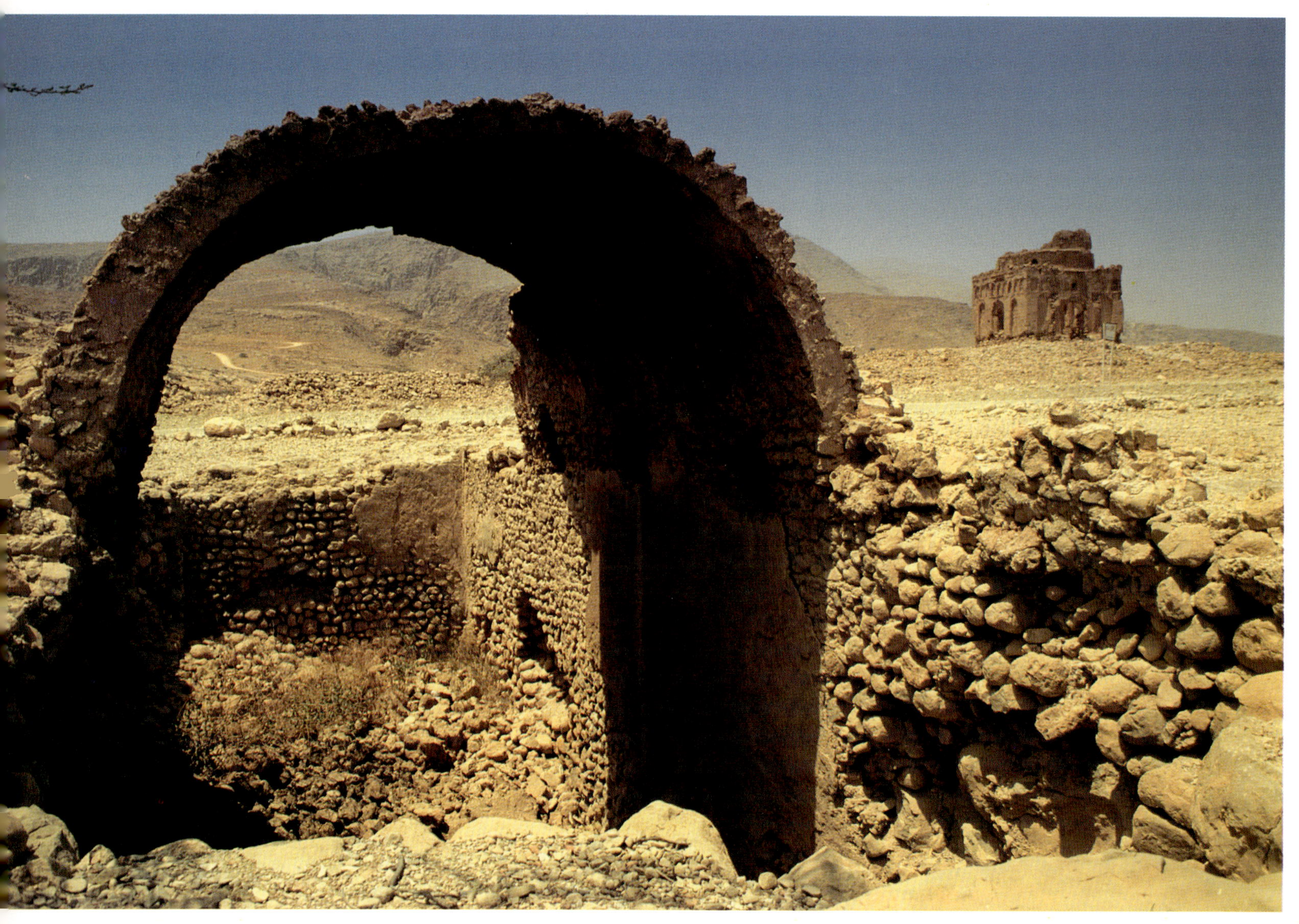

above

This stone archway that stands near Bibi Maryam's mausoleum is a dramatic gateway into a legendary past. The mausoleum's warm tones of fossilised coral and intricate plasterwork are a haunting reminder of Oman's ancient civilisation.

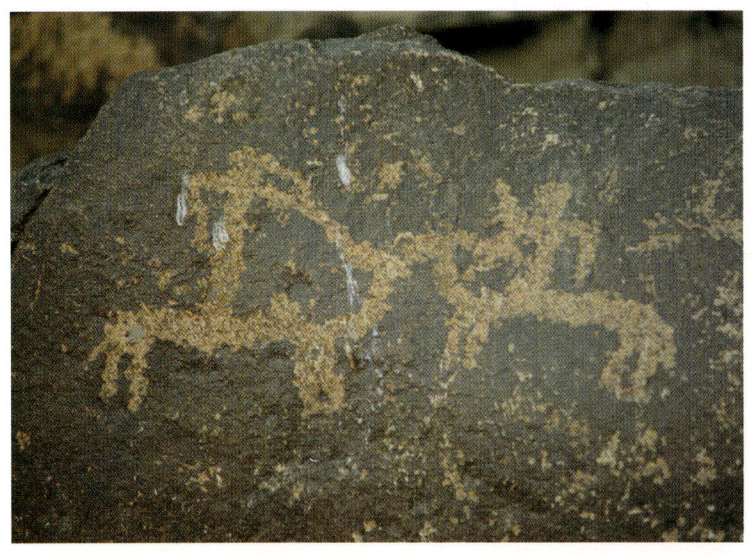

above
Ancient rock drawings have been found at many locations in Oman. These men on horseback are thought to be 1,500 years old.

Oman's ancient history and ways of life are still largely a matter of conjecture. Rock drawings, some of which are probably over 1,500 years old, give tantalising indications, with their depictions of warriors, some riding horses or camels, and bearing swords, shields, axes, bows and arrows. Some are clearly more recent, depicting guns – and even vehicles. But the cultures which produced the most ancient rock art are still largely unknown to archaeologists.

Oman's military history of the last 500 years is better documented, not least in the form of massive forts, which dominate many Interior and coastal towns and villages – and the hundreds of watch-towers, many seeming to grow straight up from sheer rock faces, which perch on crags and promontories throughout northern Oman. For example, on the strategically important route through Wadi Sumayil, which leads from the coastal plain to the Interior, through the otherwise almost impenetrable Al Hajar mountains, forts and watch-towers dominate the wadi, preventing the infiltration of an unseen enemy.

This military architecture, finely wrought in mud-brick (and in many cases, meticulously restored and renovated by Oman's Ministry of National Heritage and Culture) also had a profound effect on domestic architecture in Oman – features such as crenellated walls, walled courtyards and strong outer gates are all typical of Omani houses, old and new, with decorative elements tending to take second place to solid, defendable structures.

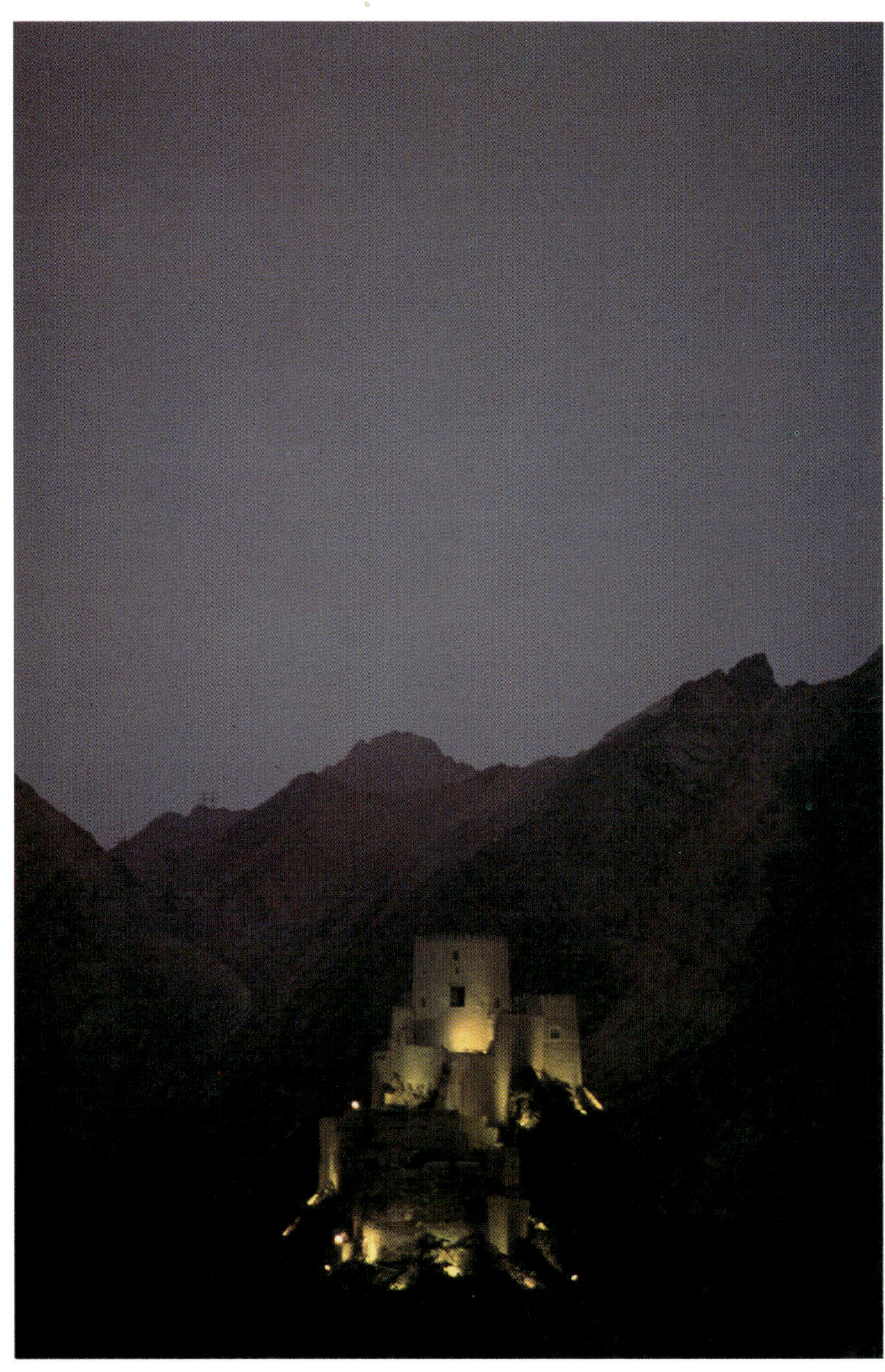

left
Standing guard over Mutrah harbour, the Mutrah fort seen here at dusk comes alive with twinkling lights, giving it an almost fairy-tale air.

below
Intricate handicrafts have earned pride of place in Omani homes. These examples of woodwork, silver and copperware and weaving are much sought after by visitors to Oman.

In Muscat and Mutrah, there are a number of examples of more delicate architecture – perhaps the most famous being the white-painted houses with carved wooden balconies and lattice-work which adorn the Corniche. Their age and history is uncertain – they are one of the happy results of the mingling of styles and cultures in a port whose deep natural harbour supported a rich maritime trade. Here too, and in nearby Muscat, can be seen fine examples of decorative plasterwork, often above windows, and finely carved wooden screens, both of which features kept a room cool and airy, while also maintaining privacy.

Traditional Dhofari houses used similar wooden or plasterwork screens, though

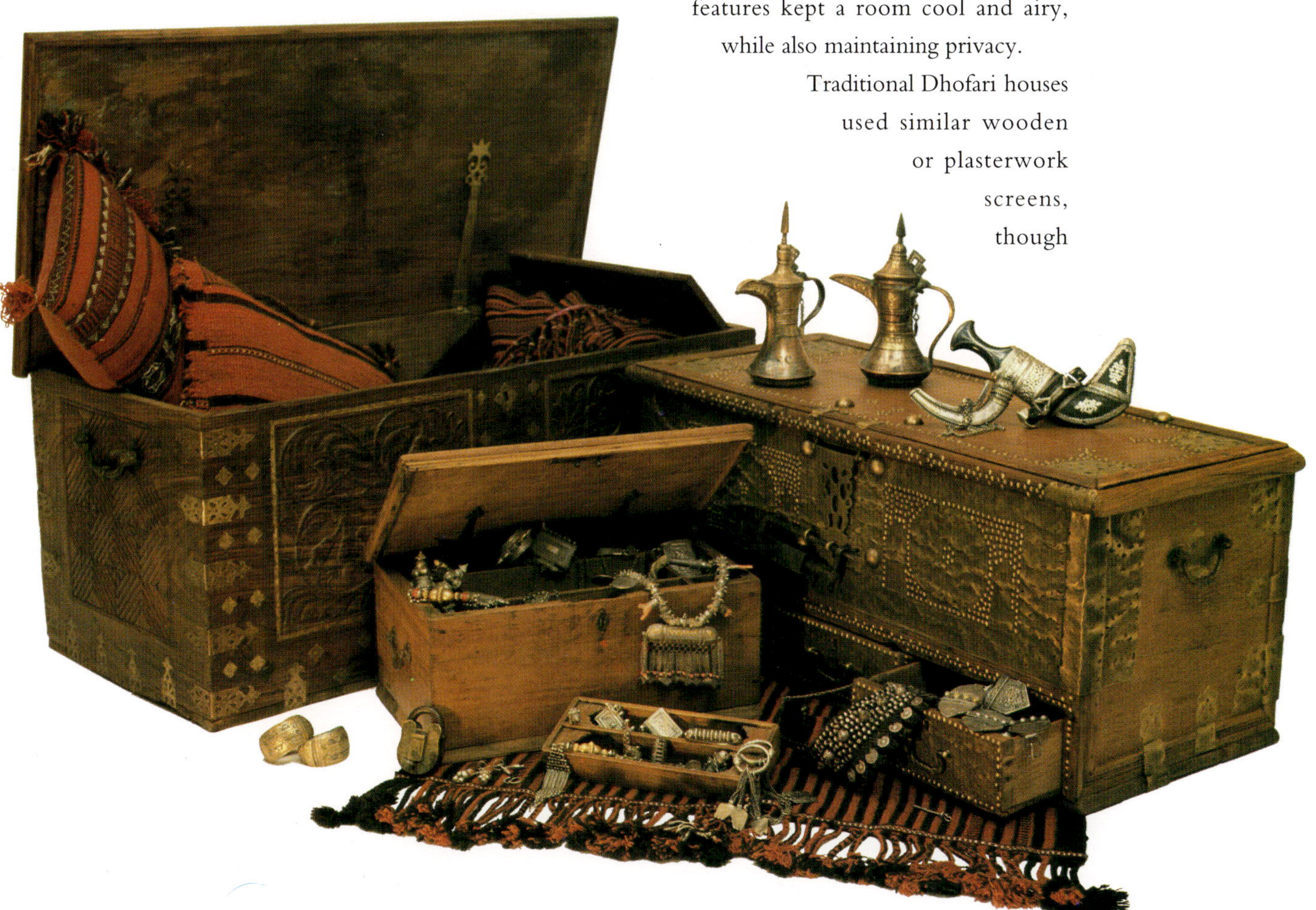

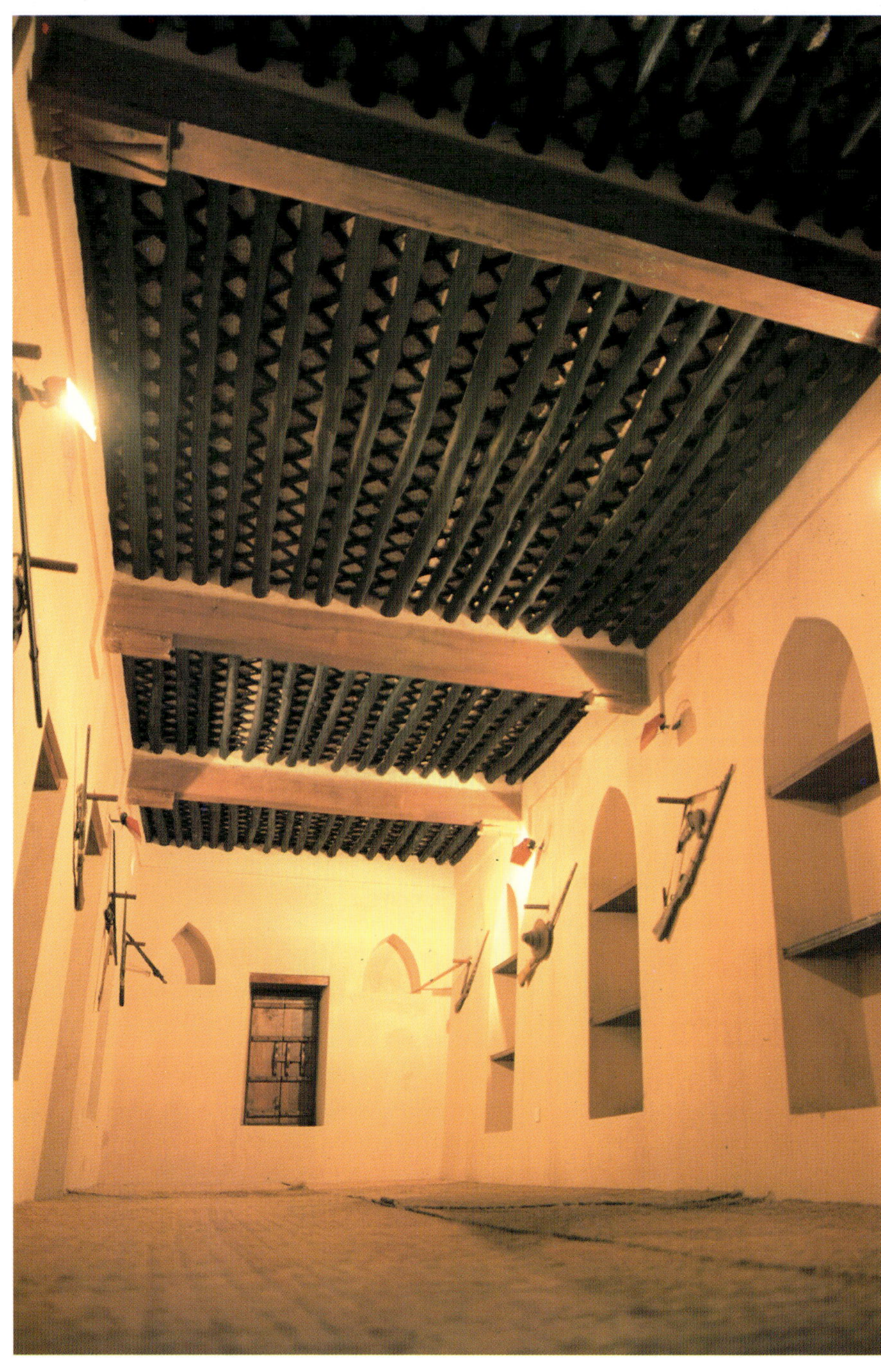

left
Forts were built on a grand scale, as the number of beams supporting this ceiling demonstrates.

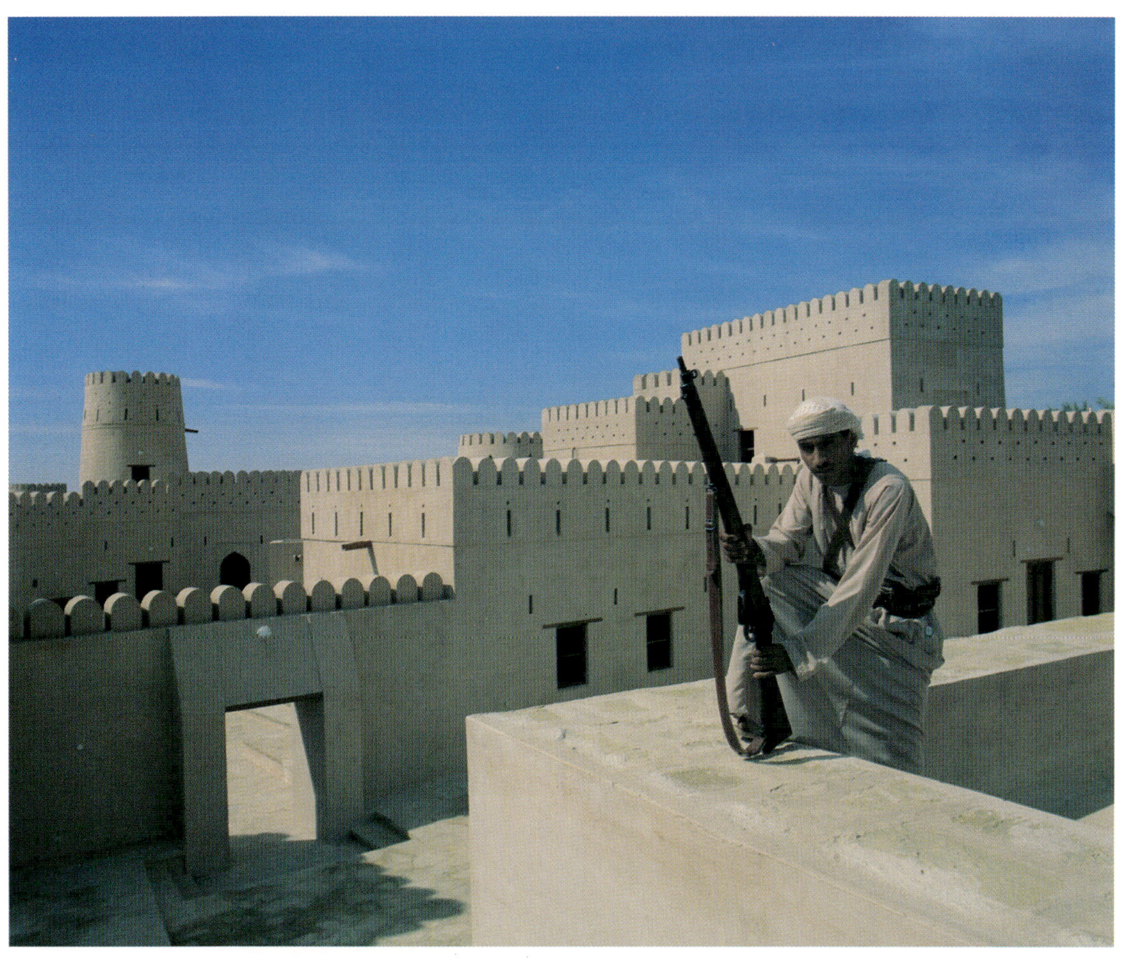

above
Living history – today, this armed guard at the Ja'alan Bilad Bani Bu Hassan fort adds to the local colour and takes visitors on guided tours as well.

in general the houses, especially the grander ones, are different from those of northern Oman. They tended to be two or three storeys high – the port of Mirbat has some fine examples of merchants' houses, evidence of the town's past prosperity. Fine plasterwork of a different kind is found, for example in the fishing village of Sadh, about 120 kilometres east of Salalah. Here, the exterior walls of some houses display, in raised plasterwork, different kinds of traditional ships – doubtless representing the source of the householders' wealth.

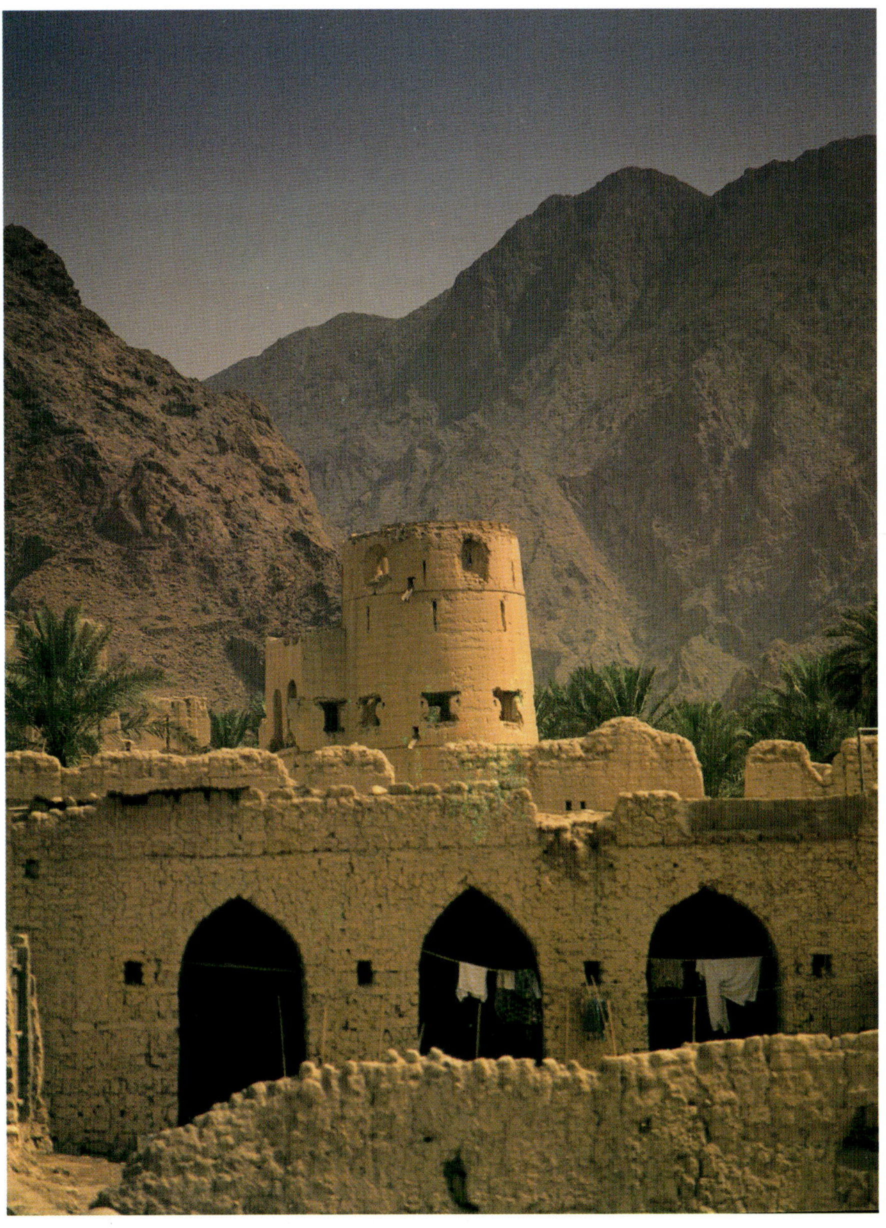

left
Forts are an intrinsic part of the landscape. They come in a variety of shapes and sizes – built with one purpose: to guard against marauding forces. Today these forts, including this one at Baushar, are of historical and architectural interest.

Fishing and trading feature large in Oman's past and present. Also in Sadh is evidence of a much sought-after delicacy which is fished in Oman's southern waters: abalone.

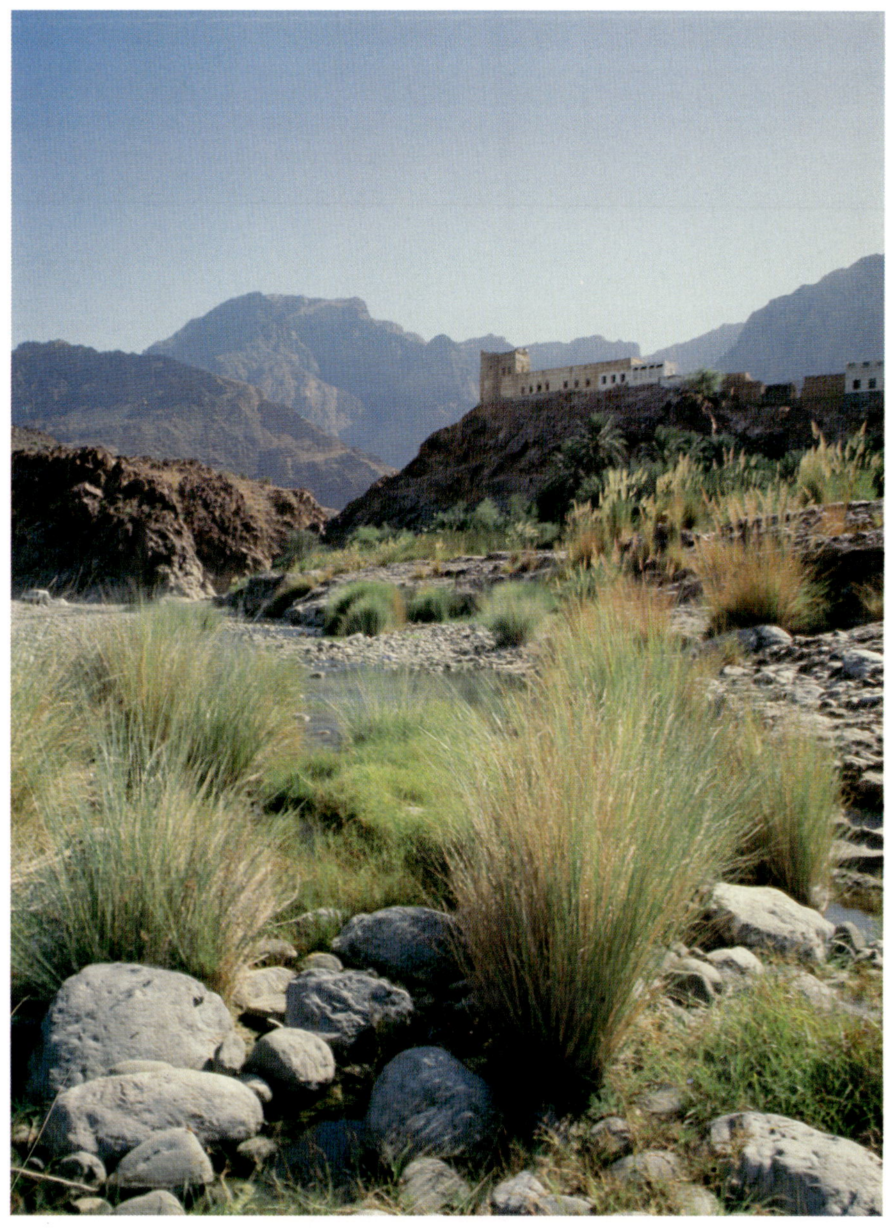

right
A scenic beauty spot which attracts visitors in droves, Mazara in Wadi Dayqah, is the ideal locale for a day out. Flourishes of green reeds and yellow gorse line a sparking stream that provides a cool and pleasant resting-spot for picnickers.

The beautiful nacreous shells are irresistible to visitors – and the fish command high prices in Far Eastern markets. Abalone fishing takes place after the monsoon, between October and

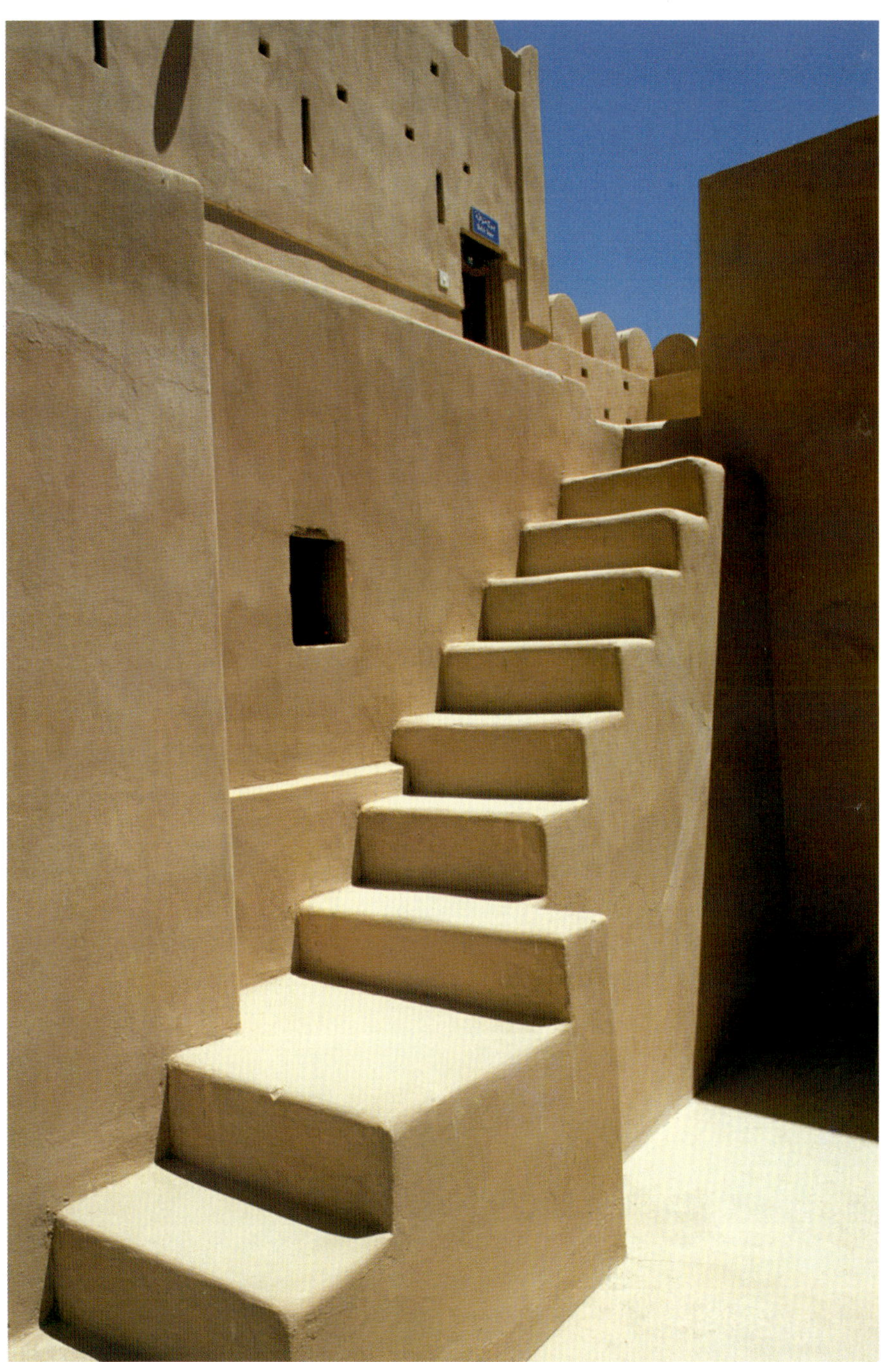

left
Many of Oman's forts have been restored over the past 25 years using traditional materials and methods. These stairs at Fort Sinesilas, which overlooks the coastal town of Sur, lead to the upper level where the tower-rooms catch the sea breezes.

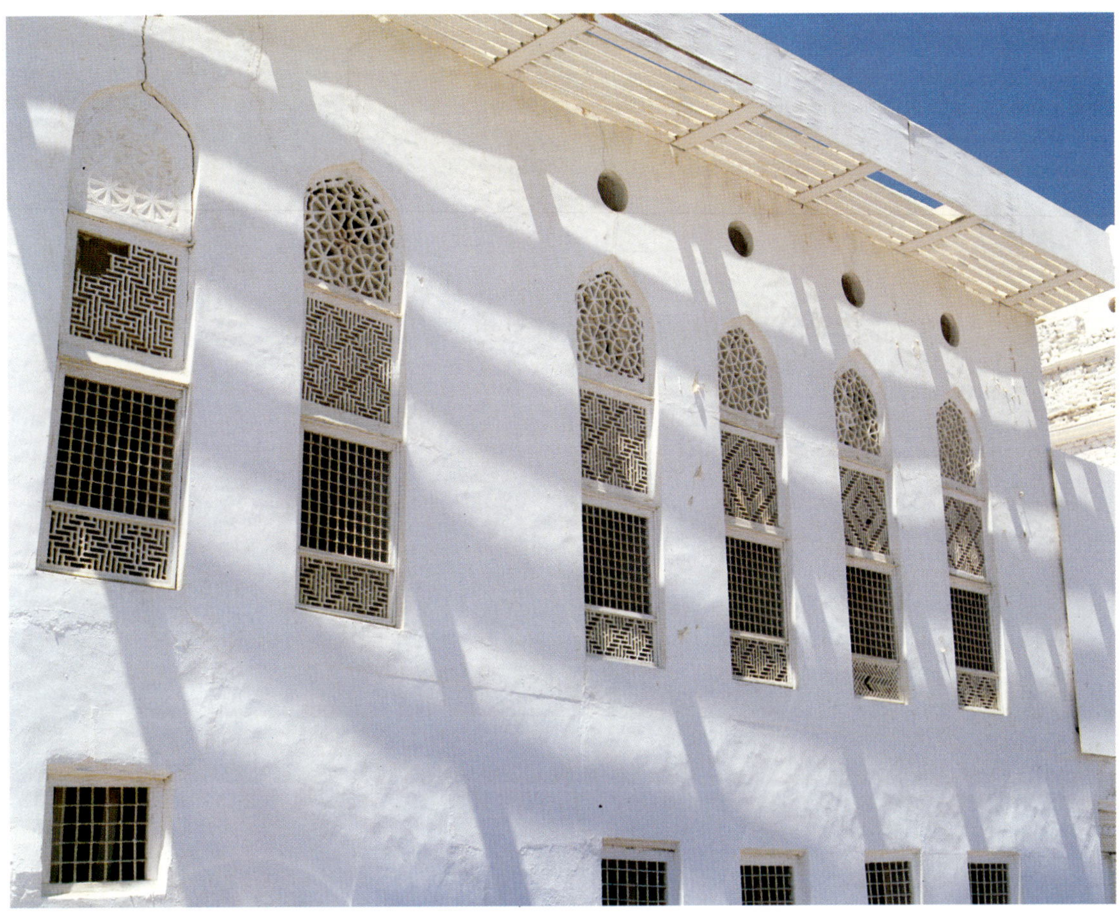

above
Local architecture is characterised by a variety of features, the most obvious being the windows which adorn people's homes. These arched windows with fretwork are typical of old buildings in the Muscat area.

March. Fishermen dive to a depth of ten metres, assisted only by a face-mask and perhaps fins. Groups of up to ten men search the sea-bed for abalone-encrusted boulders and deftly prise off the shell using a knife, before coming up for air with their catch. A good diver could collect up to 300 abalone each day, bringing short-term profitability but longer-term depletion of stocks. In recent years, the Omani government – mindful of conservation of precious natural resources – imposed a temporary ban on abalone fishing, in order to build up the over-fished stocks. Meanwhile, scientists at Sultan Qaboos University and the Marine Science and Fisheries

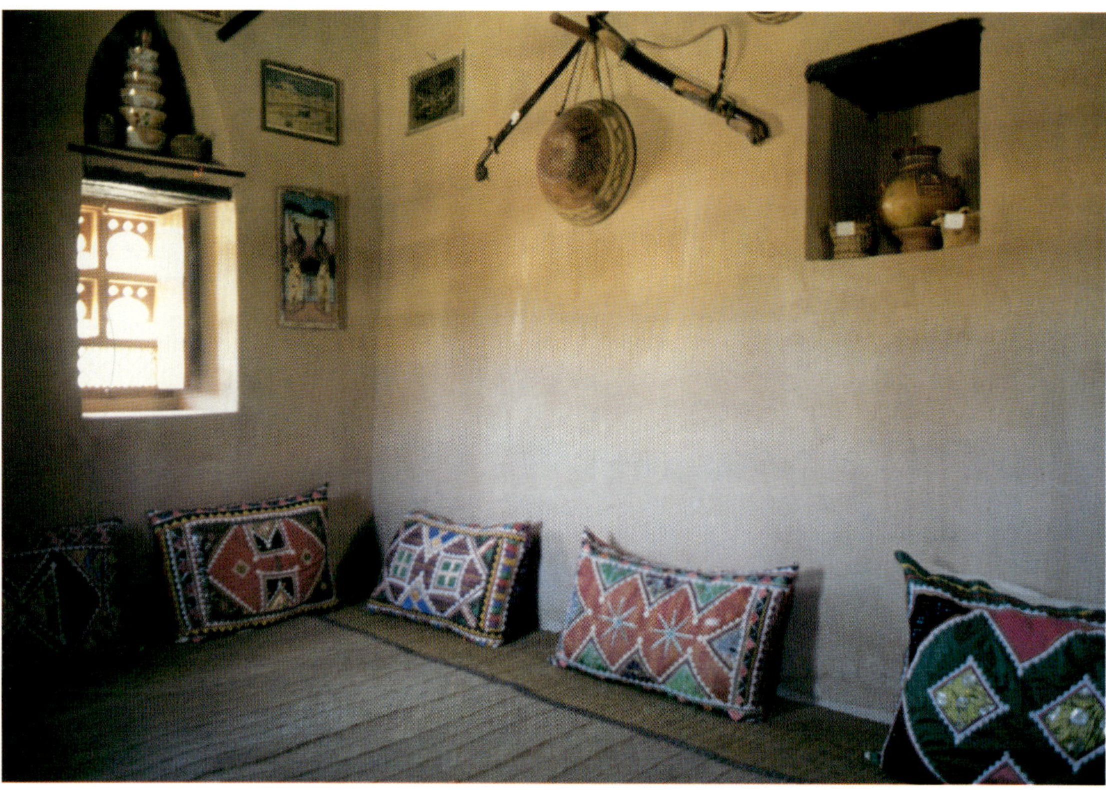

above
Omani homes were not known for being over-crowded by furniture. Omanis used to do their socialising and conduct business sitting on mats with huge cushions to lean on.

Center near Muscat are looking into the possibilities of sea-farms for abalone, which would both protect and conserve the species, along with the lifestyles and livelihoods of the fishermen.

Agriculture too continues to provide a livelihood for many Omanis, both along the Batinah coast and in the Interior. Even in remote and, at first sight, hostile parts of the country, such as the precipitous cliffs of Jebel Akhdar, splashes of bright green are evidence of the triumph of man's ingenuity and hard work. Terraced fields cling to these mountain-sides – while *afalaj* wind their way along the contours in an astonishing feat of construction. The altitude here results in a cooler climate than in much of Oman – even snow is not unheard-of – so a wider variety of crops is grown,

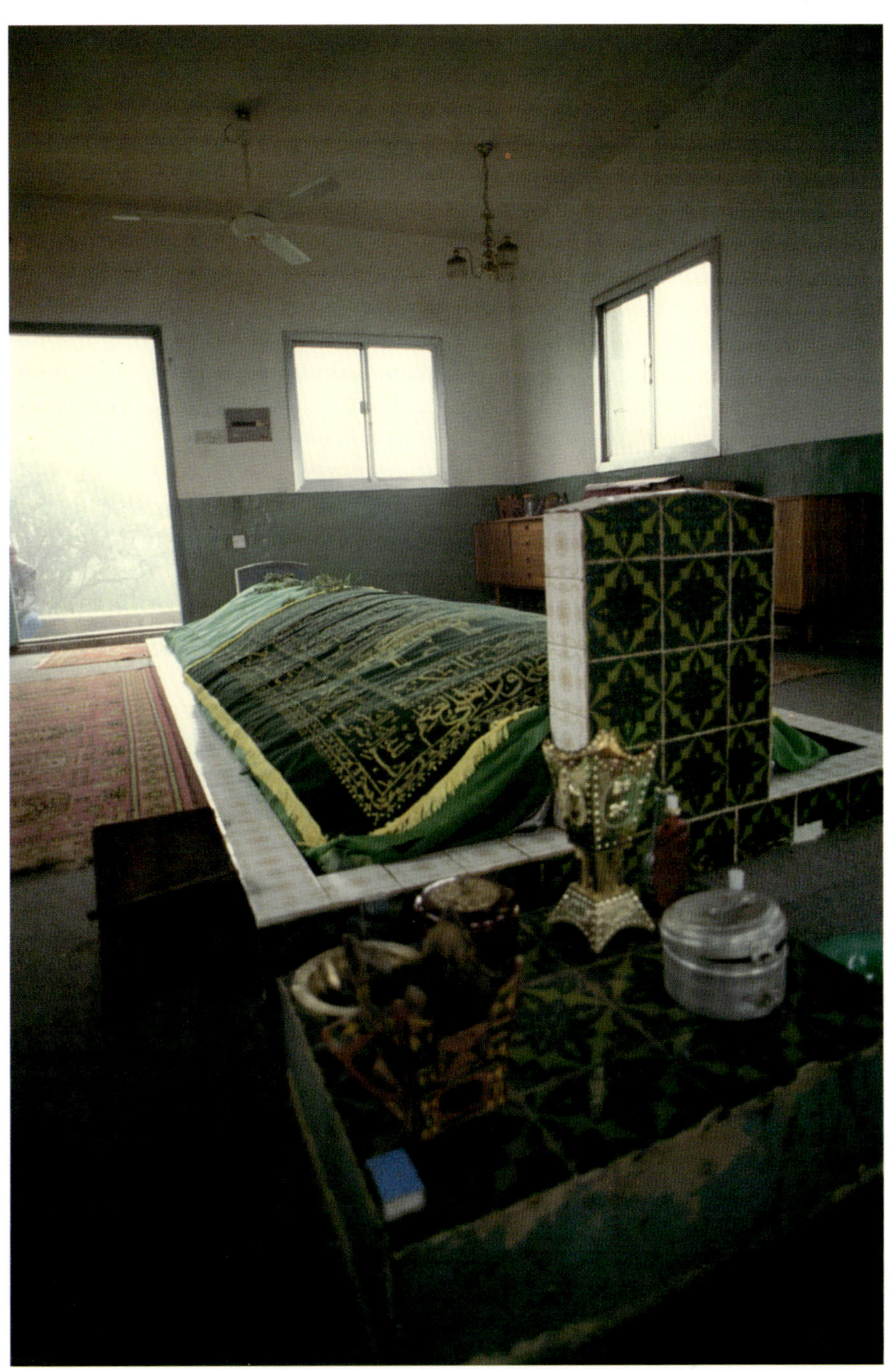

right
In the mist-laden hills above Salalah, near the village of Ittin, lie the remains of Nabi Ayoub – the prophet Job. His tomb and the carefully tended mosque alongside attract visitors from all over the Gulf and beyond.

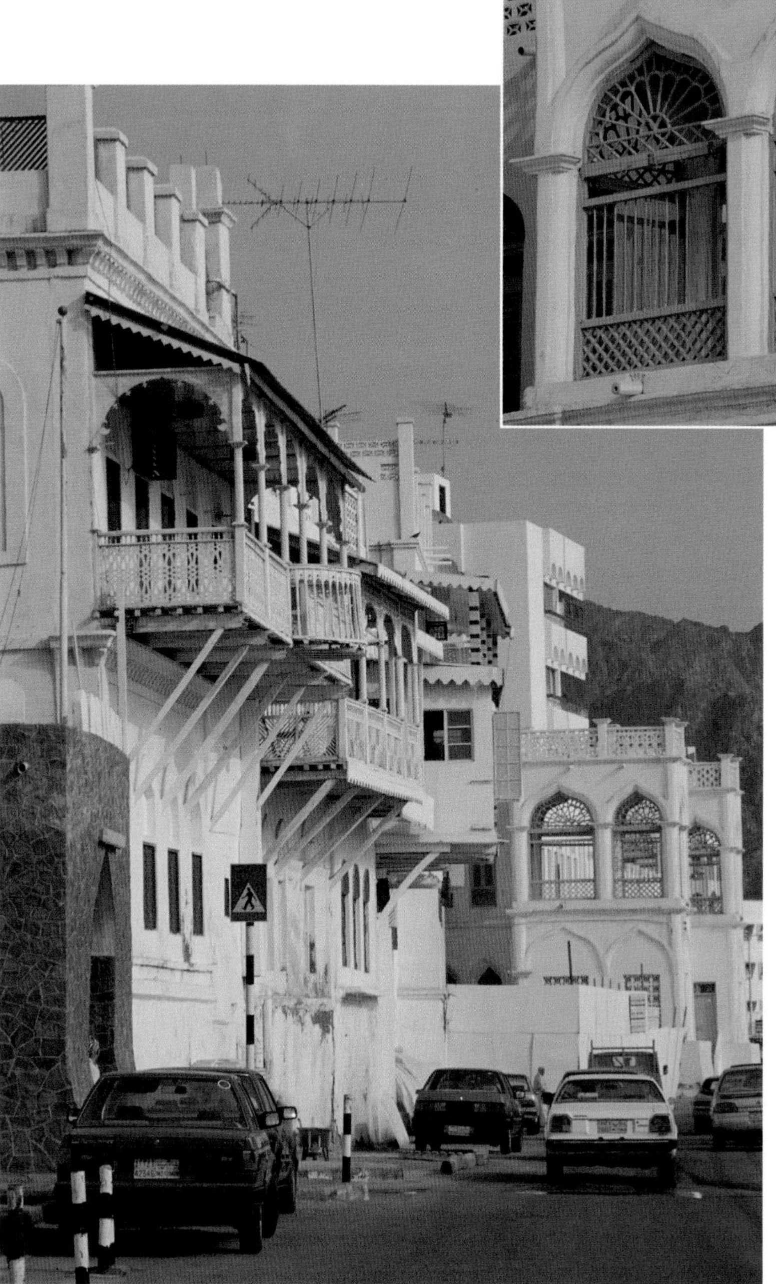

left and above
In a hot country windows play a vital role in allowing air to circulate. Naturally, builders went to some trouble decorating them, such as these which still grace the Corniche at Mutrah.

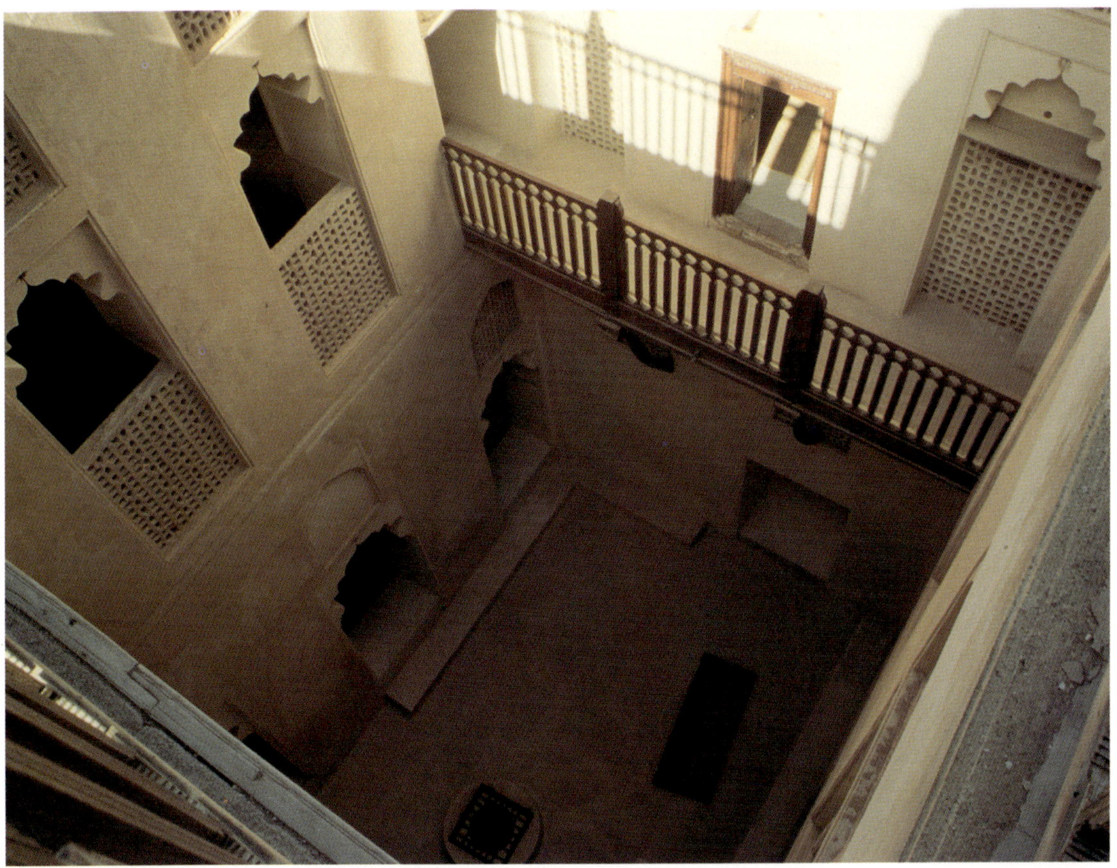

above
Most Omani homes and forts are built with courtyards. While they were used as meeting points for family and friends, they also served as ventilation shafts, as does this interior courtyard.

including walnuts, almonds, pomegranates and, perhaps most surprising of all, roses. These are harvested and brought home where a traditional (and highly successful) cottage industry has gone on for longer than anyone can remember, distilling the petals to make rose-water.

The pictures which follow give some indication of the richness of Oman's historical and cultural heritage. They may perhaps whet the appetite – for there are many more riches to be discovered there.

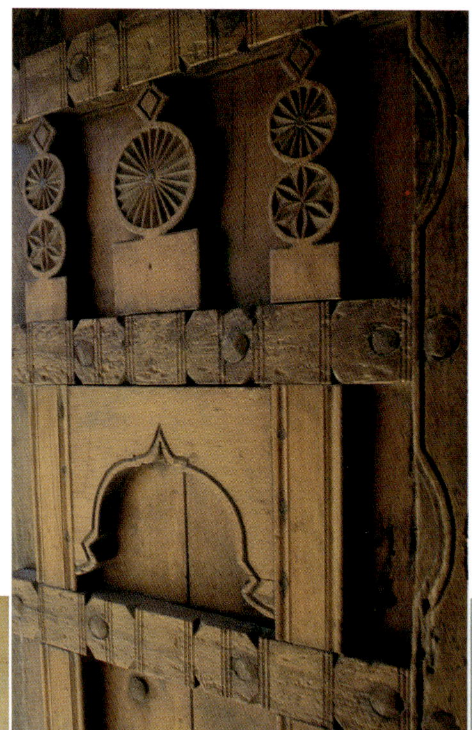

Much imagination has gone into the making of doors in Oman, whether they are modern metal painted with colourful motifs, as near Rustaq (**below**), or are intricate woodwork as in the door of the Sadh fort in Dhofar (**left**).

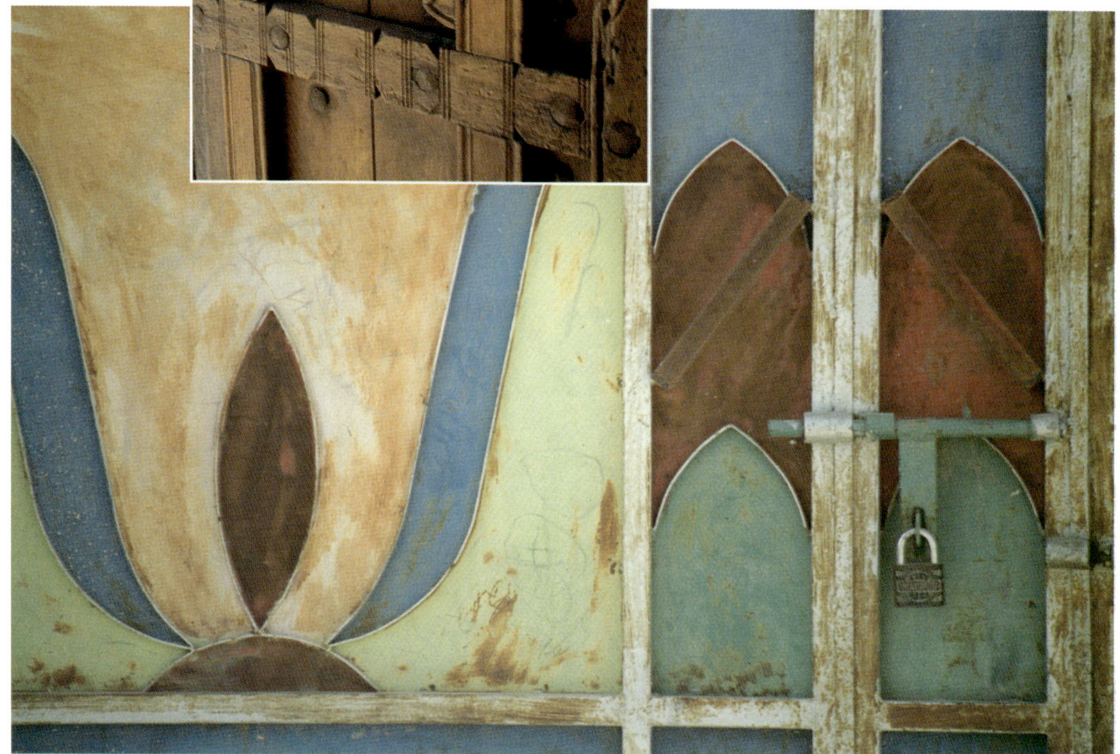

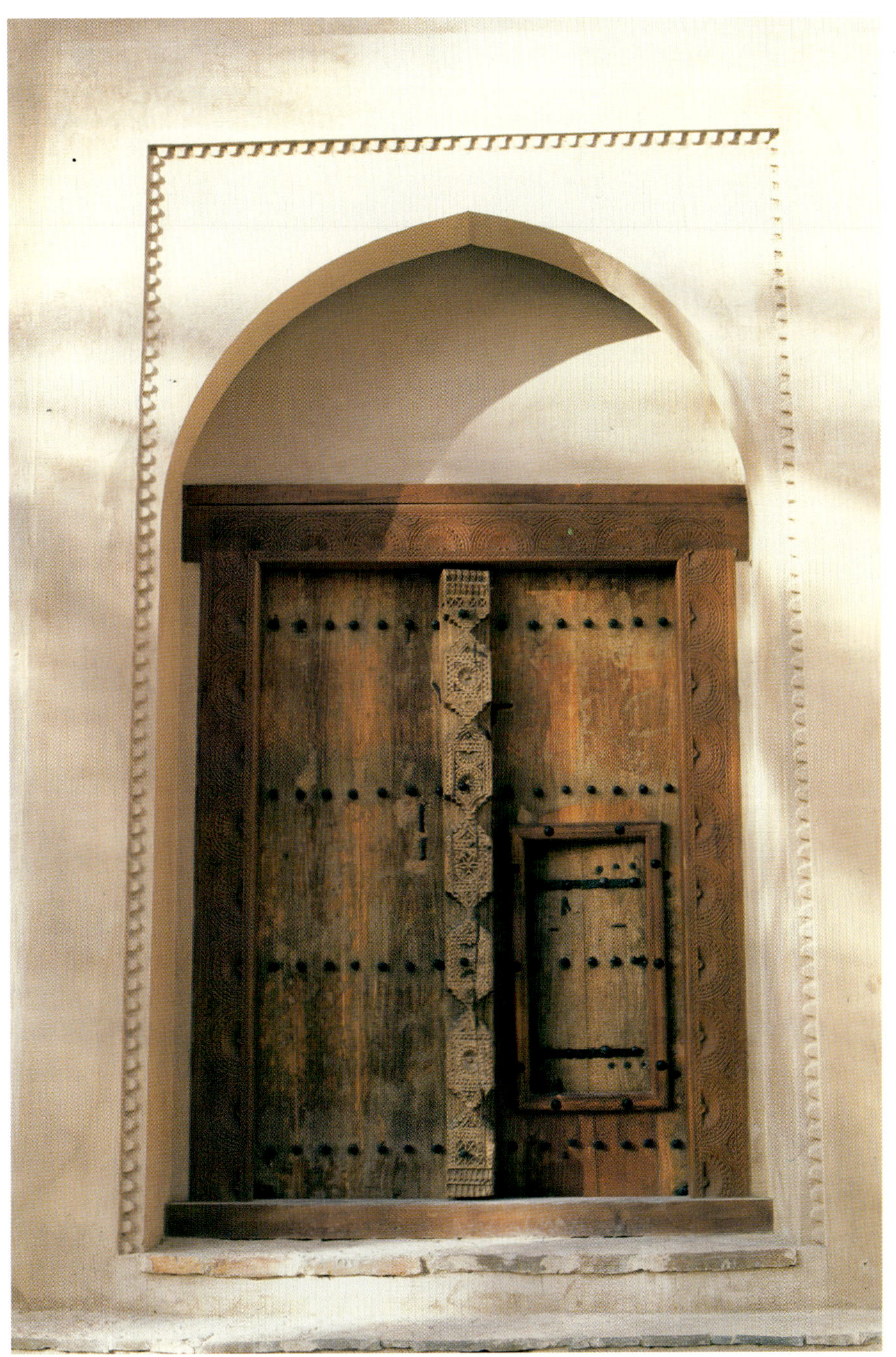

right
Omani doors come in all shapes and sizes – and range from the simple to the most intricately carved. This one at Nizwa fort leads into the main block and is typical in having a smaller inset door for daily use.

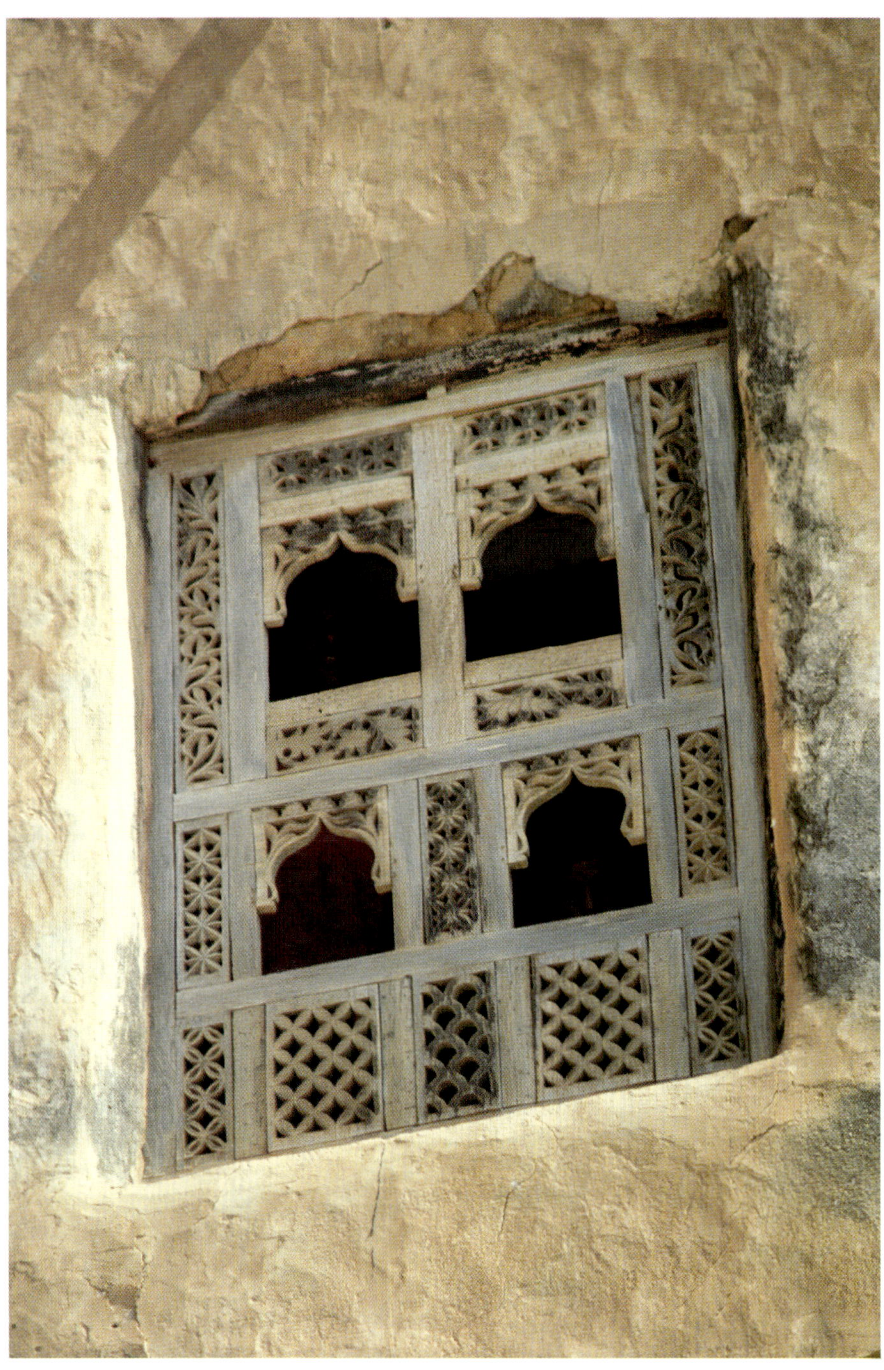

left
This window in Mirbat, like many others, is a striking example of the carver's art.

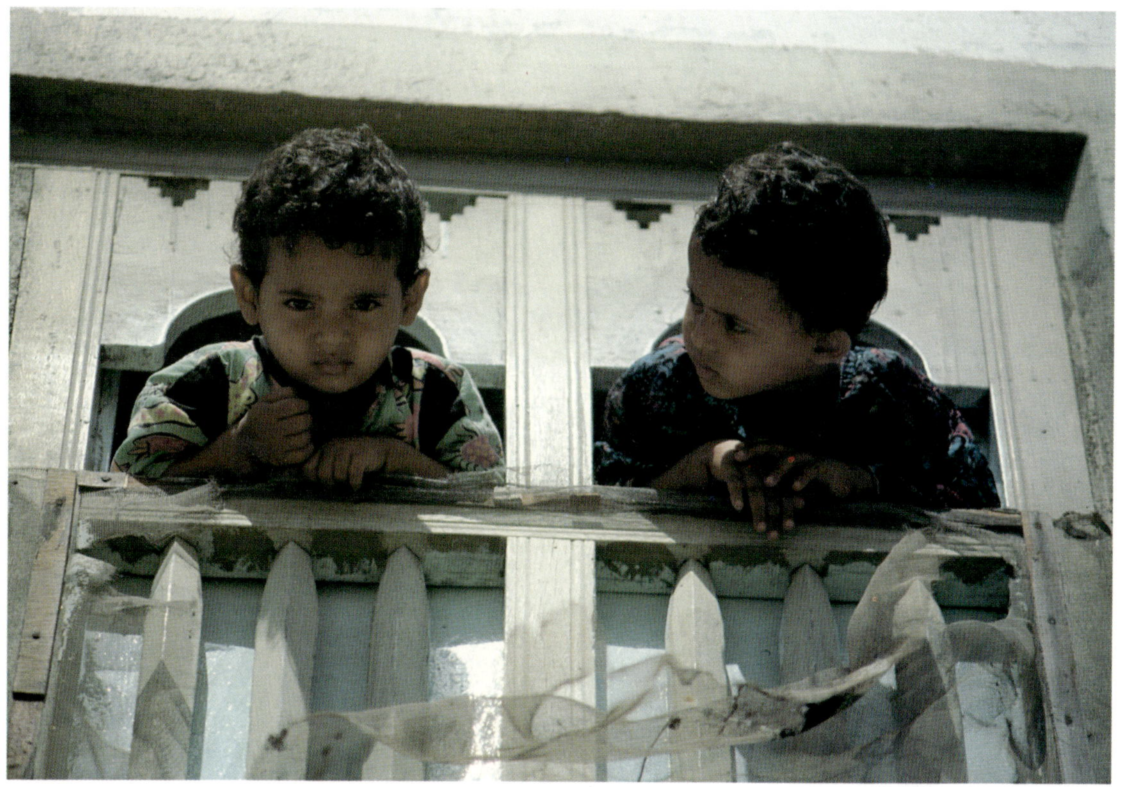

above
Leaning out of a window in Mirbat, these children can look forward to free education and a bright future.

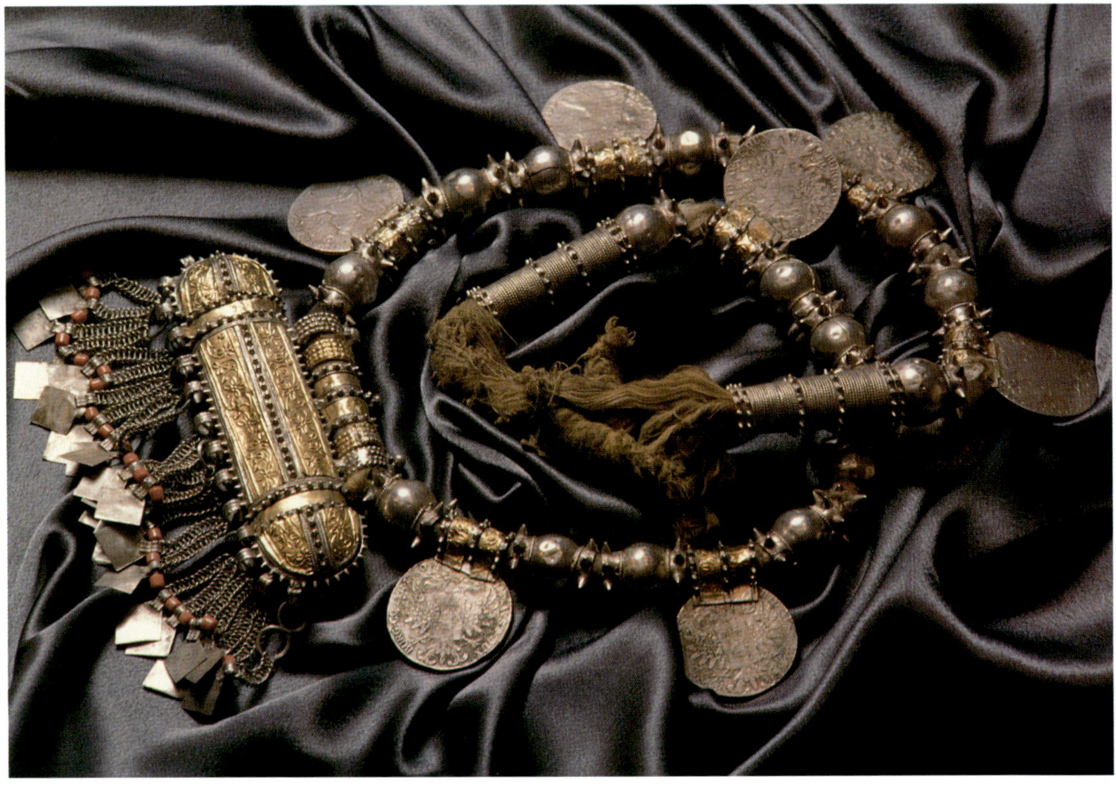

above

Oman is famed for its silver jewellery: necklaces such as this one were worn with great flair by Omani women, and are now much sought after by visitors.

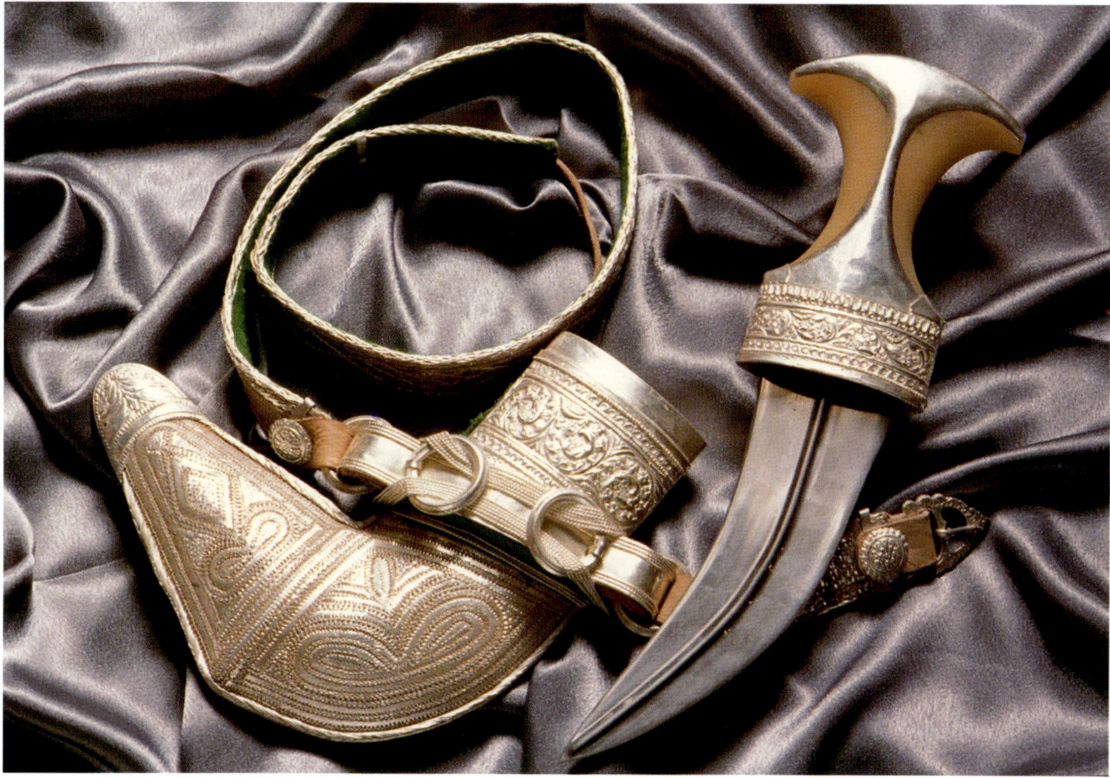

above

An ornately carved silver *khanjar* – these are worn on every ceremonial occasion. The more intricate they are, the higher the social standing of the wearer.

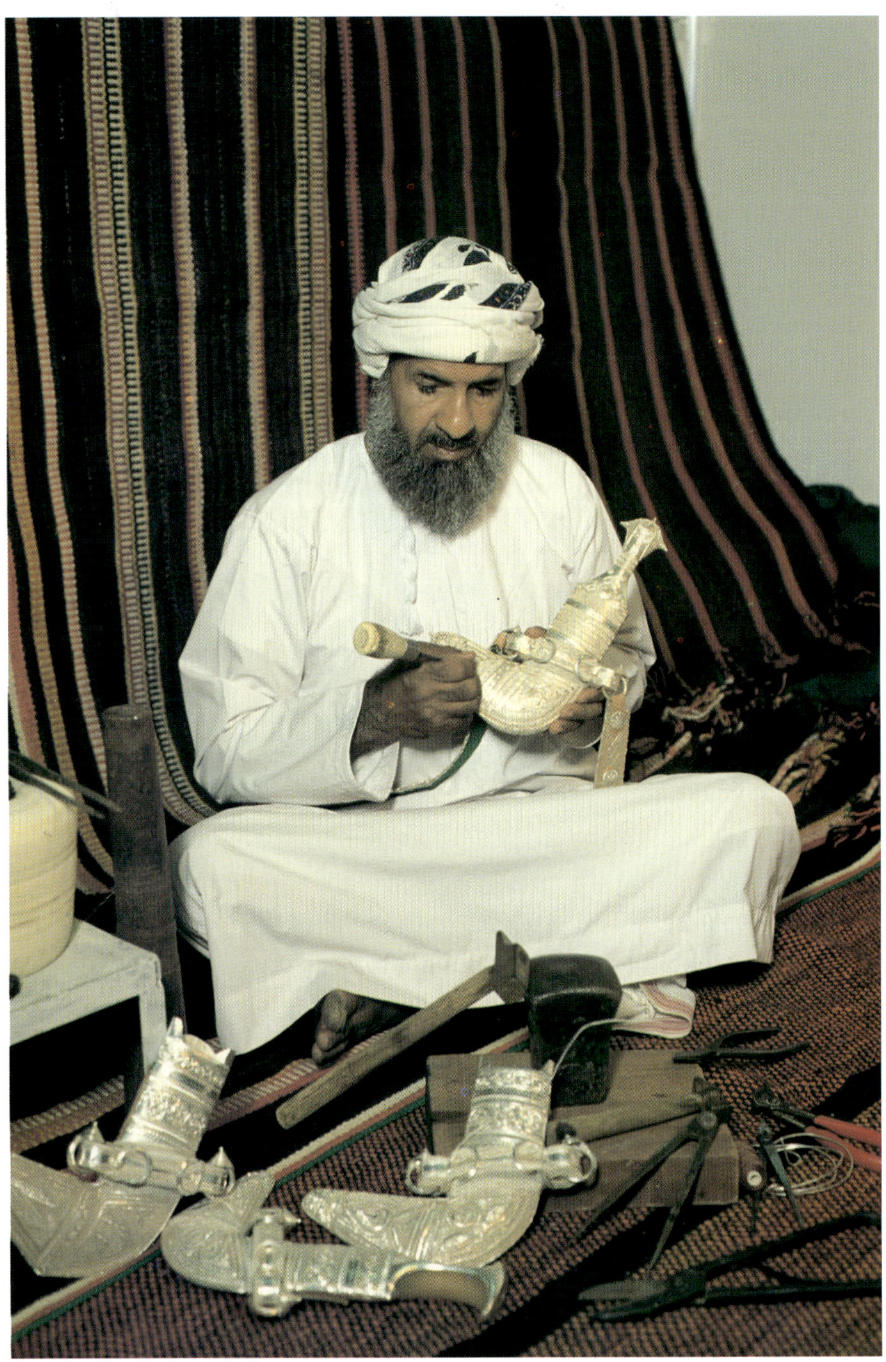

left
The tradition of silversmithing is still thriving, especially in Nizwa where, in a bustling souq, can be found not only *khanjar* but also a wide variety of silver jewellery.

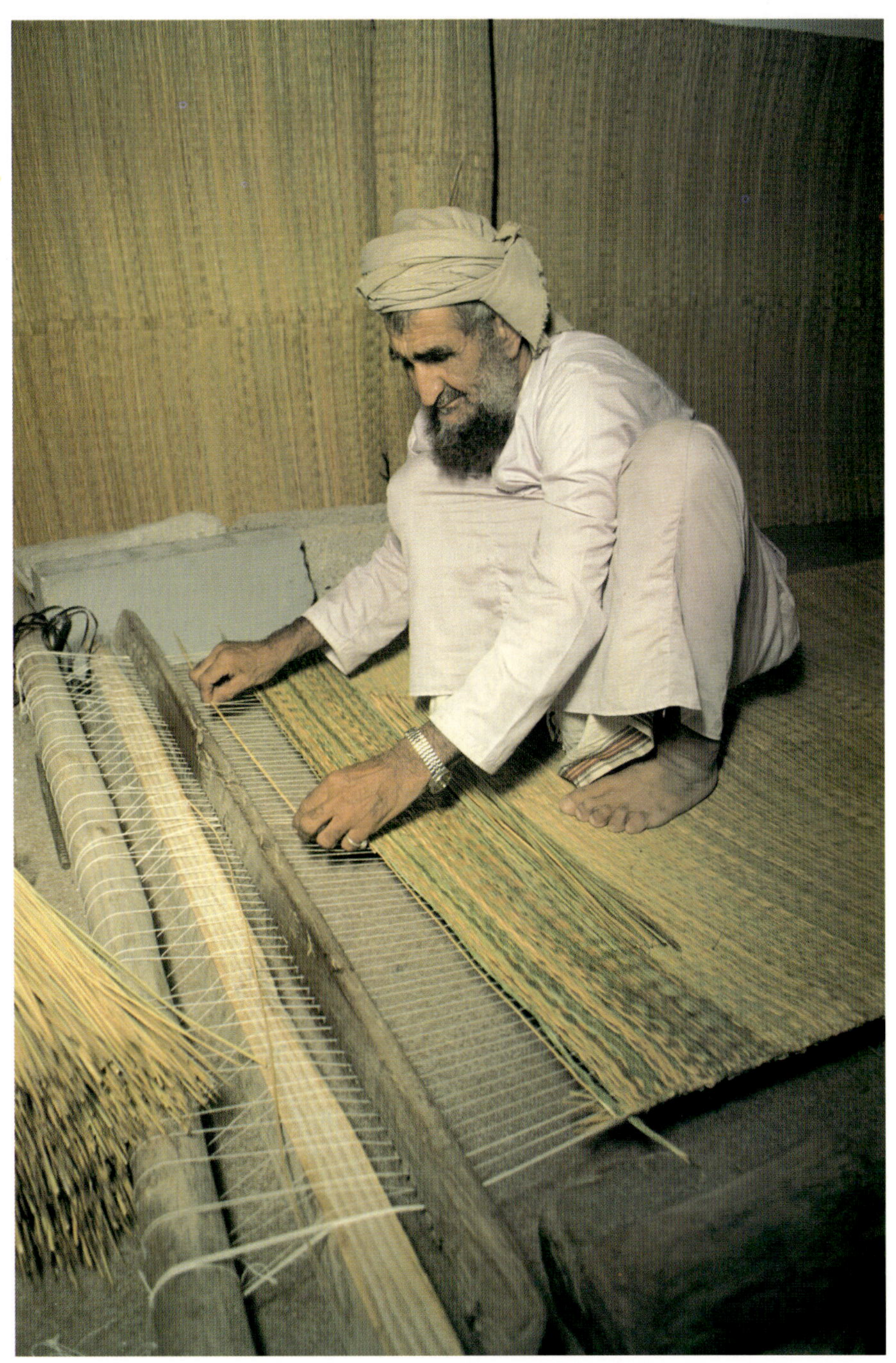

right
Practising a traditional craft which has been handed down from father to son over the centuries, the weavers of Oman turn out lengths of cool, comfortable palm matting which are still used in thousands of homes across the Sultanate.

right
This palm floor-matting and bowl, made by Bedouin women from Sinaw, are not only decorative but used in daily life.

above
Perched in the branches of a date-palm, the farmer takes stock of his plant. Farmers play an active role in pollinating these dates, which are economically important, and they are unstinting in their efforts to produce bountiful harvests.

below
Oman is rich in traditional crafts and cottage industries. And although items such as rugs and saddlebags still find a ready market, new applications for traditional skills are being explored – many involving women in rural areas.

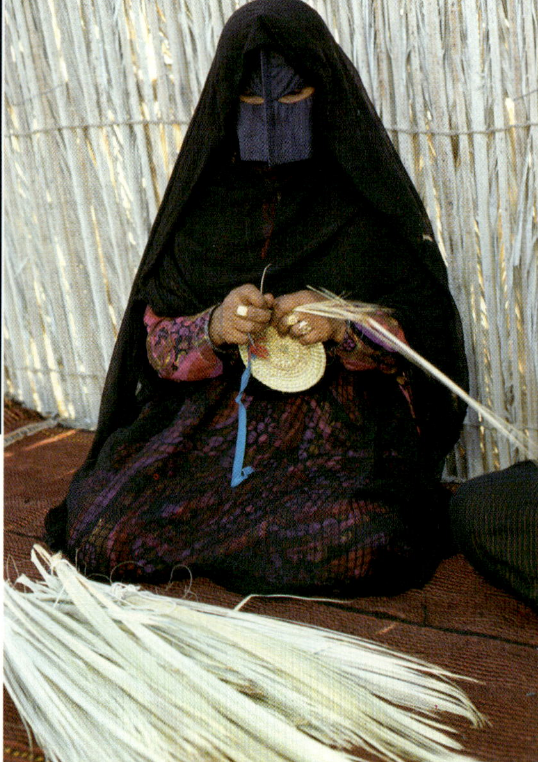

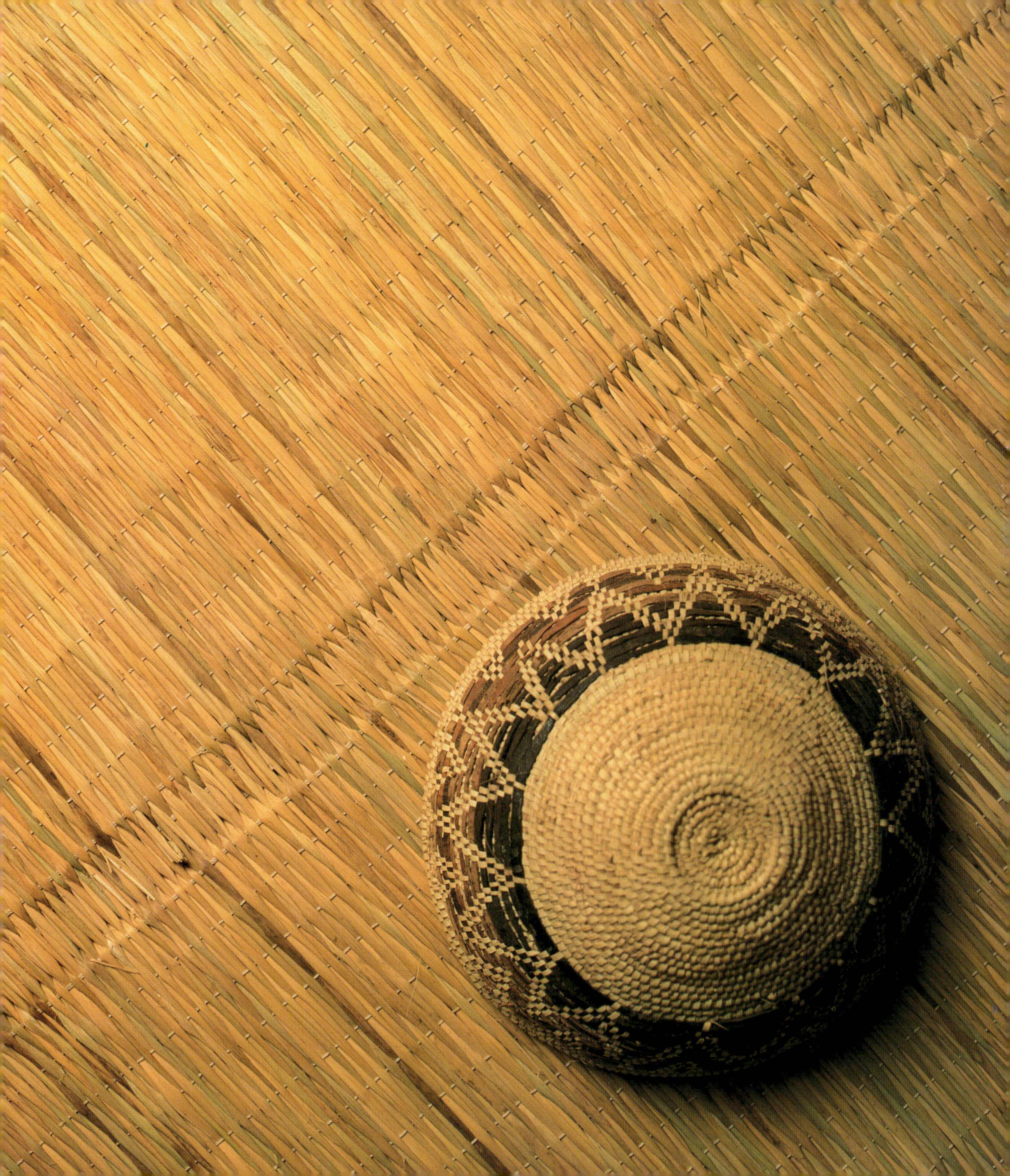

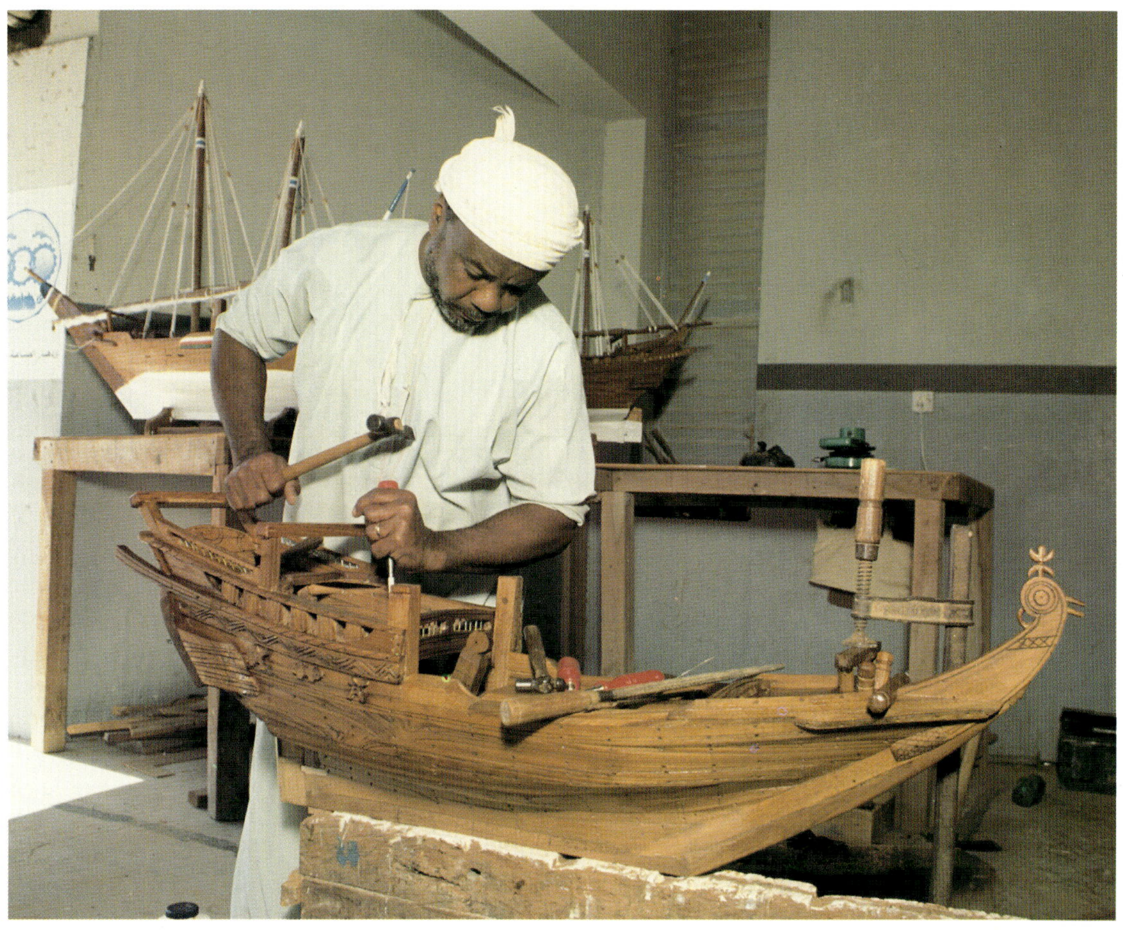

above
Highly finished models of Omani ships and boats are made by hand – such as this model dhow being painstakingly put together at the government factory in Sur.

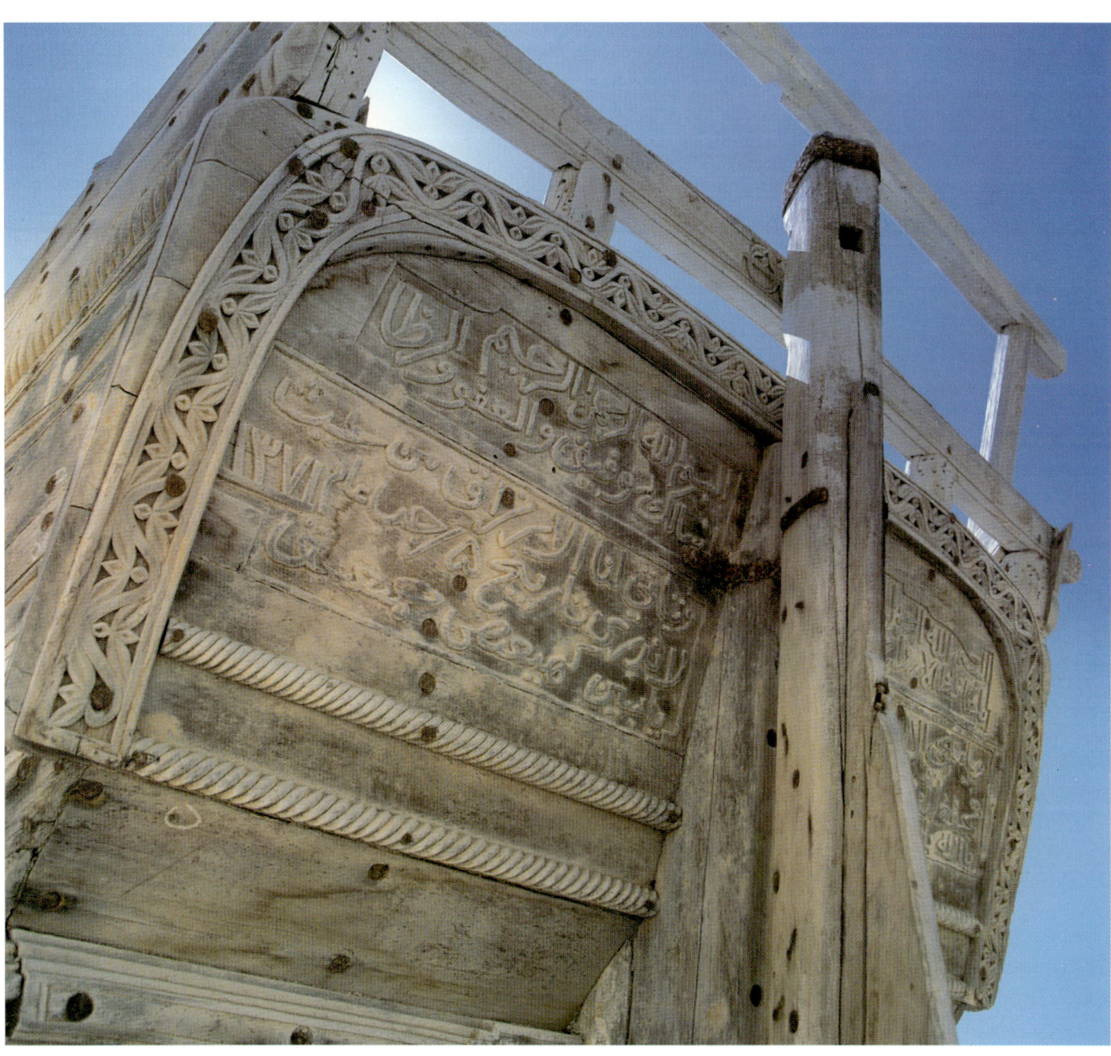

above
The Omanis have been a seafaring race from time immemorial and they have earned a reputation as highly skilled boat builders. This sun-bleached wreck of a *sambuq* is a relic found at Sadh in Dhofar.

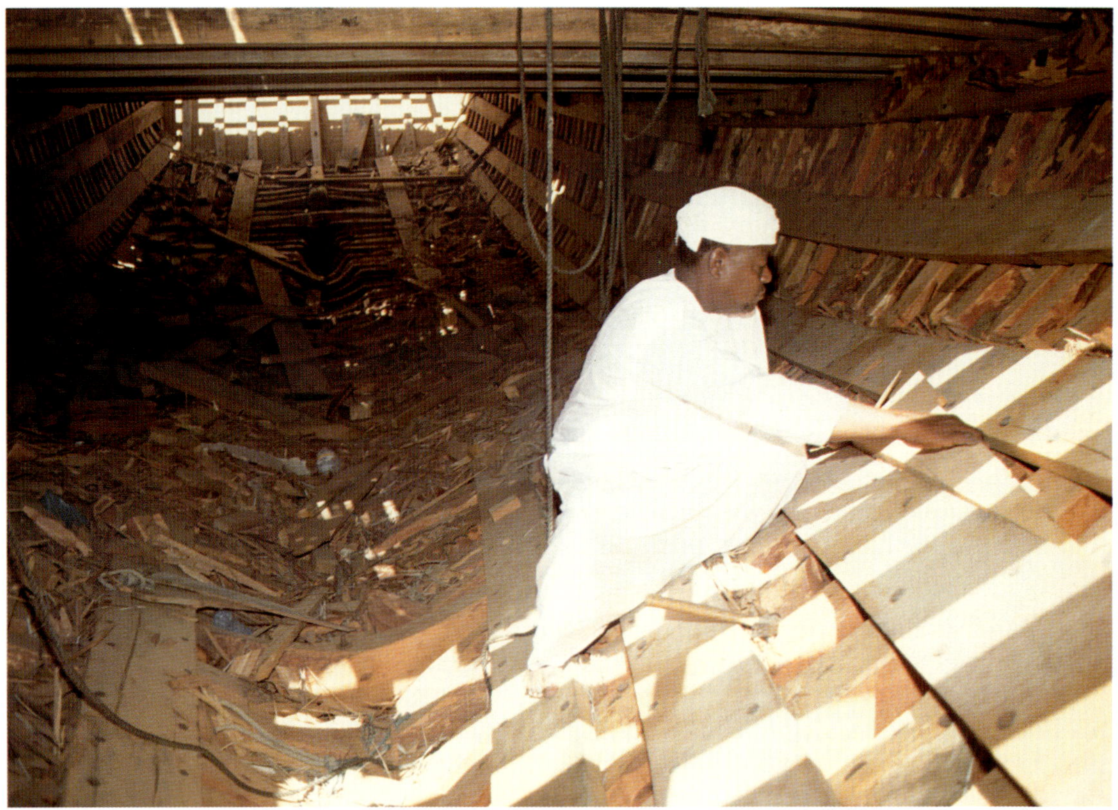

above
A traditional *sambuq* builder completes the basic shell of a vessel before finishing-work begins. Though now less busy than in earlier times, the shipyards of the eastern part of Sur still build vessels which are sold to residents of Oman and other Gulf States.

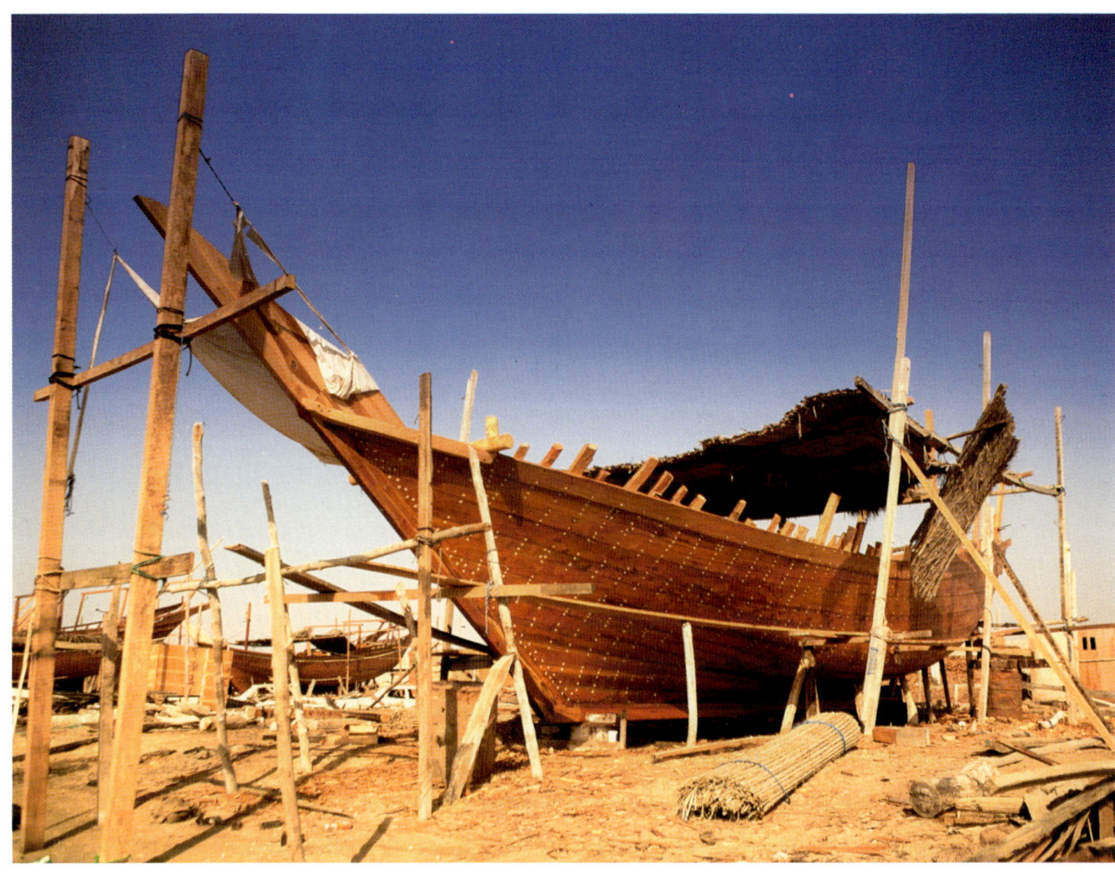

above

The pointed prow of a *sambuq* leans into the wind – as if it were straining to take to the seas. While these boats are still made to old and time-tested designs, they are now powered by modern engines.

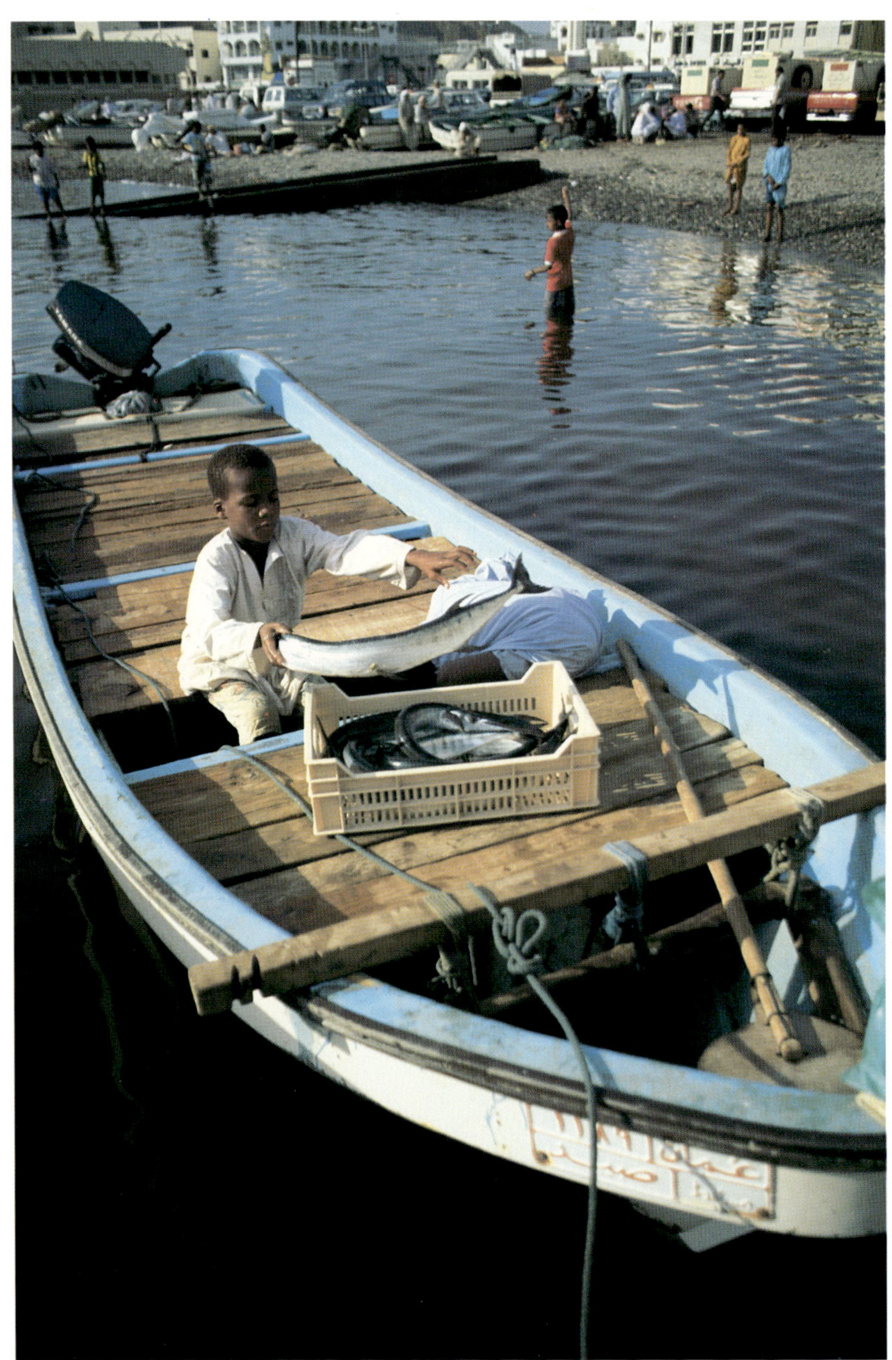

left
It's never too early to learn the family trade. And this youngster seems all set to prove he can be of help – by adeptly handling the fish brought in to the Mutrah fish souq.

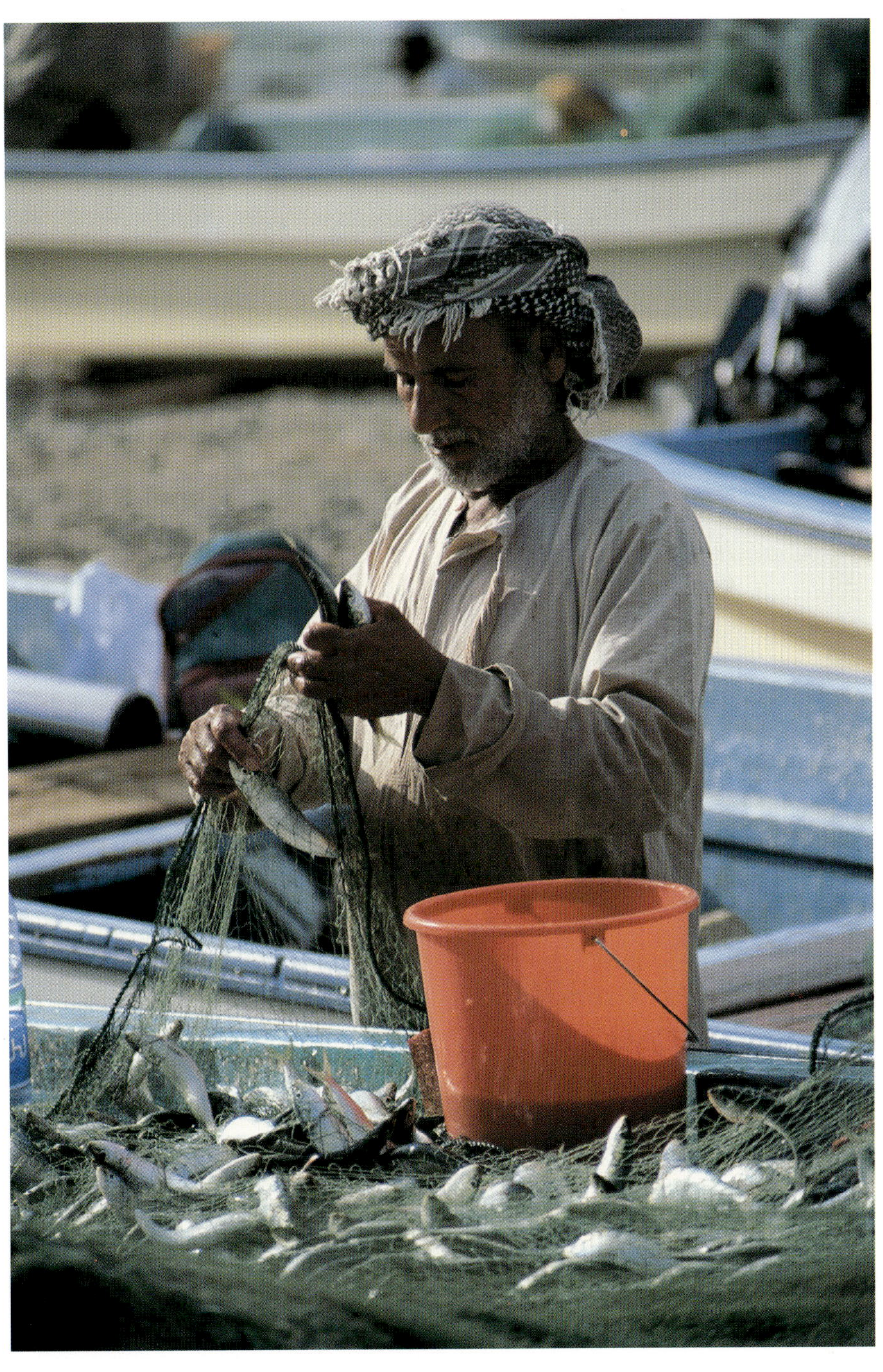

right
Every morning fishermen bring in their catch to the various fish markets. Here, silvery sardines are being pulled out of the nets at the fish souq at Mutrah.

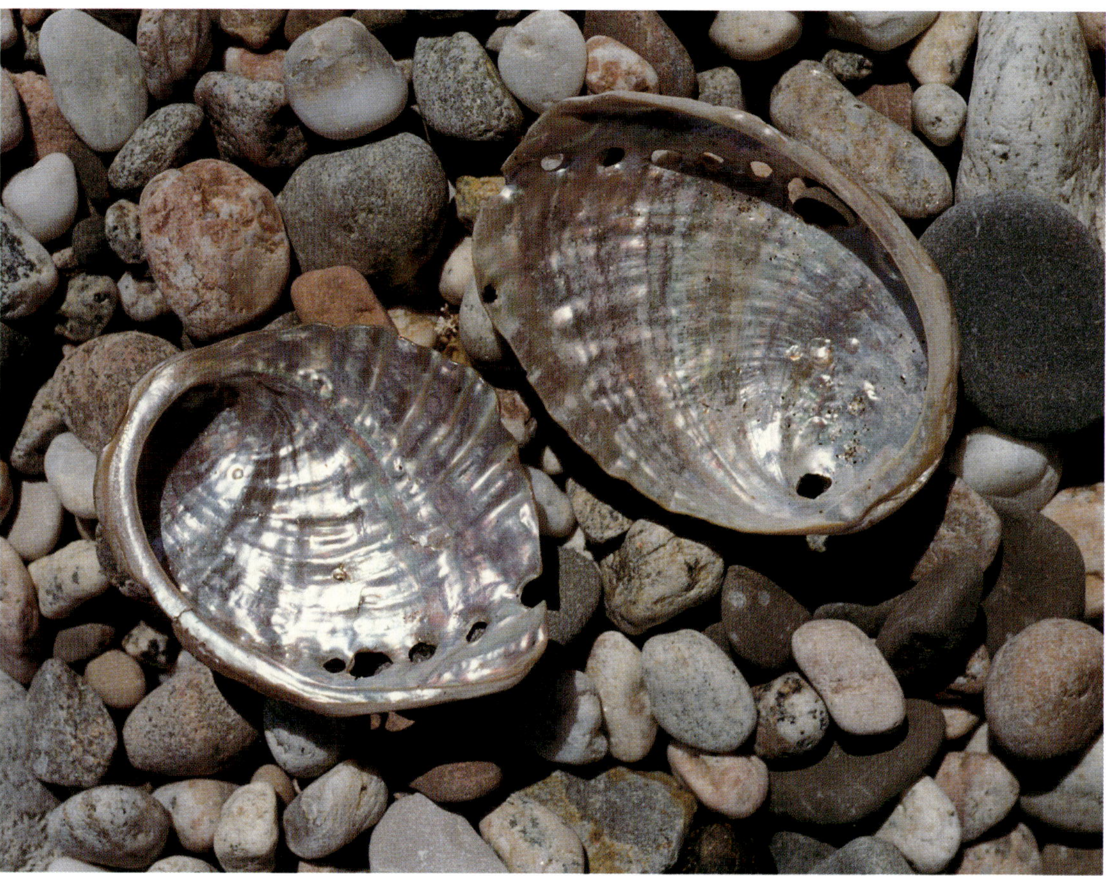

above
Abalone are in plentiful supply on the coastline east of Salalah, and are substantial export earners. These shells are from the beach near Sadh, their wonderful shells streaked with silver, glittering with a cold fire amongst the rocks and pebbles.

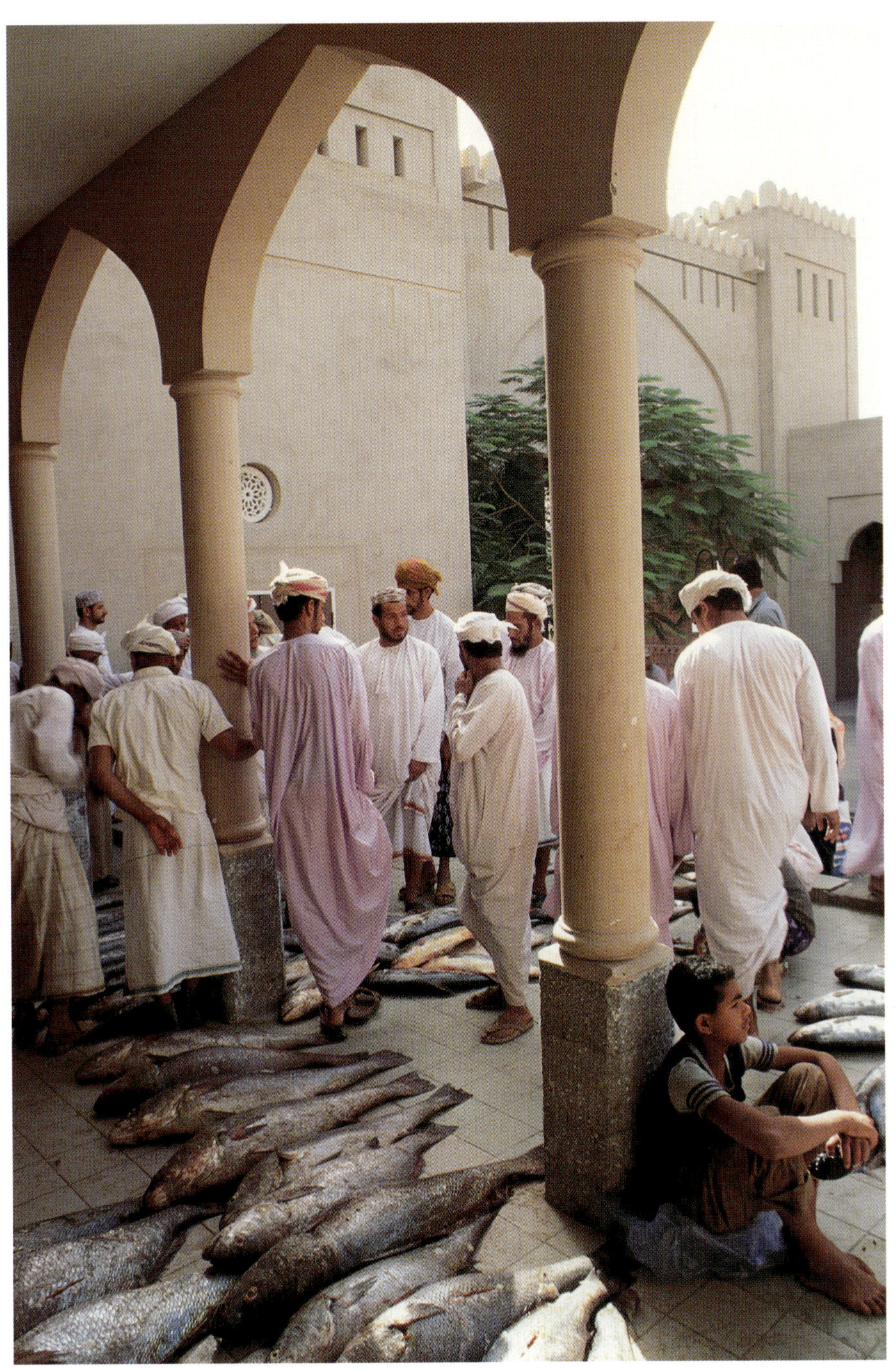

right
Thanks to the government's assistance in building ice-plants, and its investment in an impressive road network, even central market towns now have plentiful supplies of fresh fish.

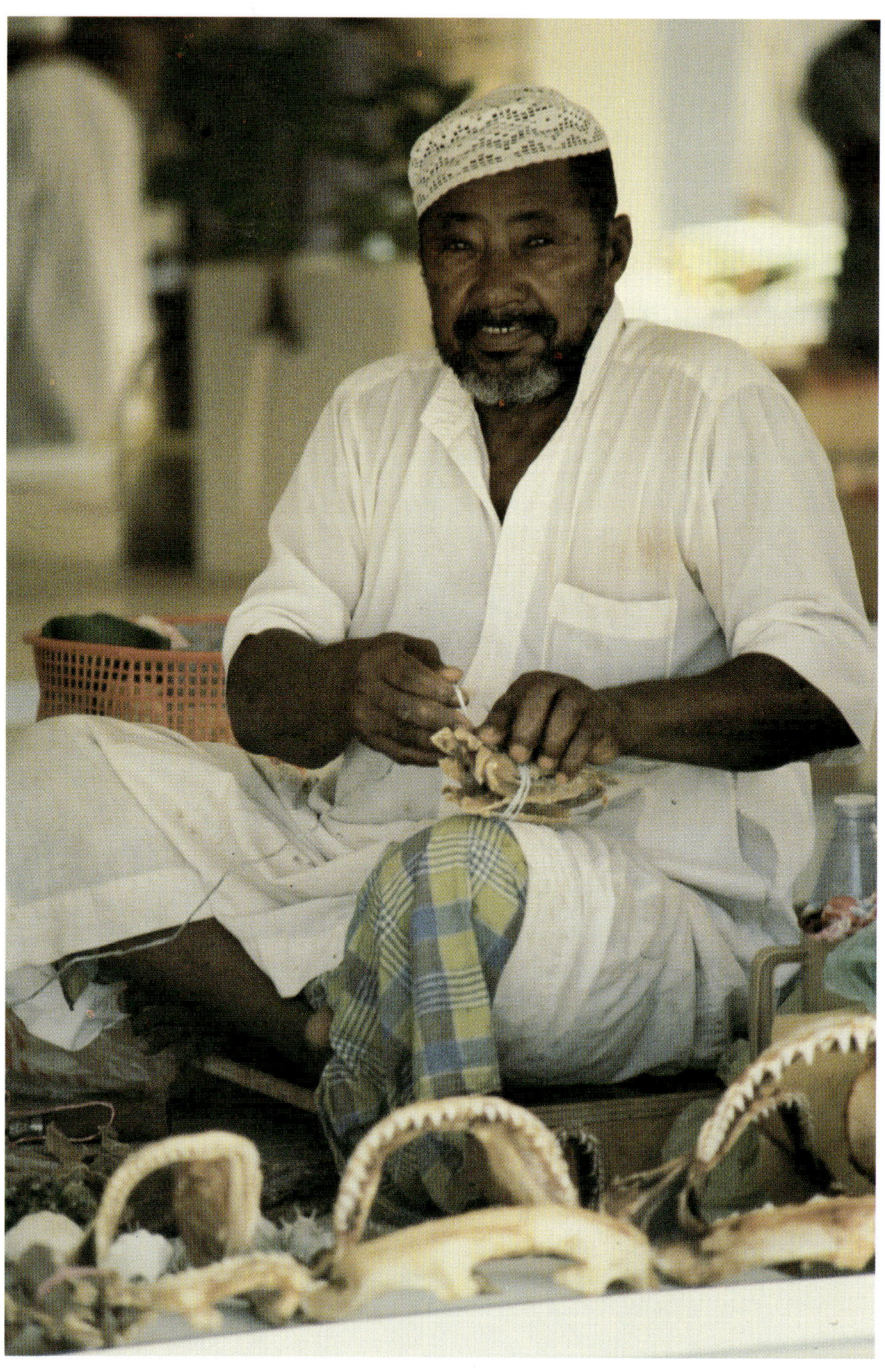

left
Dried fish, shells and sharks' teeth are displayed by this salesman in Mutrah fish souq. Many sharks live and breed in the waters of Oman.

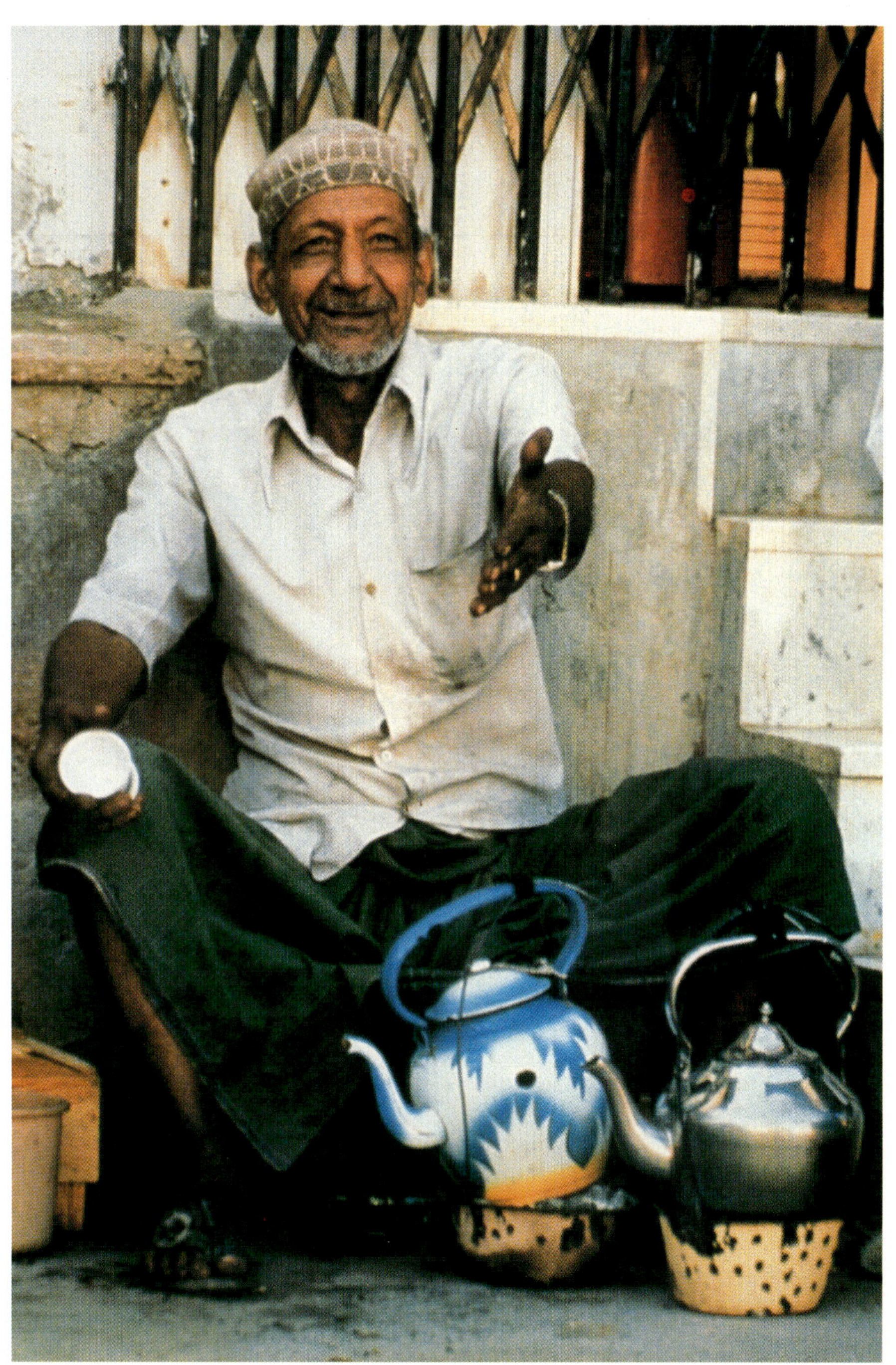

right
In the souq at Mutrah a coffee seller offers the traditional greeting of 'T'fadel' (welcome) to passers-by. The coffee, flavoured with cardamom is a refreshing hot drink as it tricks the body to cool down naturally.

above
Bull fighting takes place in Oman, though it is very different from the European version – 'bull nudging' might be a better description of this gentle and colourful display.

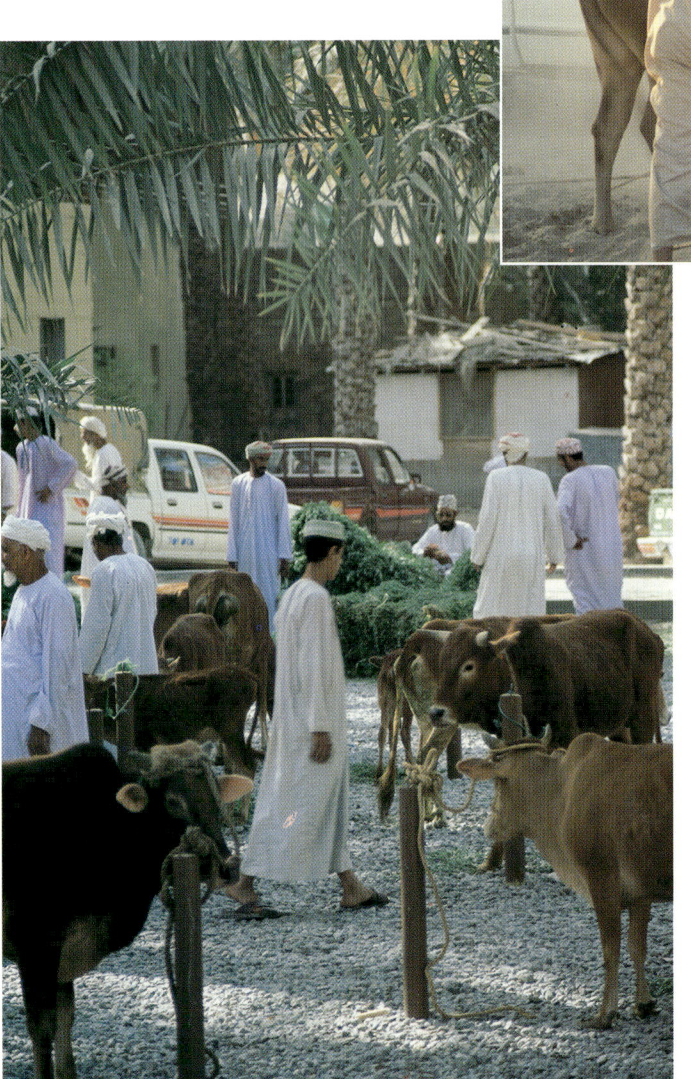

left
Nizwa has long been a major centre for cattle sales. Here, farmers have come to buy and sell at the cattle markets which are held daily.

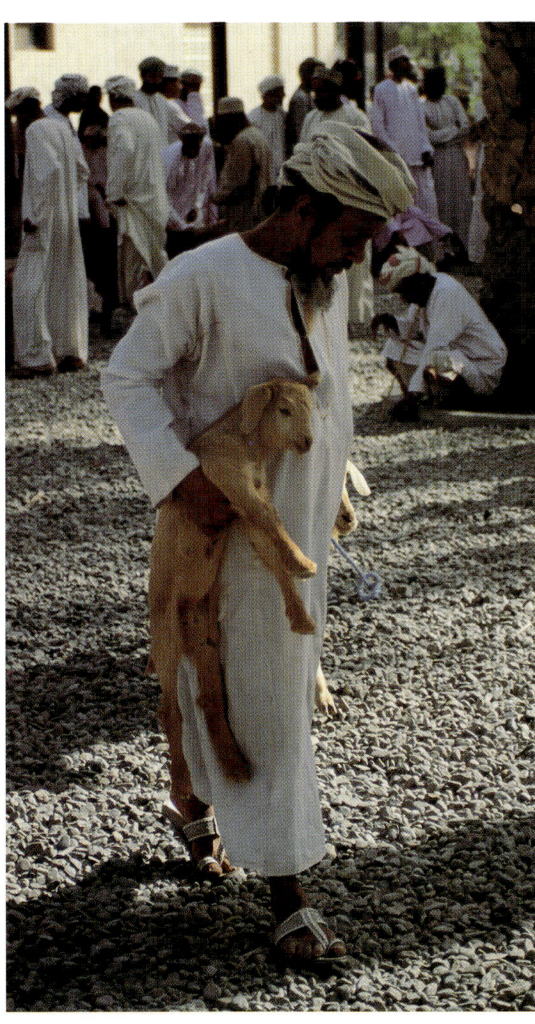

above
The choice is wide and the bargaining fierce and competitive at Nizwa market. Here cattle, goat and sheep are brought to be bought, sold or bartered.

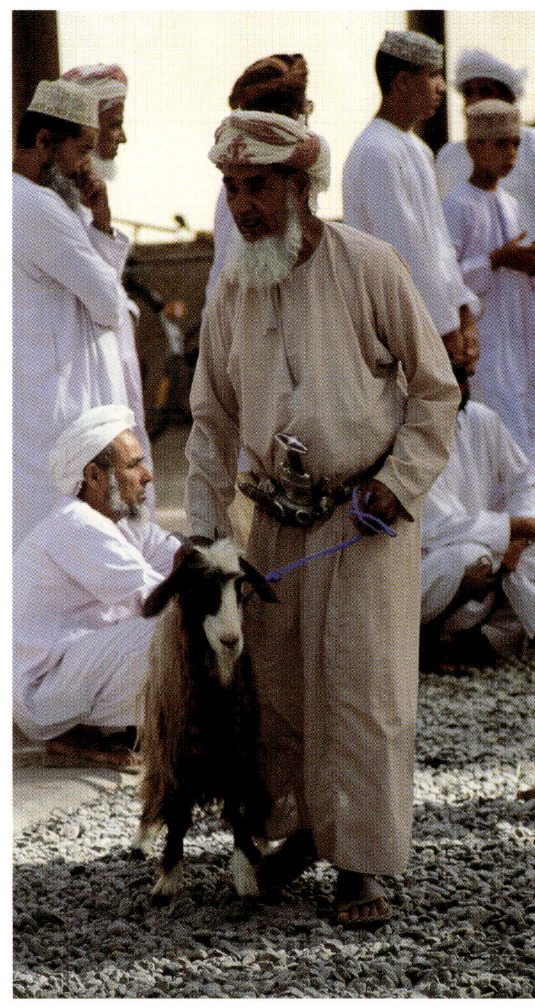

above
During Eid festivities prices of live goats and sheep rise due to heavy demand as people seek an animal for the traditional feast.

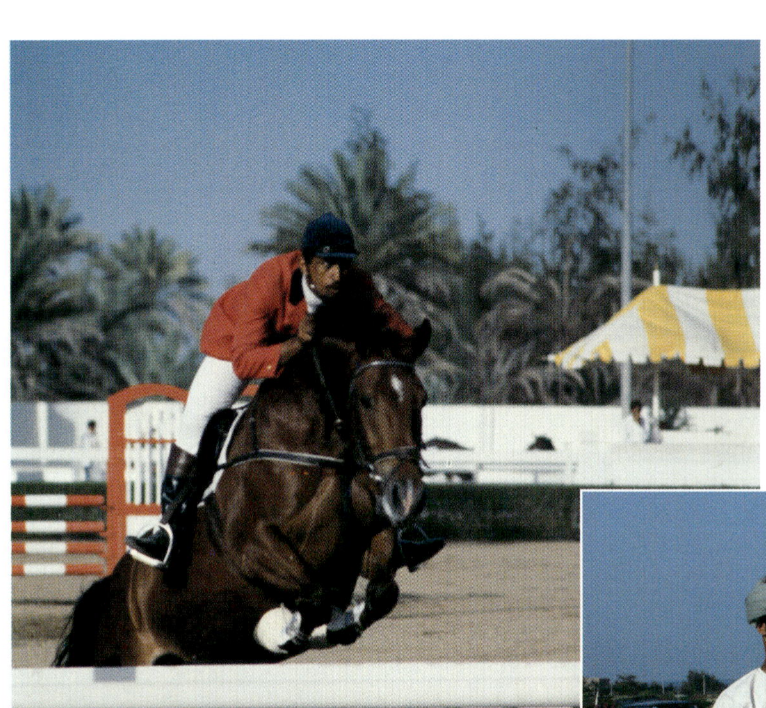

below
Proud, noble and dignified – this handsome stallion is being ridden in a parade at the Royal Stables, Seeb, before a race.

above
Arabia is famous for its horses, and equestrian events are avidly followed. This horse-jumping event is taking place at the Enam Farm, Seeb, under the auspices of the Oman Equestrian Federation.

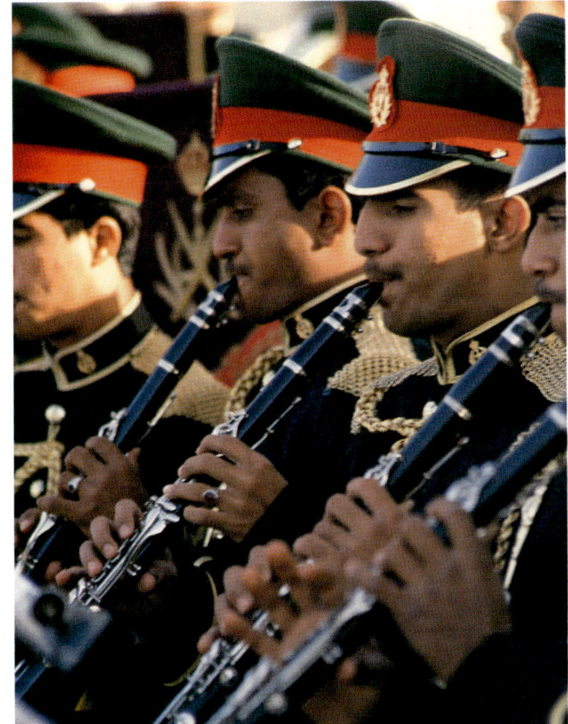

left and below

The flourish of trumpets, accompanied by the colour and pageantry of the mounted horsemen of the Royal Guard, precedes show-jumping events at the Royal Stables.

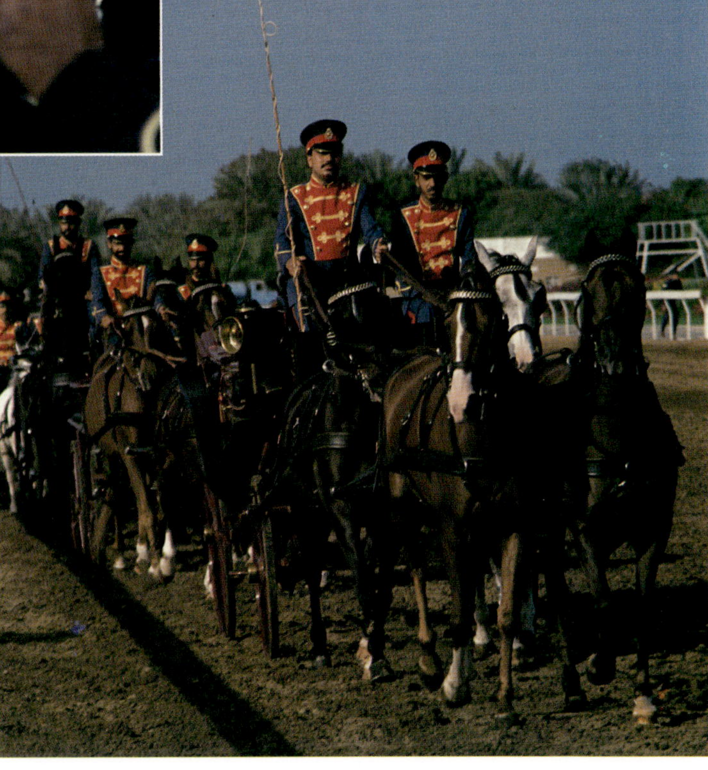

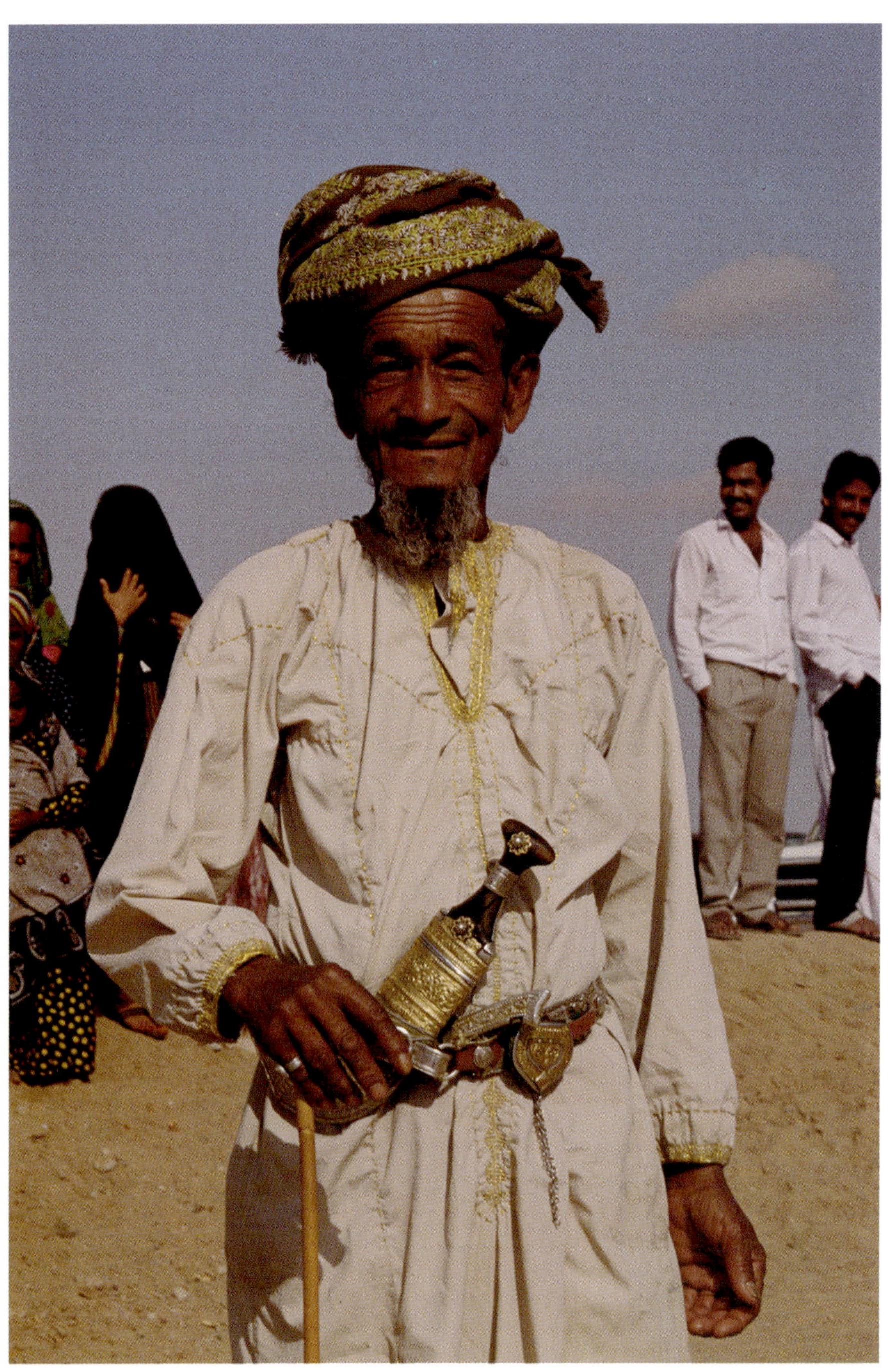

left
In Oman horse racing remains popular. There is no doubt that this elderly man is getting a great deal of pleasure out of a day's racing at Ja'alan Bilad Bani Bu Ali.

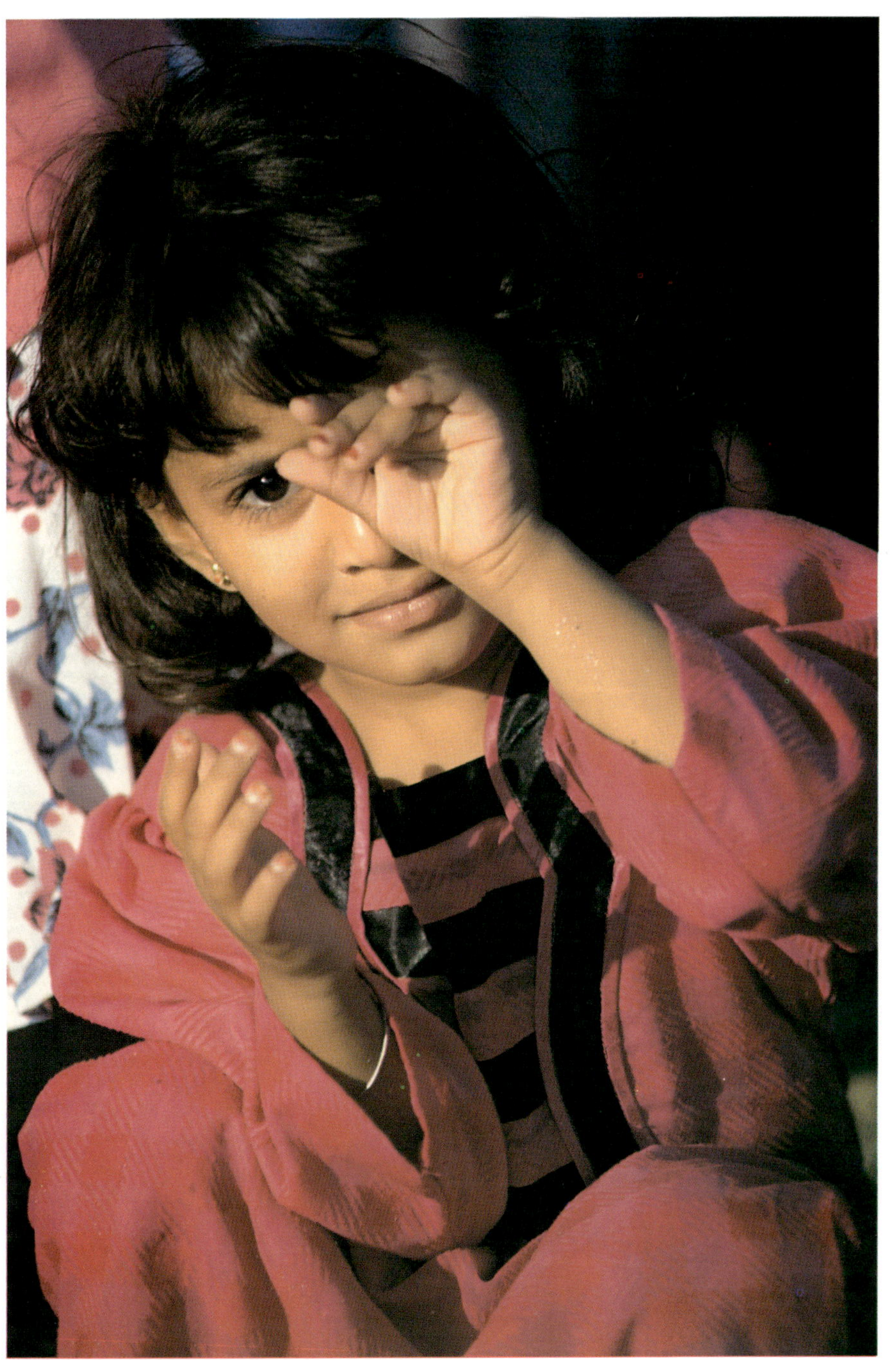

right
Oman's greatest resource is her people. This young girl, typifies the spirit of the Oman of the future.

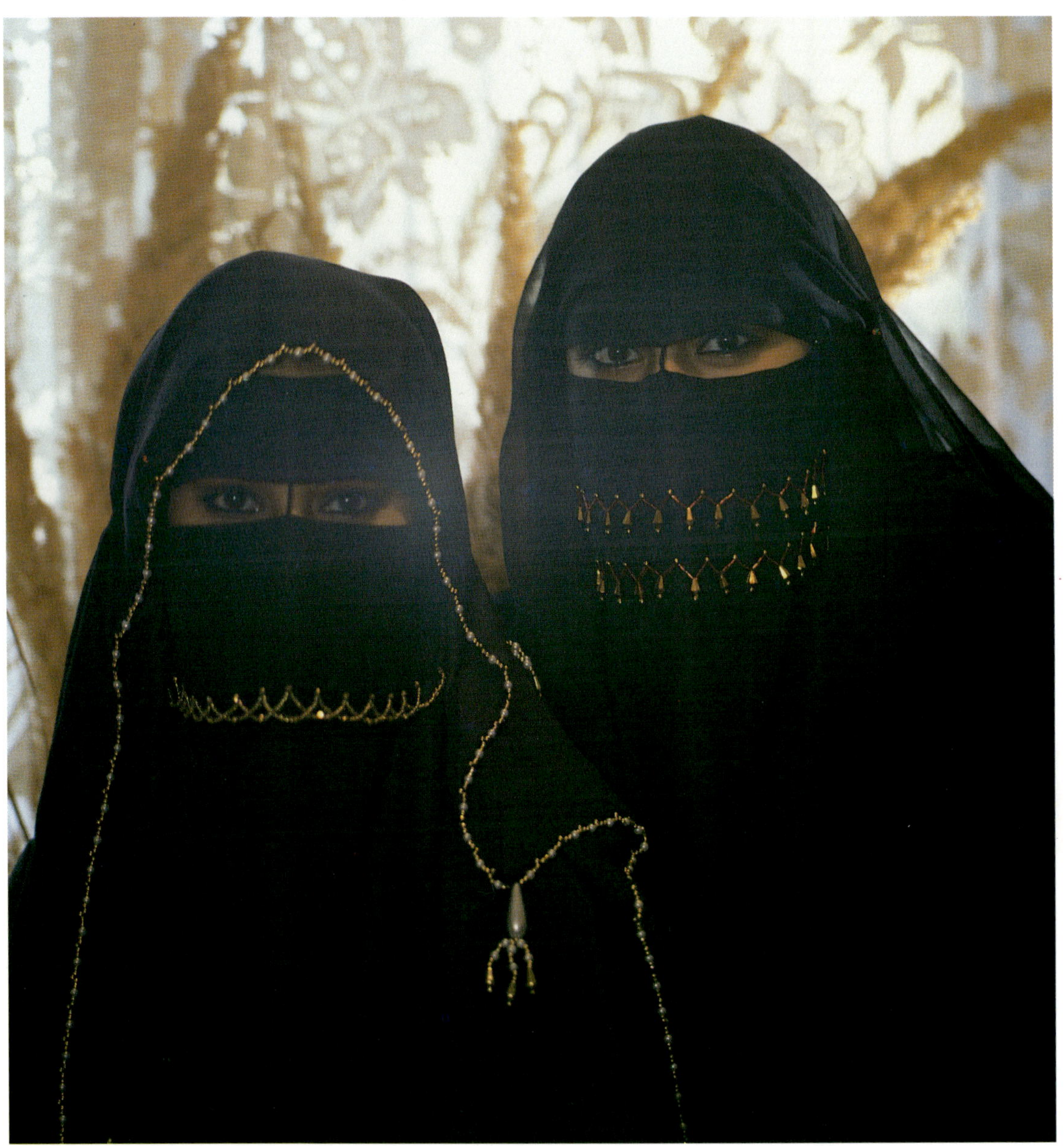

above
Beauty can be enhanced by leaving much to the imagination. These girls, traditionally covered except for their very expressive eyes, seem to radiate hidden charm.

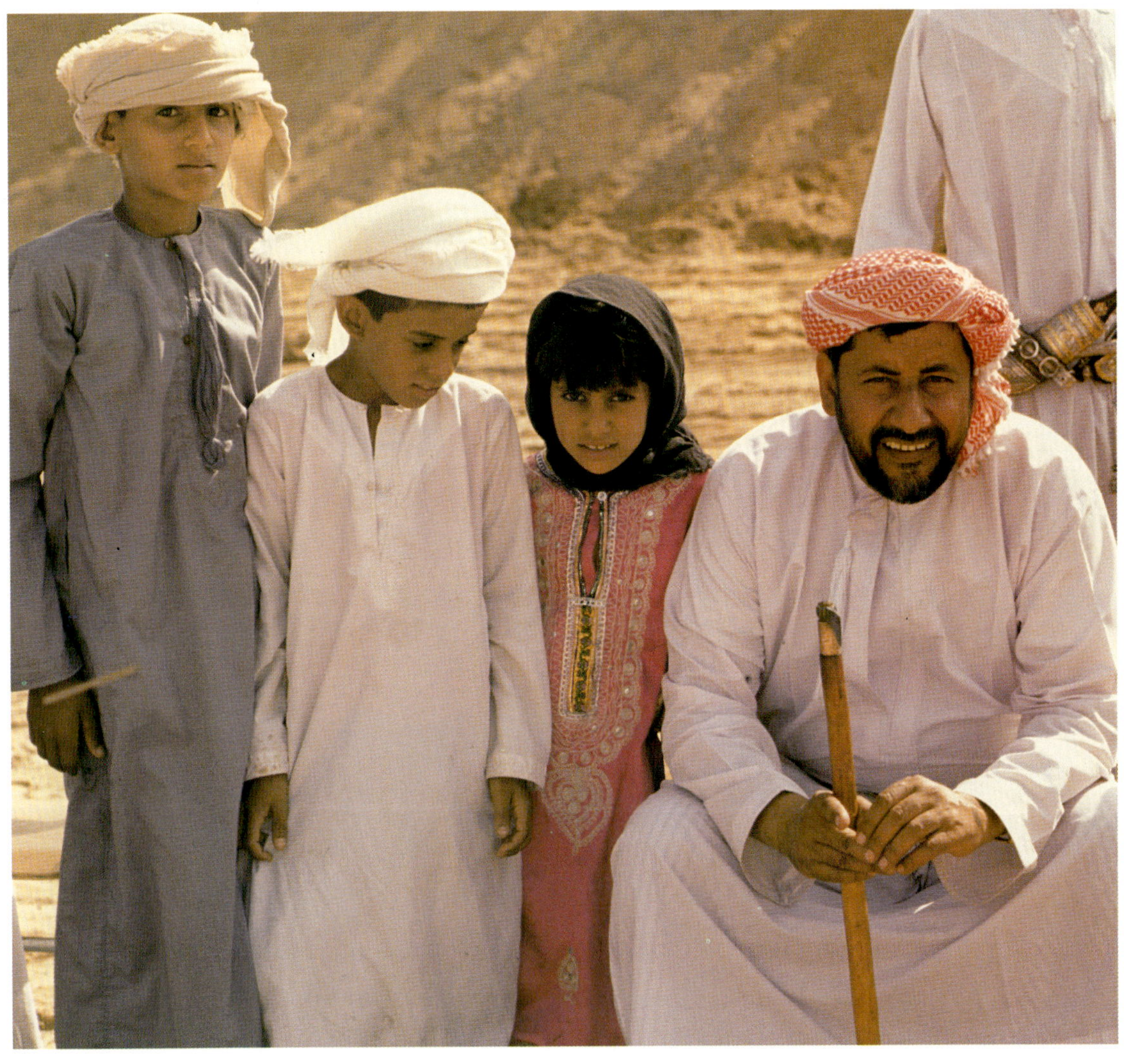

above

A trip to the local camel and horse races makes a splendid day out for this young family near Ja'alan Bilad Bani Bu Ali.

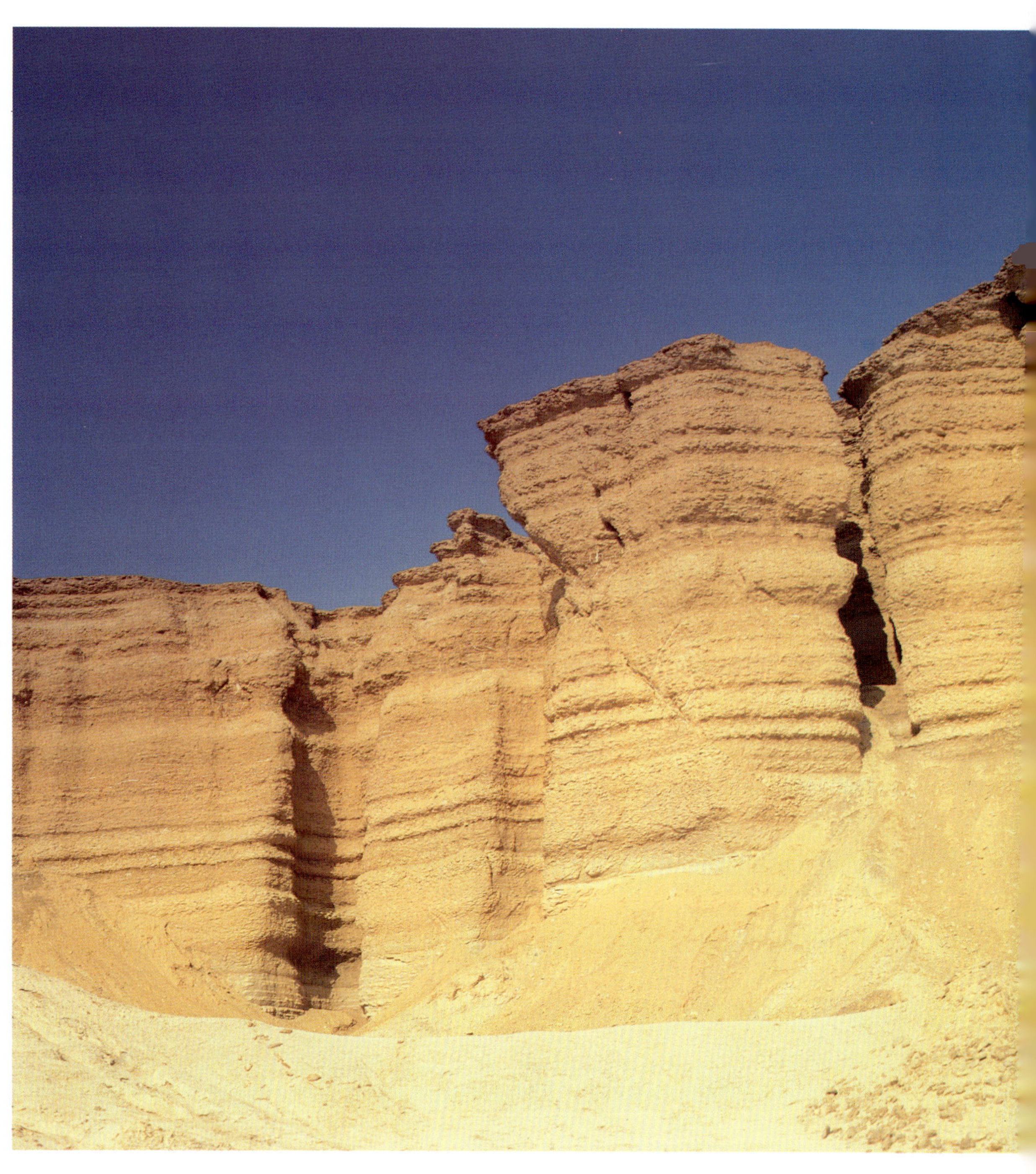

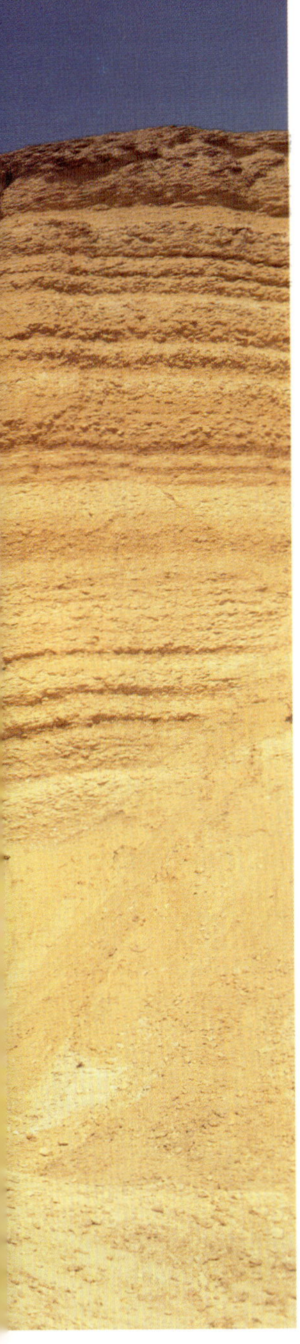

Oman's Natural Heritage

The popular imagination sees the Arabian Peninsula as a vast tract of sandy desert – an image which is rapidly dispelled in Oman, where a variety of landscapes and natural habitats brings a correspondingly wide variety of flora and fauna. Sea-cliffs and islands (especially the wild beauty of the fjord-like coastline of the Musandam Peninsula), dramatic rocky mountains, rolling grasslands of post-monsoon Dhofar, stony desert plateaux, reedy lakes – Oman has all this and more – as well as the anticipated windswept sand-dunes.

On the accession of His Majesty Sultan Qaboos in 1970, few could have thought that Oman's natural heritage would quickly become a national priority – there were other, apparently more pressing, needs for the creation of a modern infrastructure. But the Sultan himself emphasised its importance: "If we are to develop and conserve [our natural heritage] we must understand it. If we are to understand it, we must study it. Our plans for development must be based on facts; facts about our resources, our environment, our ecosystems, and facts about how we, as human beings, exist in interrelationship with the wild plants and creatures who share God's earth with us."[1]

left
In spite of the national goal of non-dependence on oil, Oman's economy is still oil-driven. These limestone rocks are behind Fahud oil township, very near the area where oil was first discovered.

---

[1] from His Majesty's Foreword to the *Journal of Oman Studies* Special Report (No. 1)

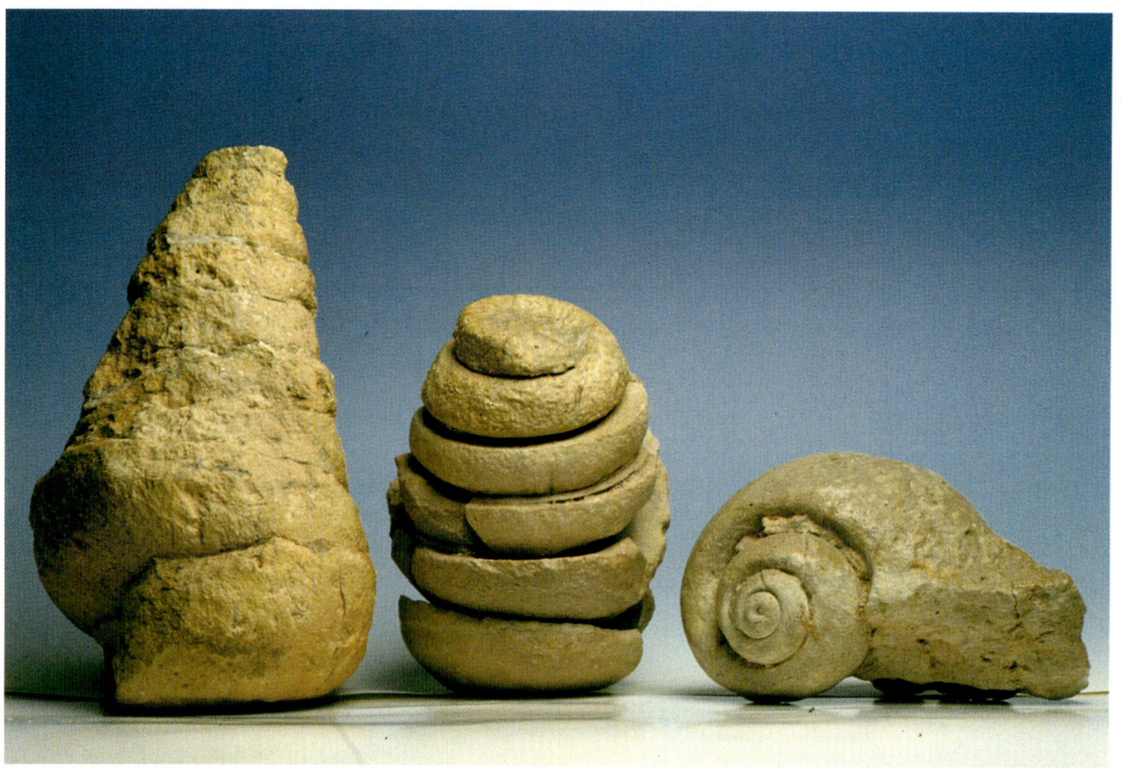

above
Fossils found in the rocky escarpments around the central oil township of Fahud show that this area was below sea-level many millions of years ago. It was here that oil was first discovered in Oman.

Some examples of this approach have already been mentioned in the Introduction (pp 14–17): another fine example of conservation in action in a precarious ecosystem is the *khawrs* of Dhofar. *Khawrs* would, in a wetter climate, be river estuaries; in Dhofar, they are lagoons found at the mouths of wadis, and separated from the sea by a sand-bar – and they act as a focal point for many kinds of wildlife. Underwater plants support a rich and diverse fauna of tiny crustaceans and insects, which provide food for birds such as the flamingo, which filters food from the sediments with its specially adapted beak.

Such is the richness of bird-life on the *khawrs* – with 186 different species recorded at Khawr Rawri, and as many as 2,500 birds counted in March 1992 on Khawr Dahariz

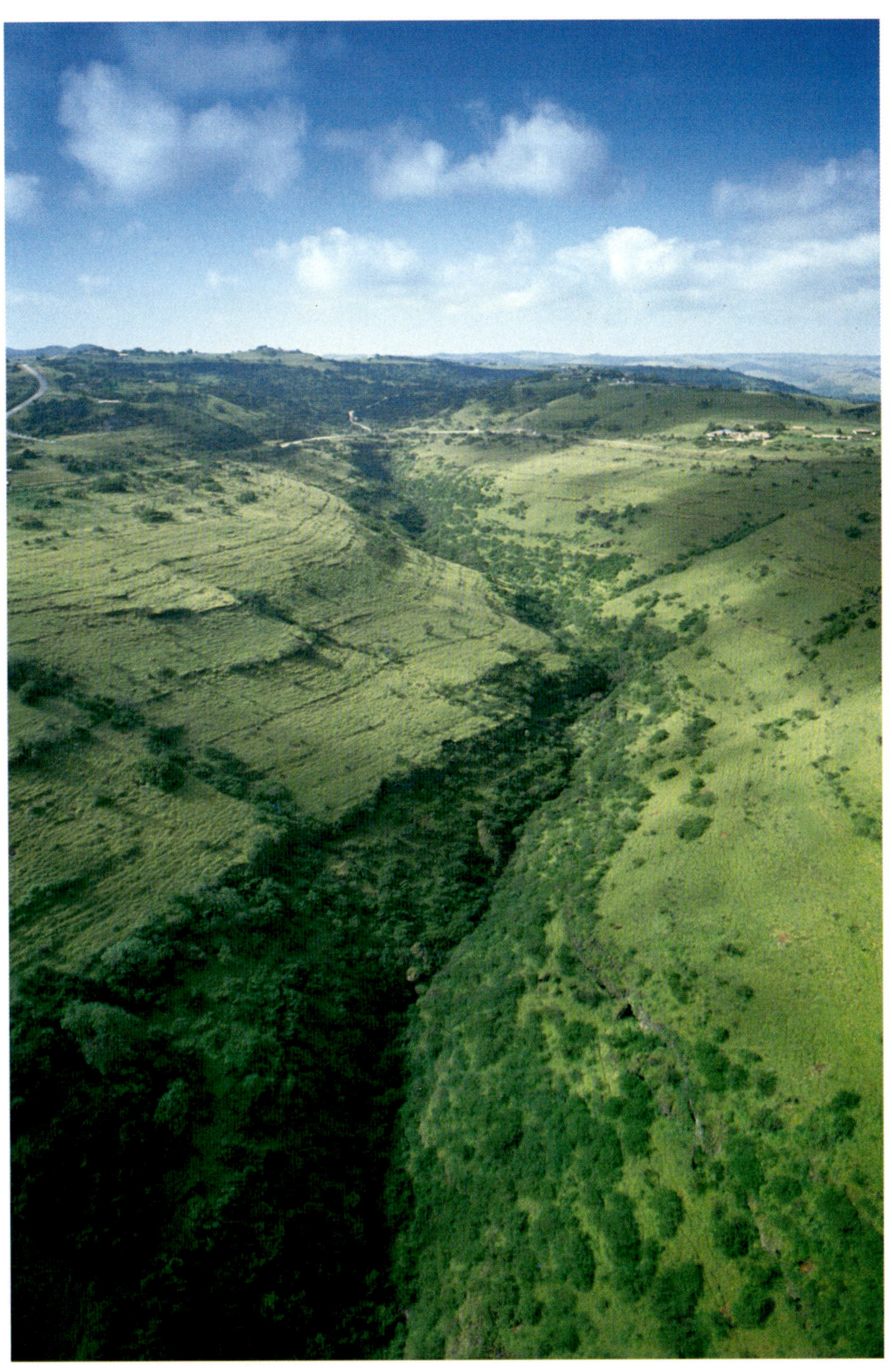

right
Lush greenery is a natural by-product of the monsoon season in Dhofar. The moisture-laden winds blanket the coast and mountains with mists from the end of June to August. Fertile hills and cool temperatures add up to the perfect conditions for nature to run riot.

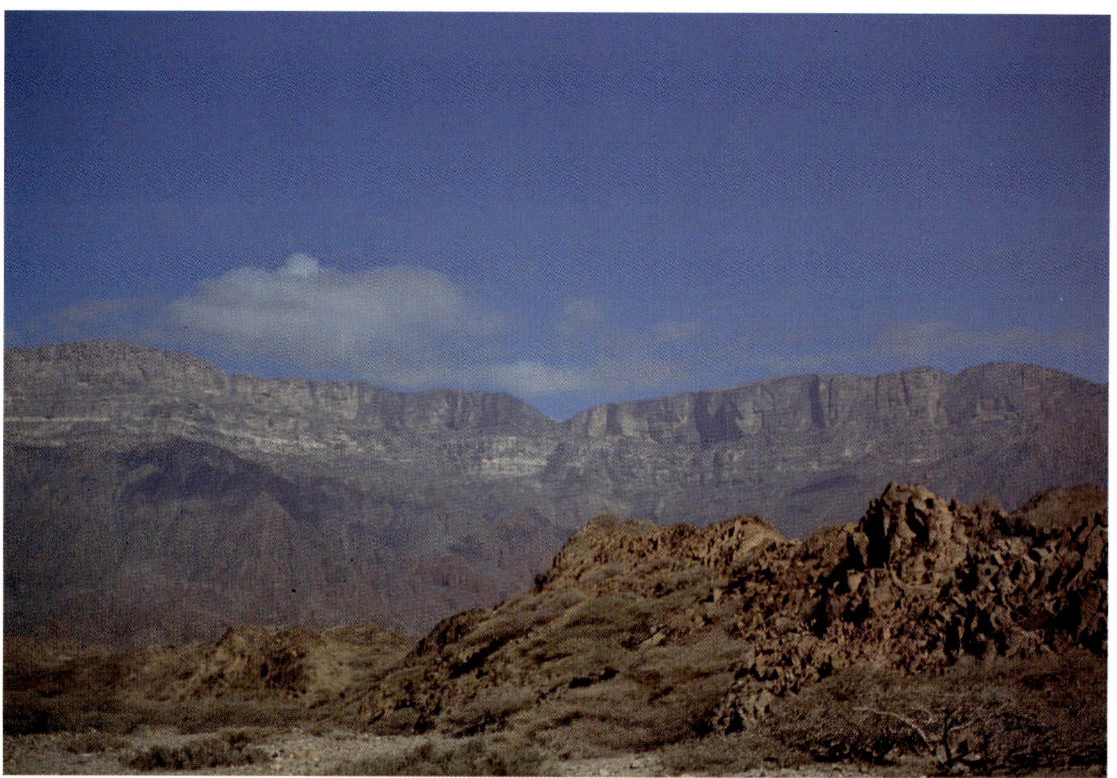

above
The soaring mountains of Jebel al Qara stretch across the horizon, forming a backdrop behind Salalah. From the roads leading up into the mountains, the traveller is treated to the most spectacular views across the coastal plain and wooded hillsides.

alone – that Khawr Salalah has been managed as a bird sanctuary for many years. Many of the birds are migrants travelling to European breeding grounds in the spring and returning to Africa in autumn to escape the cold northern winter. The Land Use Plans for the Southern Region have now designated many of the *khawrs* as nature reserves.

Khawrs are only one of Oman's many natural wonders: more immediately obvious are the high and craggy mountains, many of which are composed of limestone, formed from the skeletons of tiny marine animals which collected on the bed of a warm, shallow sea some 50–250 million years ago. The movements of the restless earth are well illustrated in Oman, where fossil marine organisms, which once gathered on the sea-floor, now lie at an altitude of over

right
In dramatic contrast to the rocky highlands are the shifting dunes of the Wahiba Sands. Roughly 400 kilometers away from the Capital Area, this desert stretches down to the Arabian Sea. These sands consist of quartz, carbonate and ophiolitic grains blown in from nearby eroded rocks and marine sediment – and move inland at about 10 metres per year.

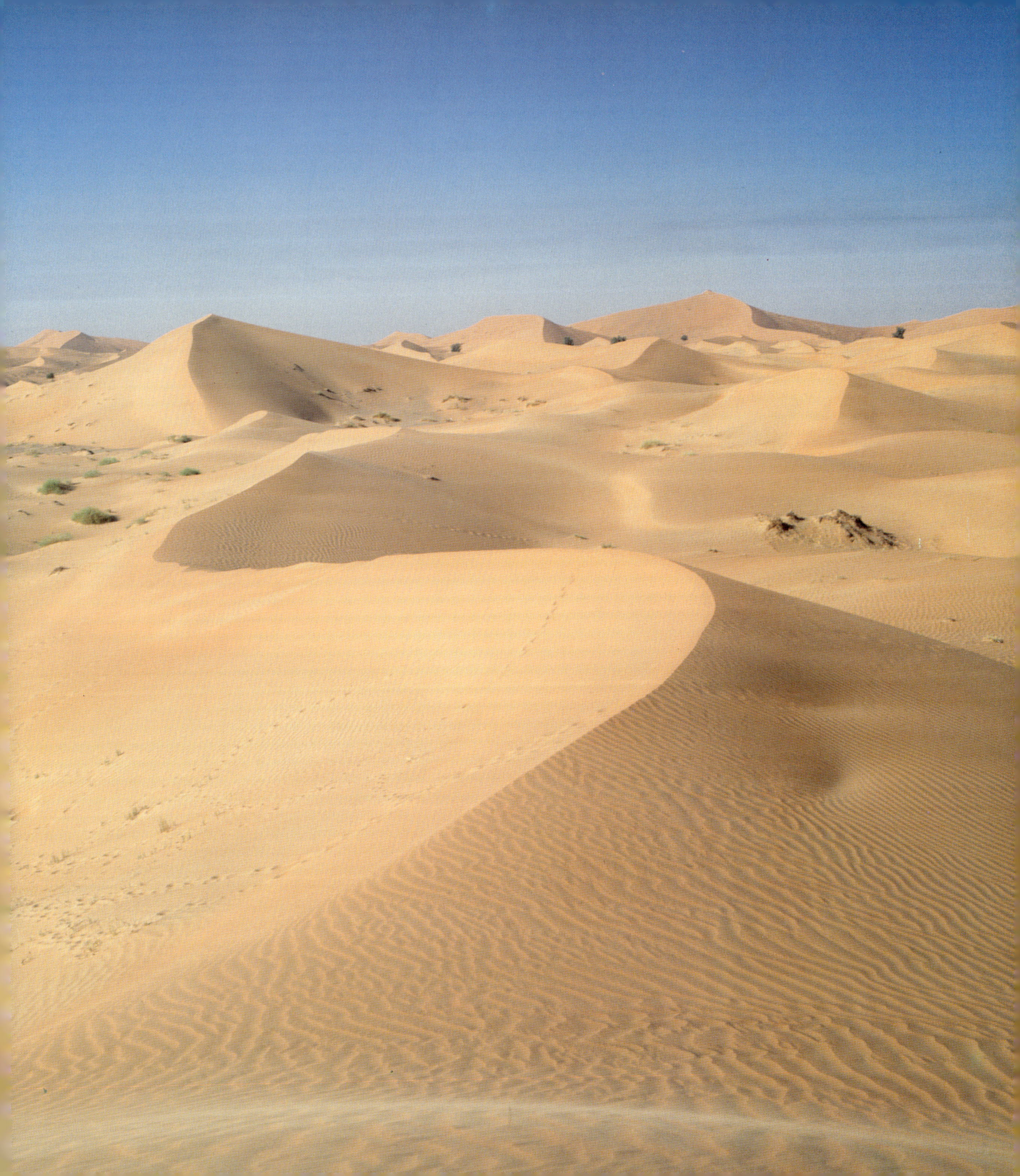

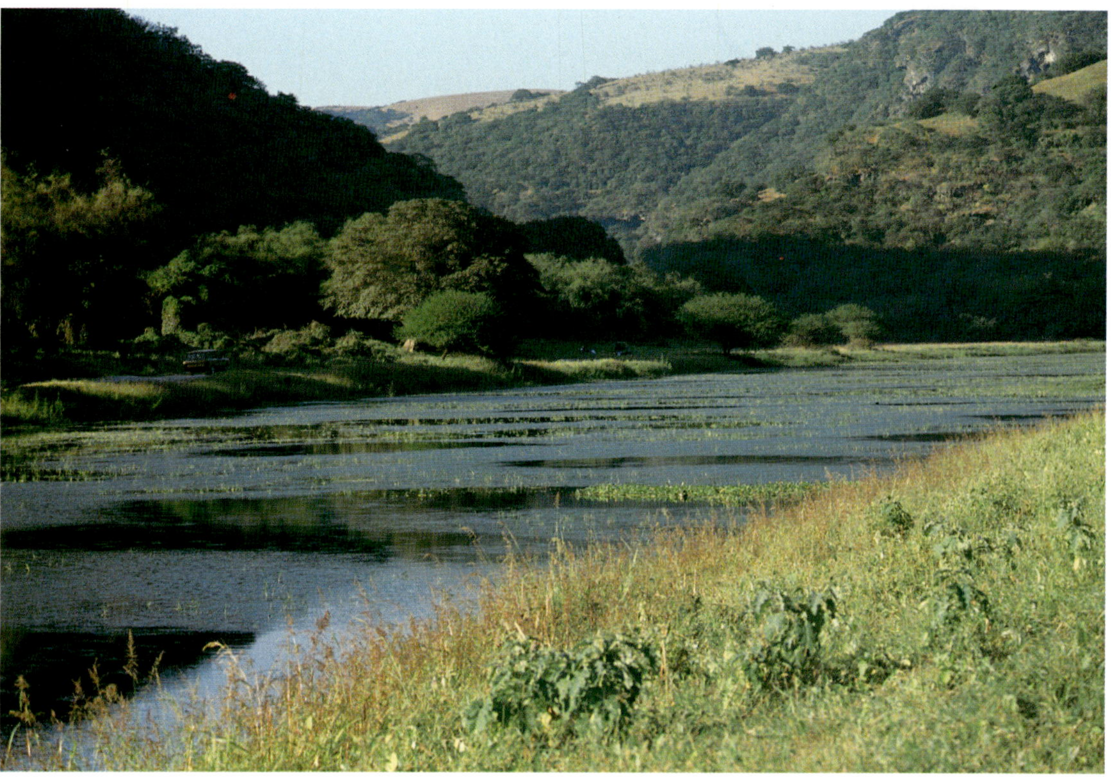

3,000 metres, at the crest of Jebel Shams, the highest point in Oman. Over many thousands of years, rainwater has changed the shape of the terrain, both on the surface and underneath, creating cave systems and large underground chambers. One of these, the Majlis al Jinn ("Meeting Room of the Spirits") cave is the second-largest cave-room in the world, with a floor area of 58,000 square metres and a volume of four million cubic metres. That's nearly twice the height of the Oman Sheraton Hotel in Ruwi!

Wadis, or dry river-beds, penetrate deep into the heart of Oman's mountain ranges. Many of the graded roads in Oman follow the course of a wadi – and travellers on such roads find much to delight them: villages built of mud-brick, date plantations, palm-fringed streams, pools, ancient watch-towers and

above
After seasonal rains or monsoon mists the permanent lake in Wadi Darbat, in Dhofar, is surrounded by greenery.

right
To the visitor exploring the wadis of Oman is a very significant part of their stay. Wadi Bani Auf, shown here, is one of the more delightful discoveries.

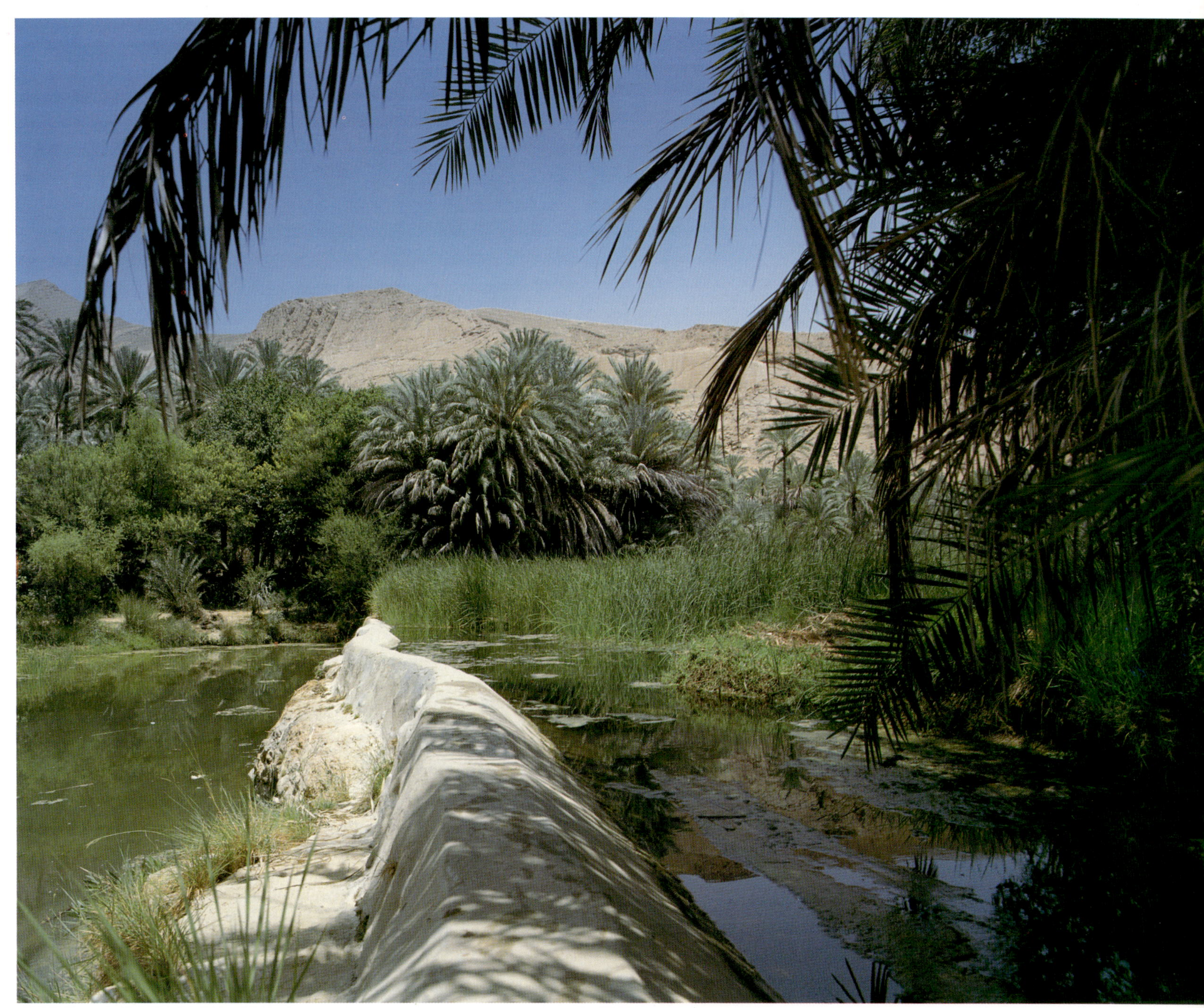

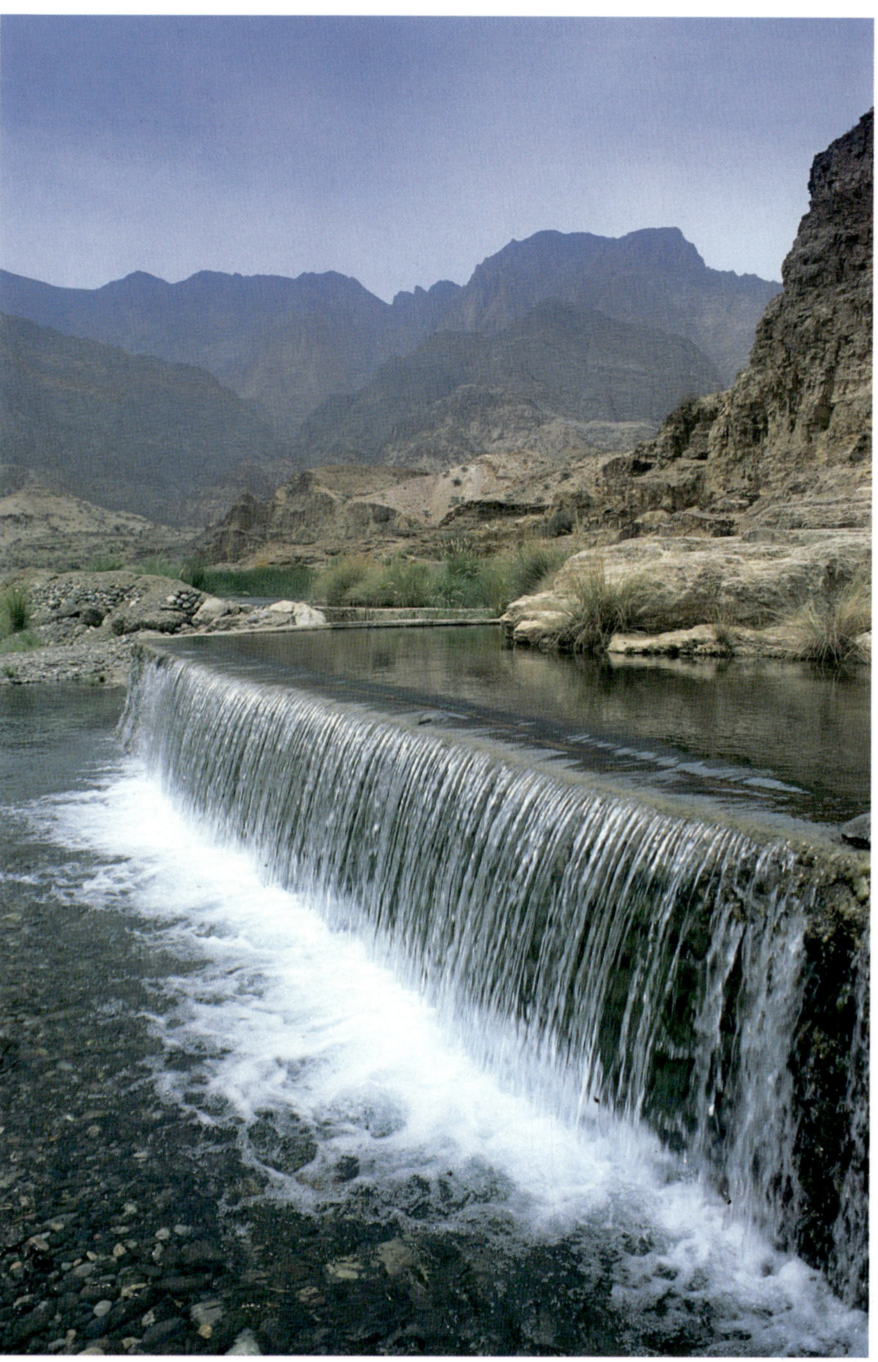

left
After recent rains, the dam near the village of Mazara in Wadi Dayqah turns into a small waterfall. With a large catchment area in the Eastern Hajar mountains, this wadi is fortunate to be a perennial water source, which at weekends attracts many campers and picnickers.

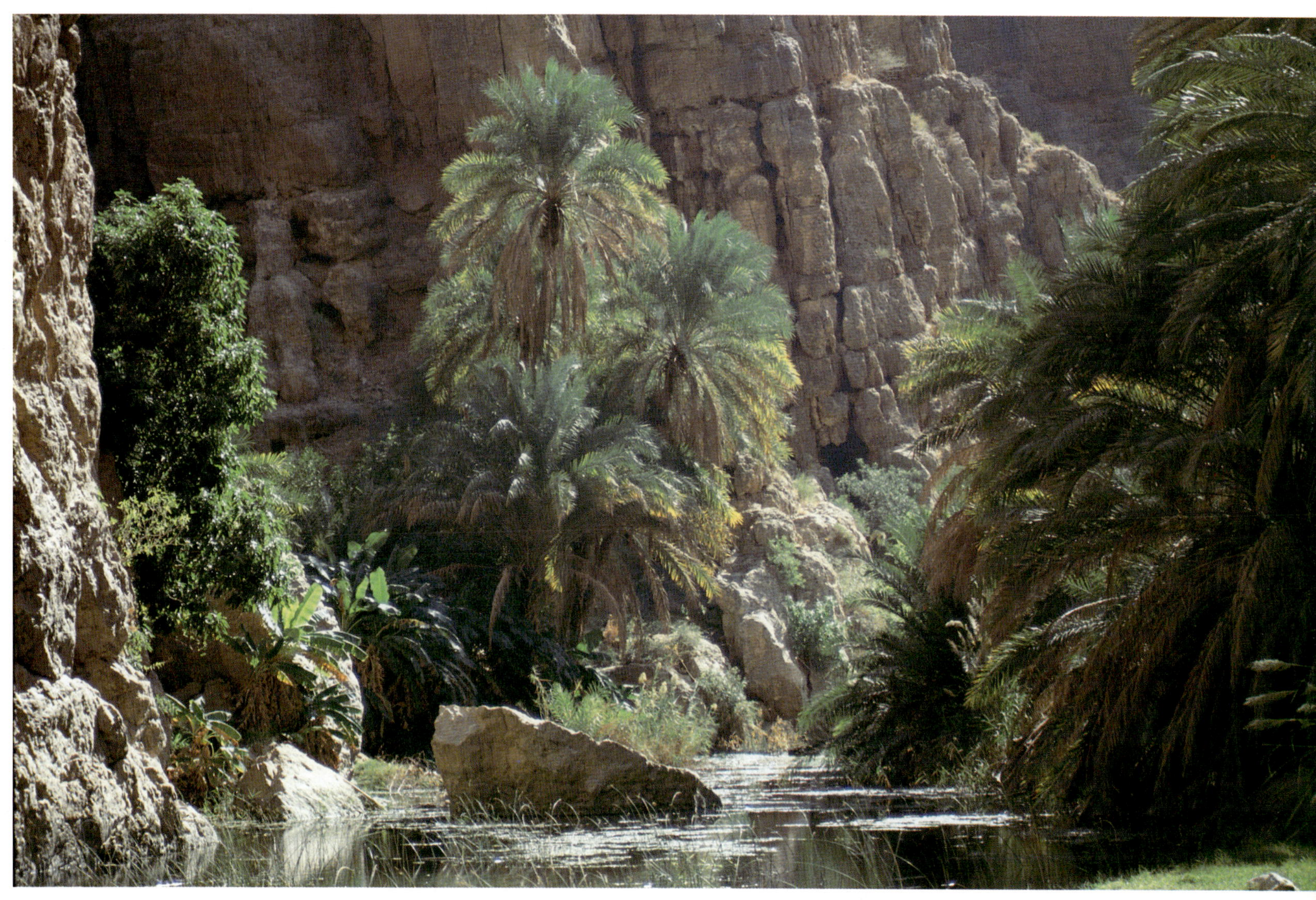

above
Very few wadis can match the drama and beauty of Wadi Shab. Cutting its way inland from the mouth of a wide creek, the wadi presents the intrepid explorer with quite a challenge. The rocky walls loom overhead, the canyon floor is covered with scattered boulders and stretches of rushing water demand fairly high levels of human endurance.

falaj channels, and the ubiquitous goats. Sooner or later, most wadis become impassable to motor vehicles – villages and homesteads beyond are supplied by pack animals, and donkey trains are still a frequent sight in, for example, Wadis Shab and Bani Khalid.

Perhaps one of Oman's most astonishing natural sights is

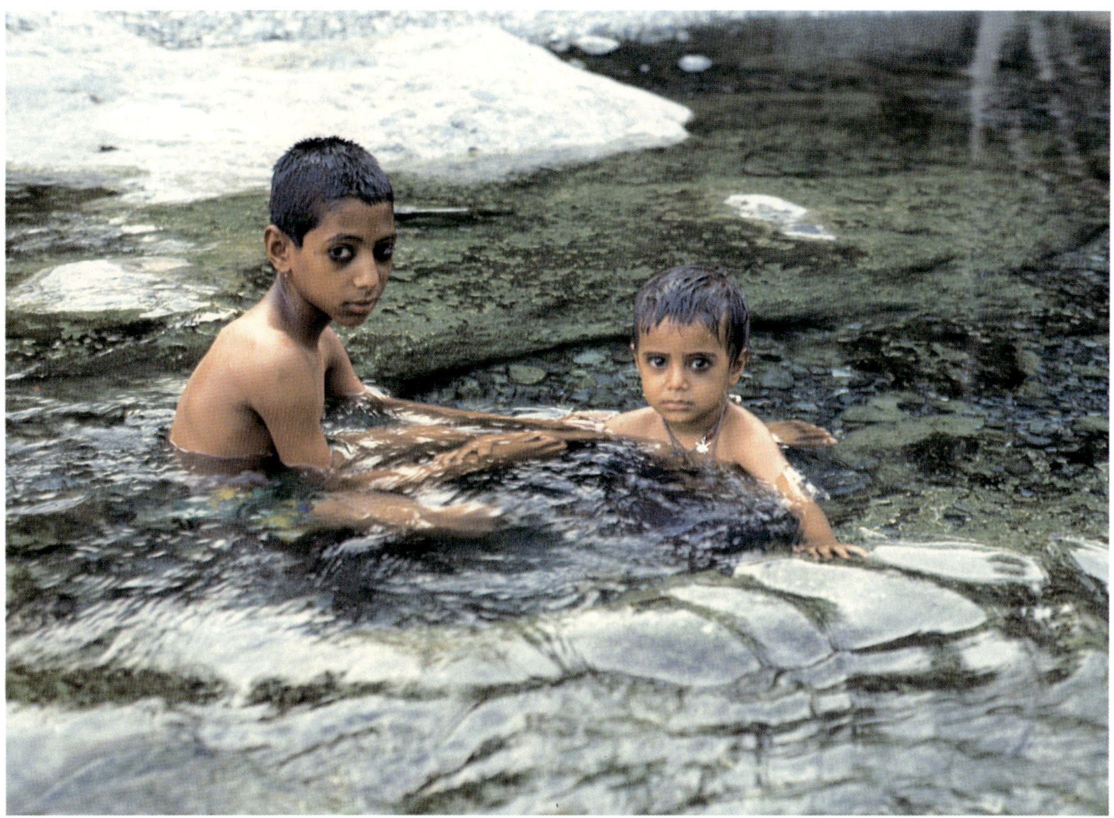

above
Oman also has its share of health spas. The hot springs where these children are playing are near Nakhl, and are now a major tourist attraction.

Wadi Darbat, in the Southern Region. At a distance, its most remarkable feature is the 200-metre-high cliff wall, eroded by wind and water into delicate patterns. Every few years, this precipice becomes for a few short hours a waterfall – the result of a sporadic cyclonic storm – and described in the 1950s by Wendell Phillips, American oil-man and explorer, as "one of the world's magnificent natural phenomena . . . unique in Arabia and must be seen to be believed".

The track down into the wadi itself is precipitous and rocky (and wholly impassable during the monsoon season), descending into light woodland, from which it emerges on the shore of a long reedy lake. "Such a scene as this we never expected to witness in Arabia", exclaimed nineteenth-century

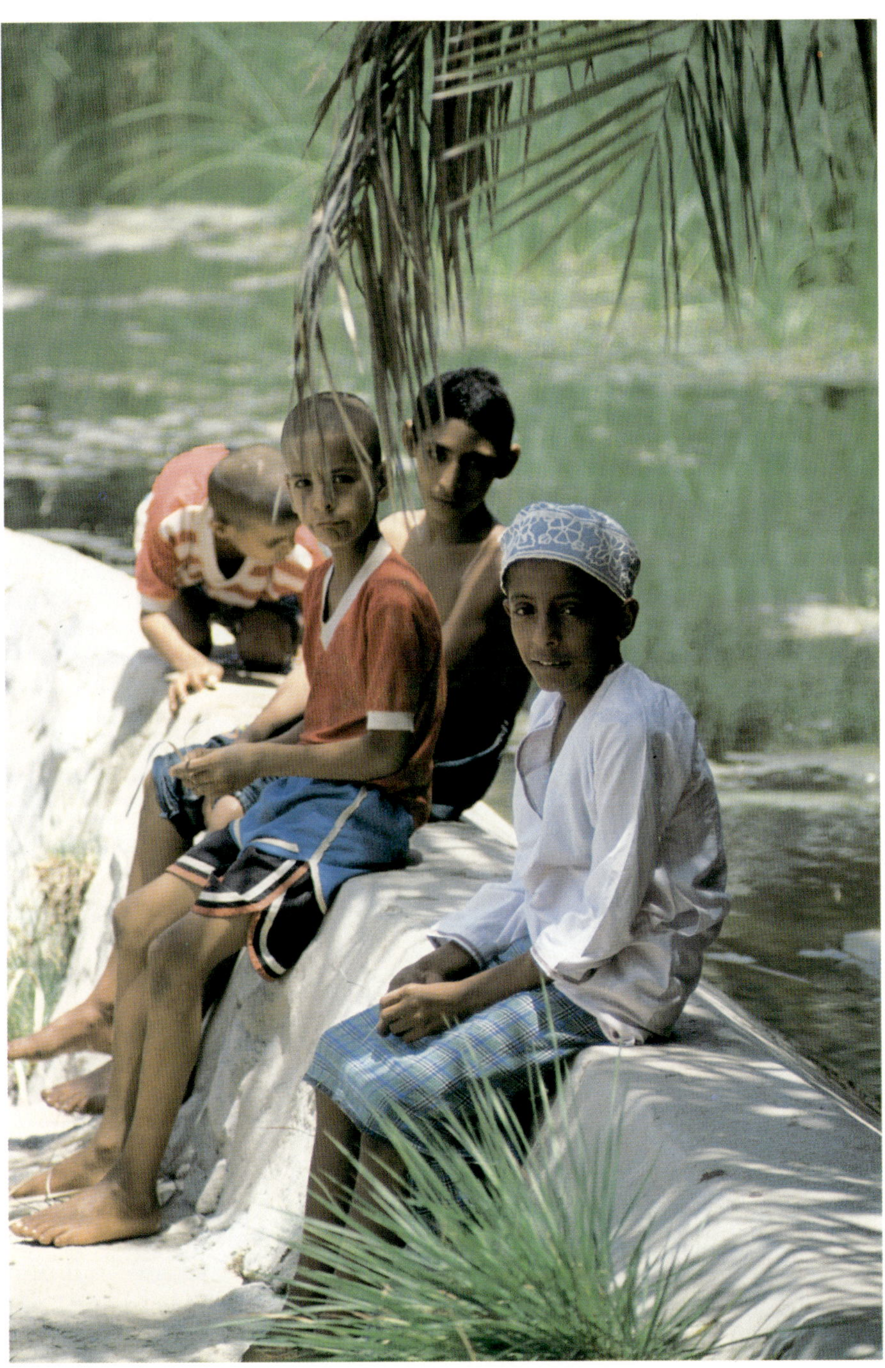

right
One of the most frequent destinations for explorers is the Wadi Bani Auf. The first 10 kilometres of road run through a narrow canyon with steep-sided cliffs. Water flows in interrupted streams along the canyon floor – a peaceful rural scene.

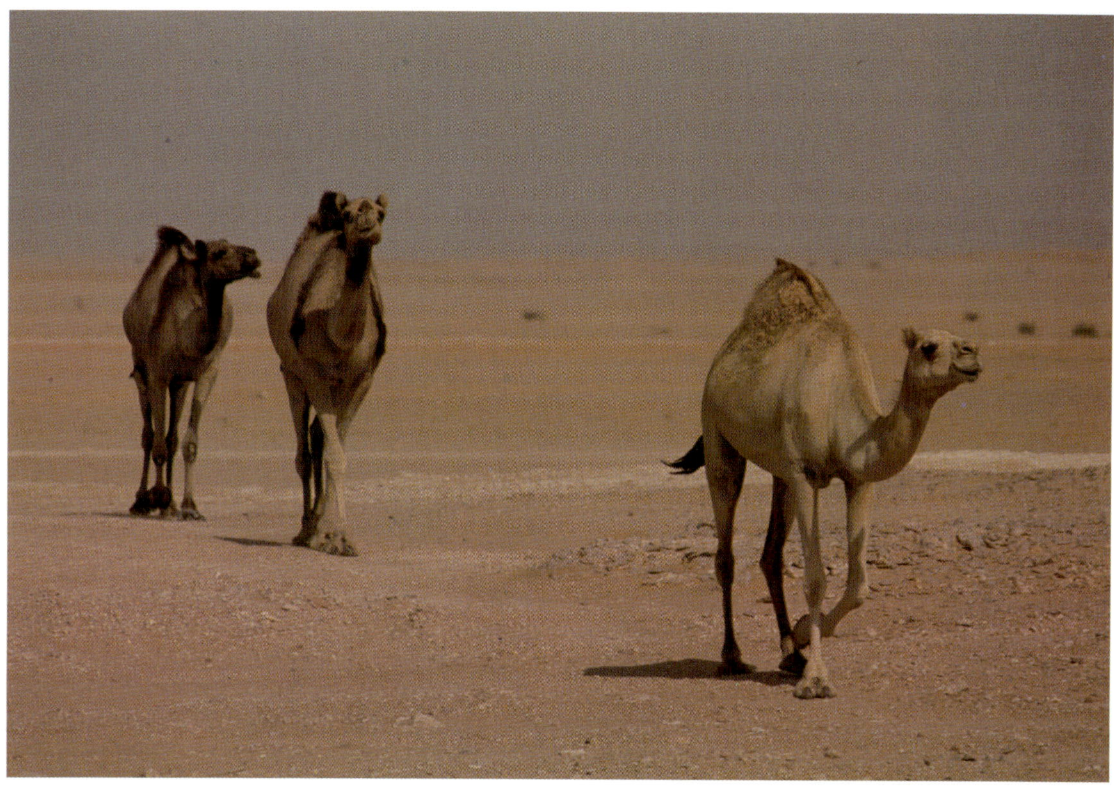

above
Camels are found all over Oman. These, near Thumrait, make light work of the rocky desert they are strolling through.

explorers Theodore and Mabel Bent – and their amazement was well-founded. Water-birds are plentiful, and the bushes and trees beside the lake are hung with the tiny, almost spherical nests of Rüppell's weavers. These exquisite nests are built by the male bird as part of the courtship ritual – if his mate doesn't like the nest, she tears it apart and he must start again, until he provides a bower in which she is happy to lay her eggs. Few people now live in the wadi, though it provides fine grazing for camels, cattle and the small, short-haired Dhofari goats.

This section would not be complete without a return to where we started: Arabian sands. In taking note of Oman's natural variety, it must also be said that two of the world's great sand-seas are found partly or wholly within the borders

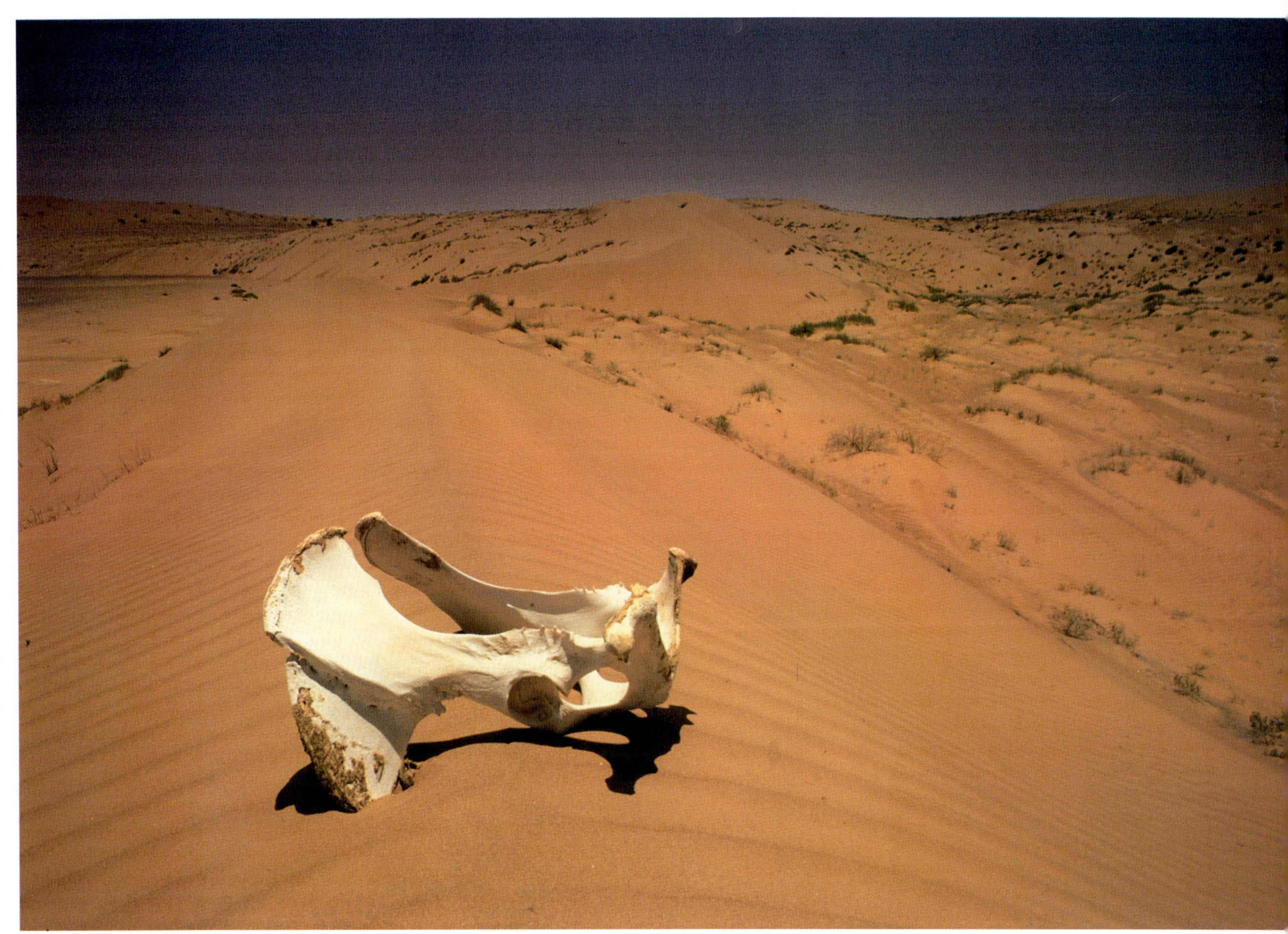

above
A camel hip-bone bears silent testimony to the extremely harsh arid conditions of the Wahiba Sands. The sand-sea, recently the subject of a major environmental study, has a temperature range between 55°C during the day and near freezing point at night.

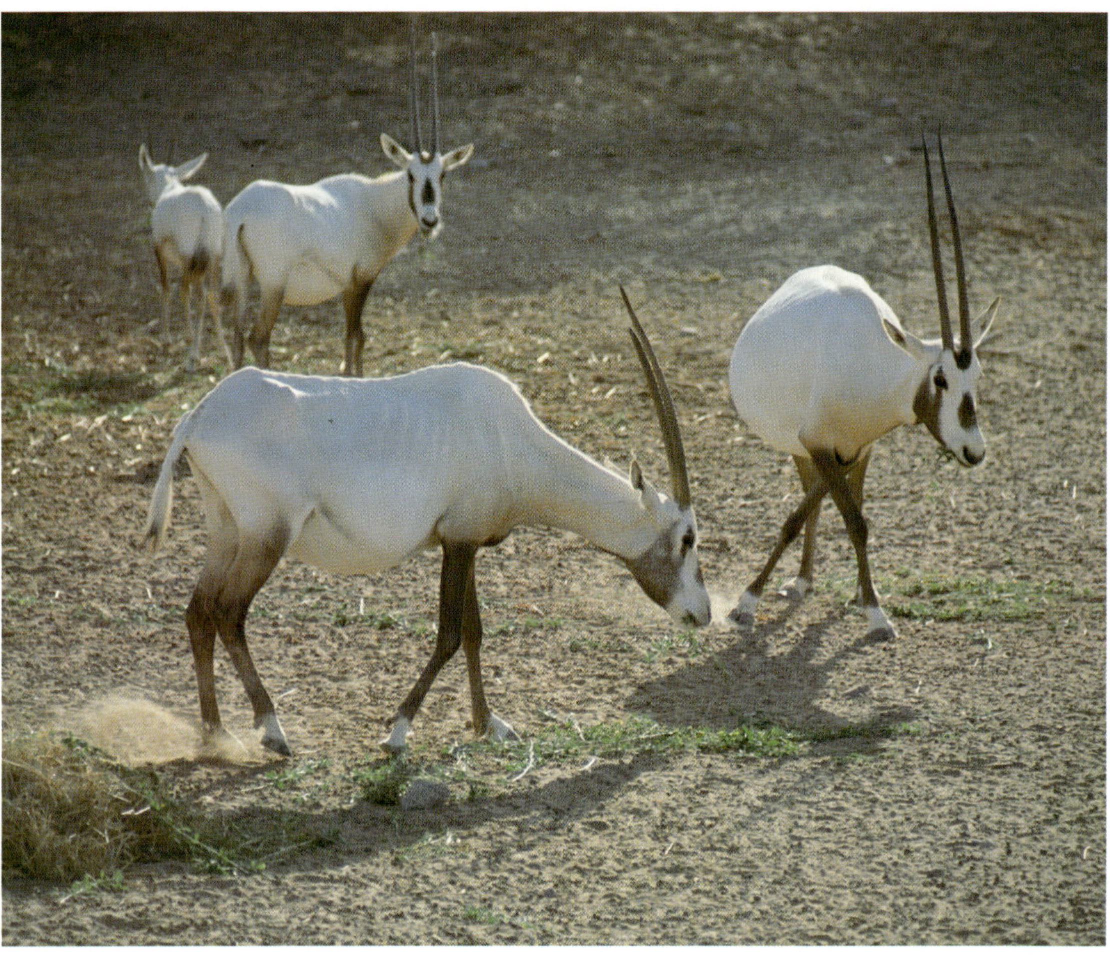

above
Sleek and swift, graceful in movement and beautiful to look at, the Arabian white oryx is a native of Oman – and a species that was given a new lease of life by the Government's White Oryx Project. The Arabian white oryx, an antelope, is specially adapted to life in a harsh desert environment where they now roam the gravel plains in increasing numbers.

of Oman: the Empty Quarter (Rub al Khali), over which explorers such as Bertram Thomas and Wilfred Thesiger trekked, and the Wahiba Sands, a small (10,000 square kilometres), isolated "perfect specimen of a sand-sea", as it has been described. An intensive five-month study of the Wahiba Sands was carried out by Britain's Royal Geographical Society, in conjunction with the government of Oman, and involving 35 international scientists and more than 500 other people. Among their discoveries were 150 plant species; an ecosystem surviving on dew; woodlands of *ghaf* trees which

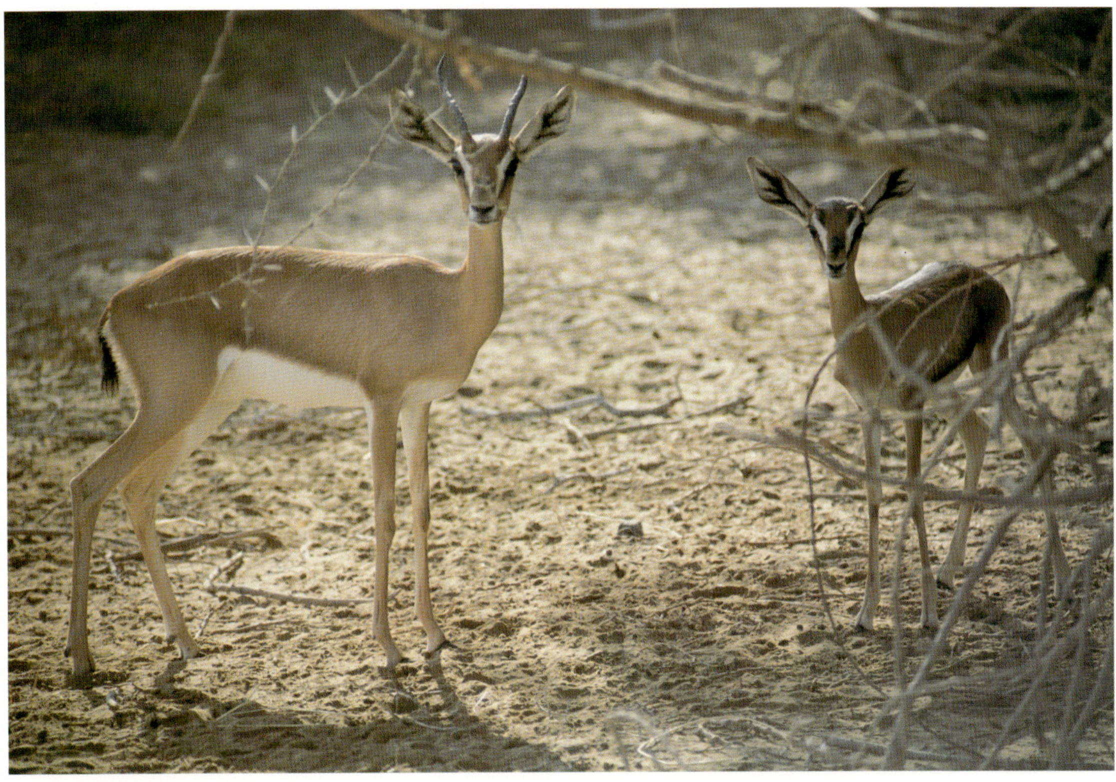

above
Arabian gazelles are very much a part of Oman's wildlife. These doe-eyed, slender-legged creatures don't often show themselves to inquisitive visitors. However, those who have ventured into the Interior report seeing these graceful animals moving at some speed across the plains, sometimes even close to major towns.

are home to over 200 species of mammals, birds, reptiles and amphibians; the largest cemented sand-sea in the world; and 16,000 invertebrate specimens, including a dew-drinking beetle previously found only in Africa's Namib Desert.

So despite their barren appearance at first sight, even the most inhospitable areas of Oman are teeming with life, not all of which has yet been fully understood or investigated.

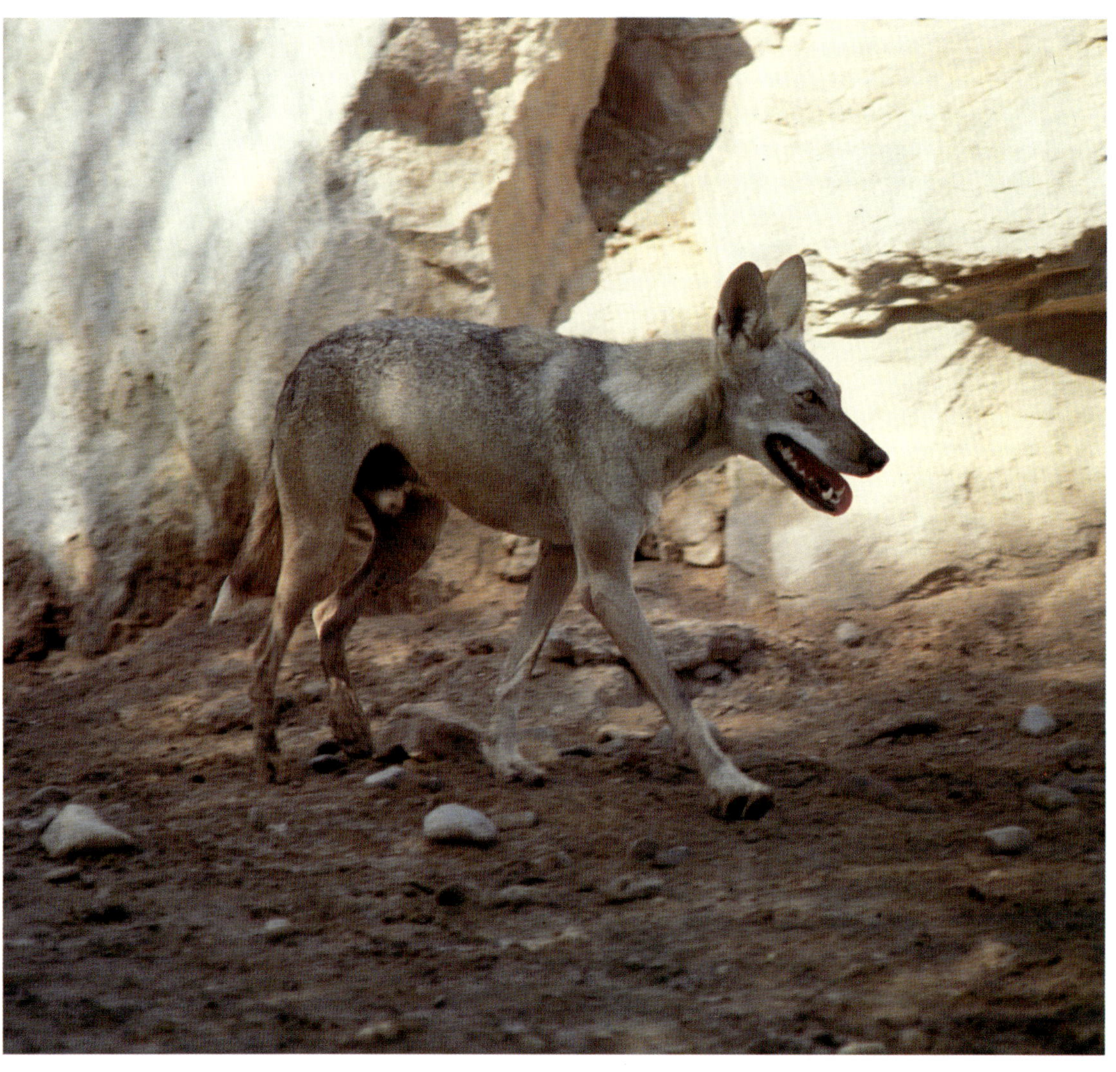

above
Most people do not associate Oman with ferocious wildlife. But some species are native to Oman – such as this Arabian wolf on the prowl.

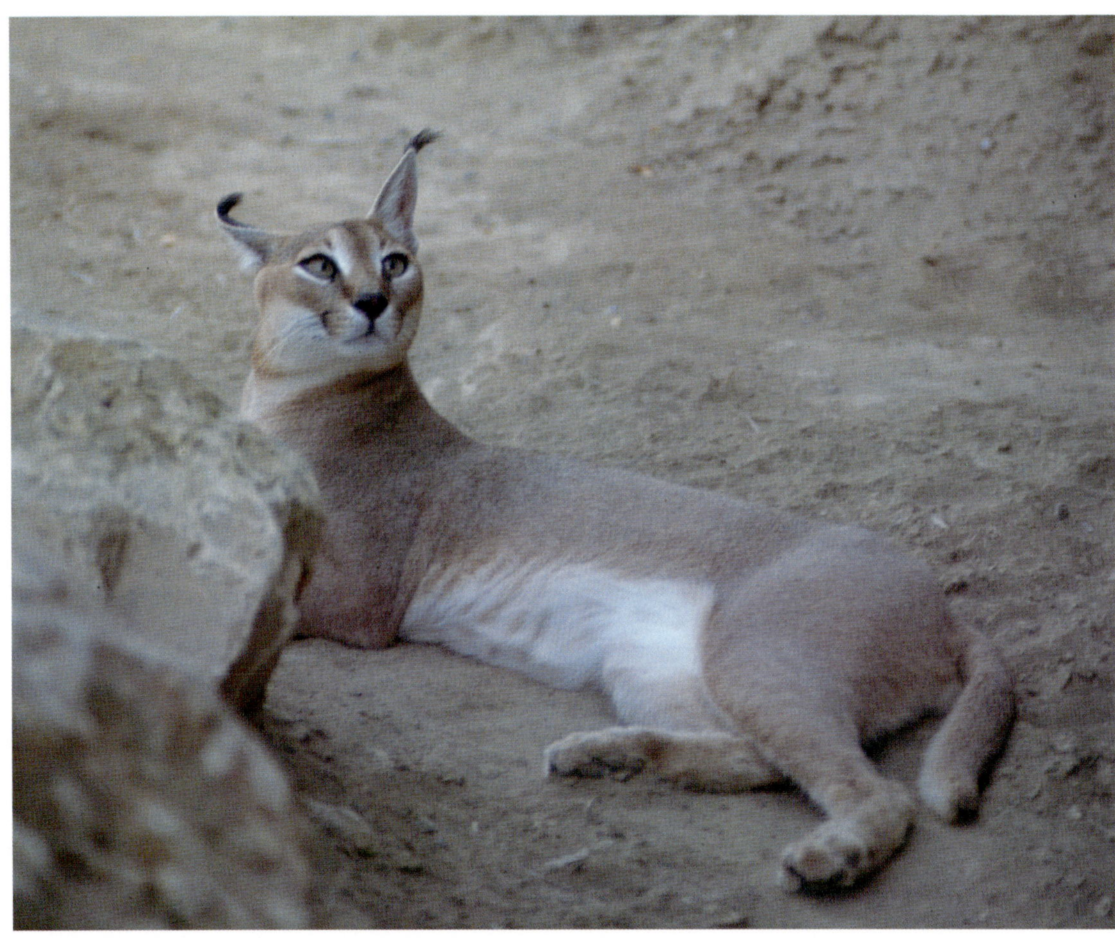

above
An almost human look of enquiry seems to shine out of the eyes of this caracal lynx. While here it is seen at peace with its world and very restful in its demeanour, this member of the cat family can move at lightning speed.

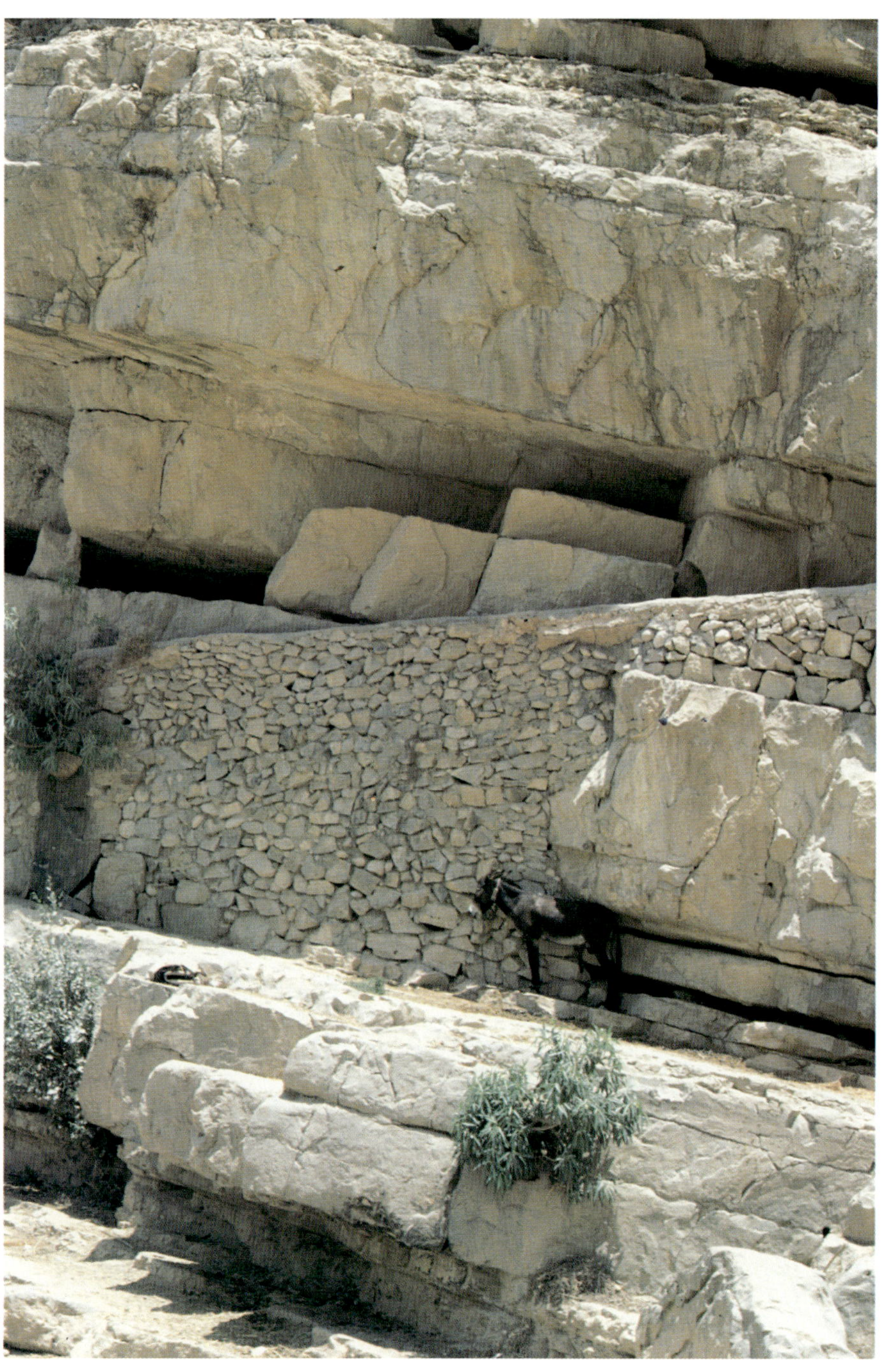

left
These wadis once contained the rushing waters of rivers that ran deep and wide. Today, they are parched river-beds whose rocky walls bear mute testimony that life-giving waters once flowed between them. Along these wadi walls, man has laboured to build pathways that link up far-flung rural communities.

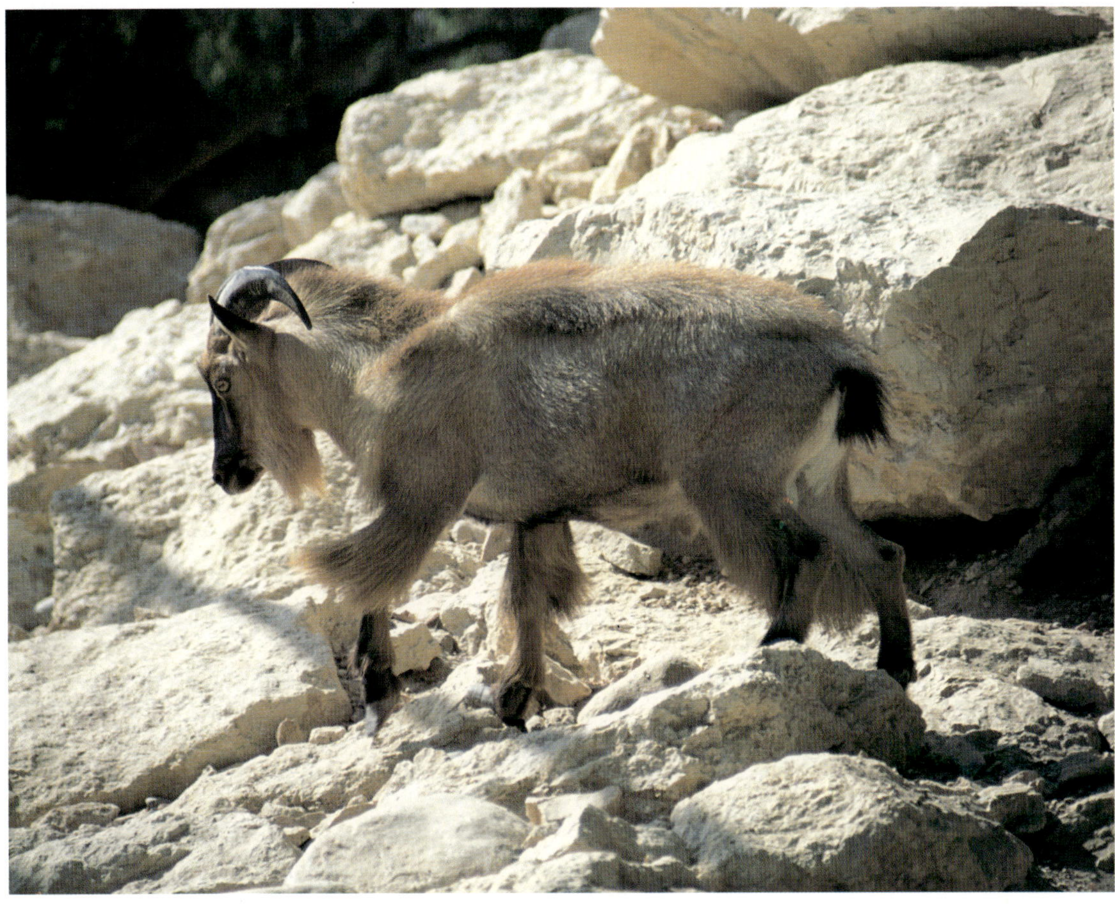

above
The government's conservation programmes have done much to save many species of wildlife from becoming extinct. Amongst those which flourish today is the *tahr*, a kind of long-haired half goat.

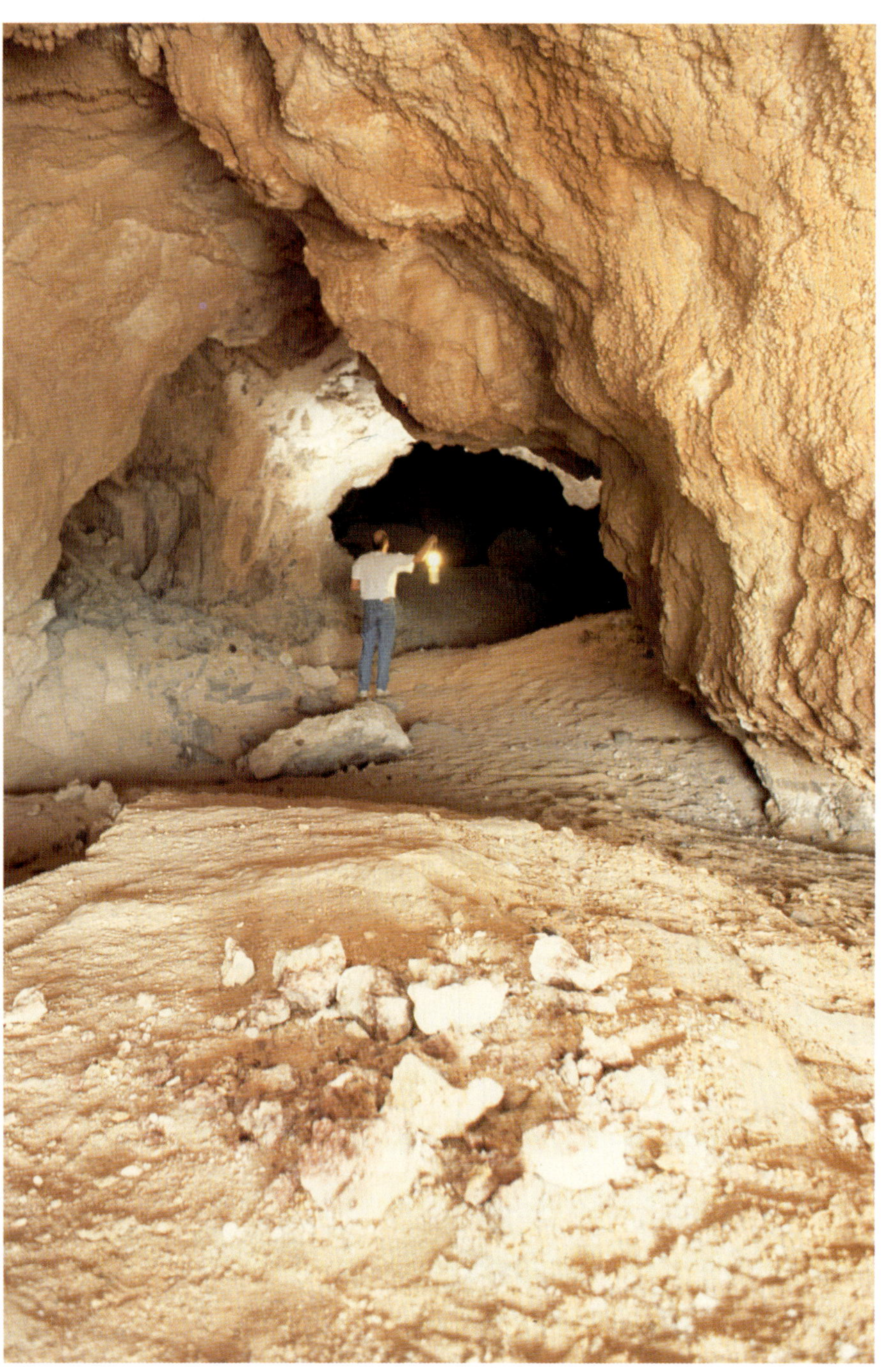

left
For many centuries the Bedouin relied upon the ancient salt mines of Qarat Al Milh and Qarat Al Kibrit. The salt domes, here being explored by the photographer, are caused by salt in the rocks migrating upward and being eroded by natural process. It is probable that sulphur, which was used as a treatment for camel sores, was also found in the area.

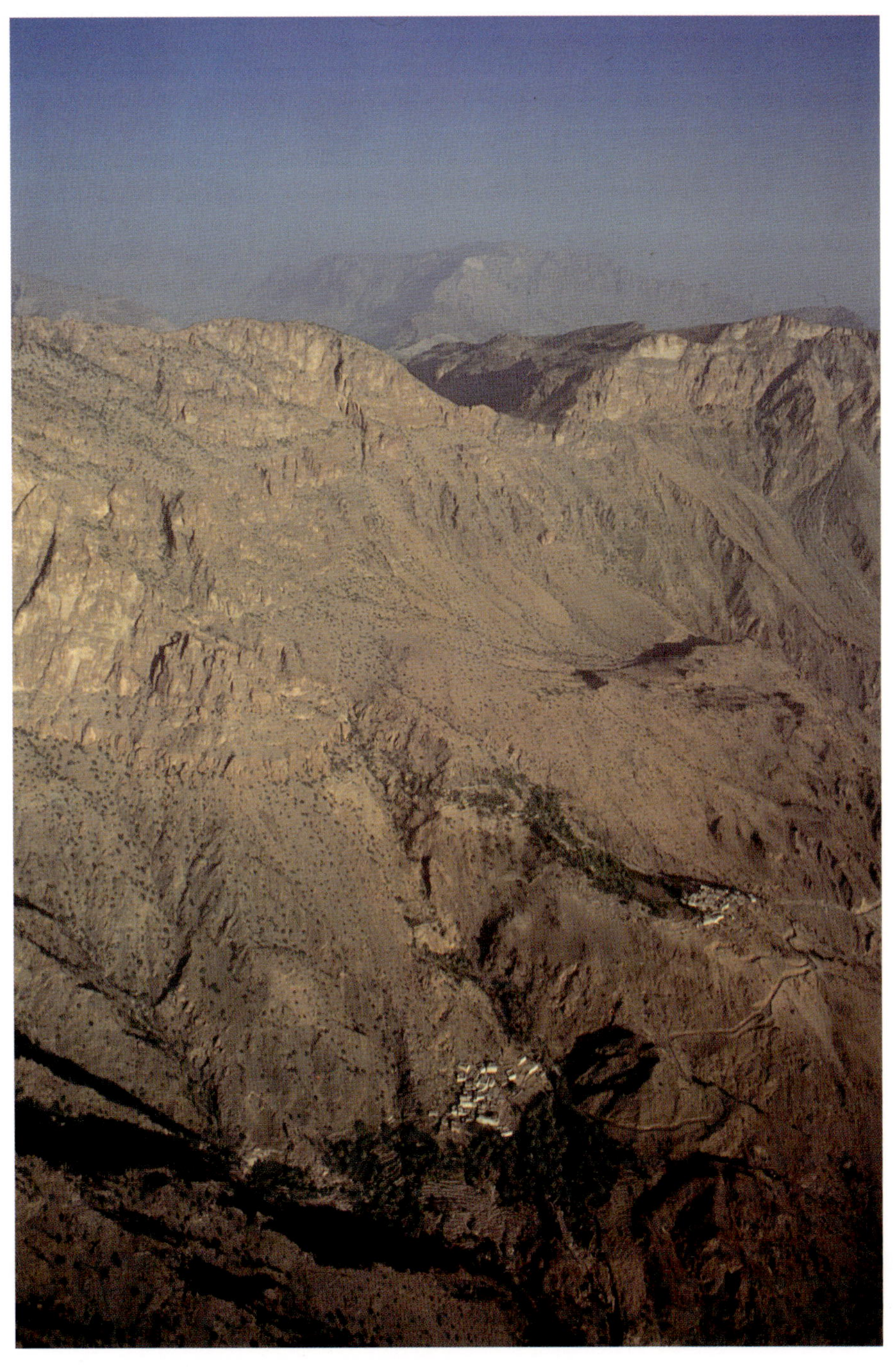

right
In a land where drama is intrinsic to the landscape, this little hamlet, called Wakan village, is huddled high up in the protective embrace of the Ghubrah bowl – a natural rock formation near Rustaq.

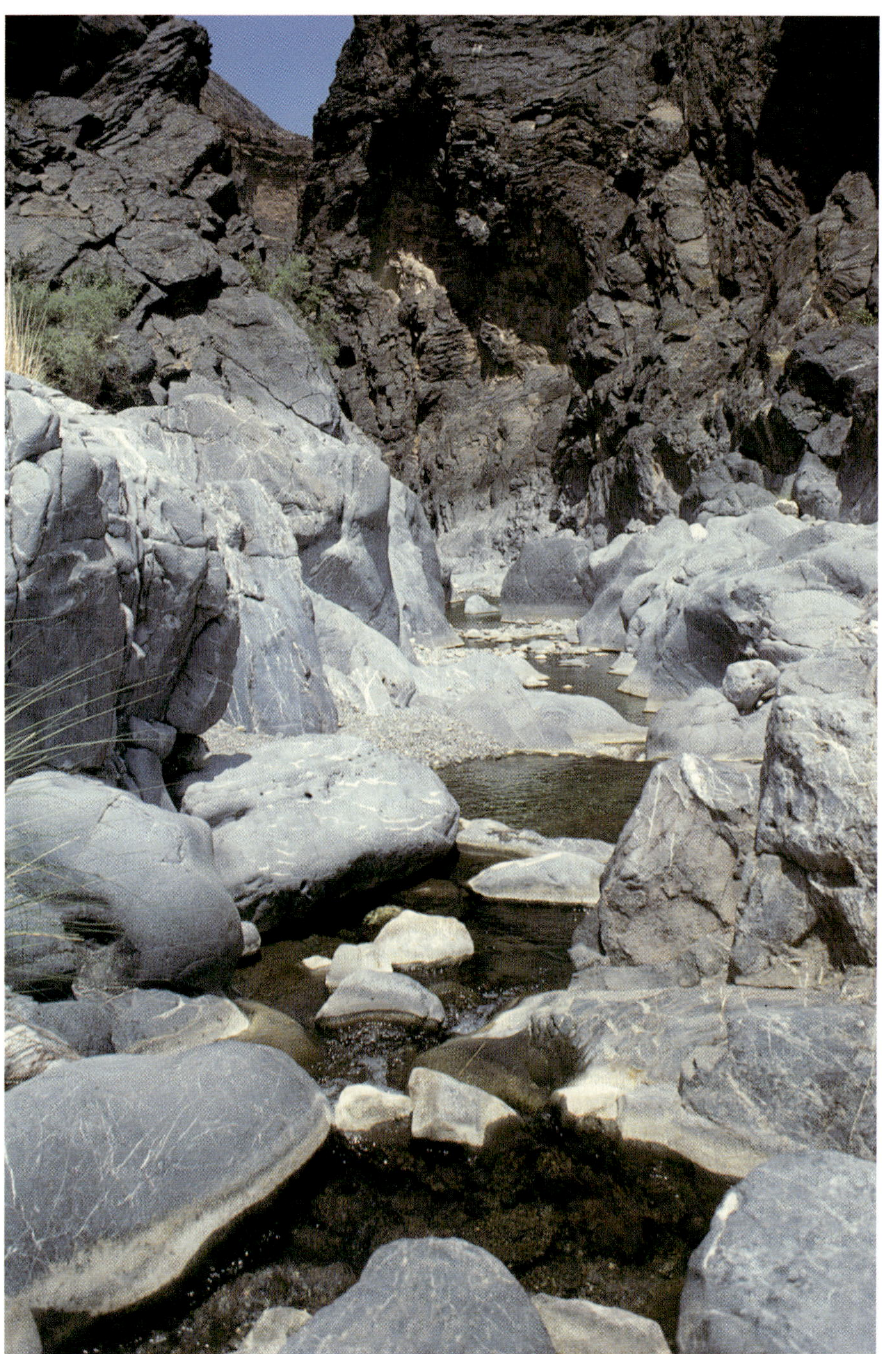

left
A section of Wadi Bani Auf, which is also known by some expatriates as the snake gorge, is littered with massive boulders and pools of water – connected by small waterfalls. Most of the day the gorge is shaded, providing a cool and refreshing stop for explorers. The snakes that give this its name usually disappear before they are seen, like most animals in Oman.

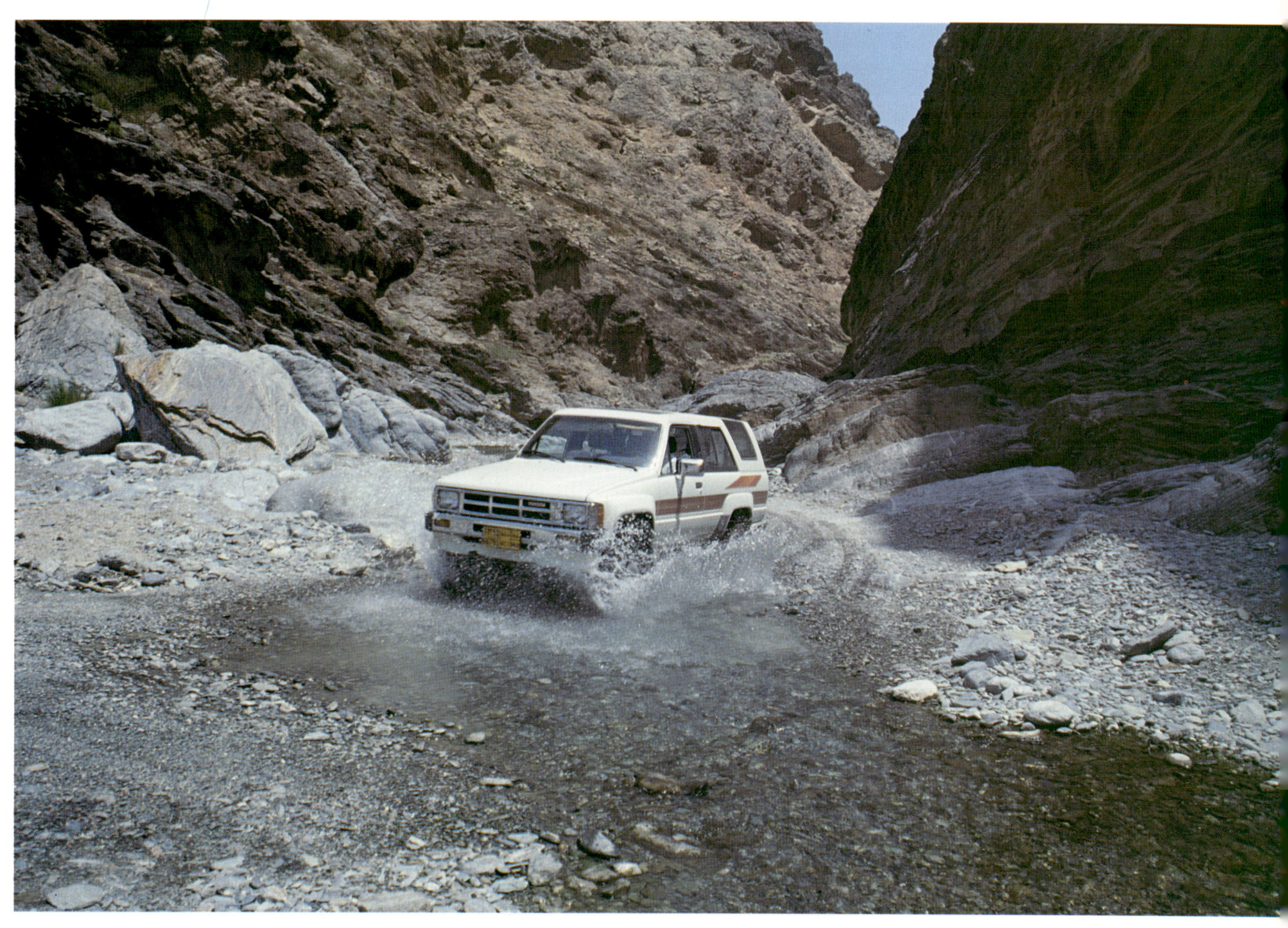

above

During the cooler months of the year, groups of families and friends can be seen taking off into the Interior in a variety of four-wheel drives and pick-ups – all set for a weekend out in the wild. Amongst the more frequented spots is Wadi Bani Auf – where the canyon presents a host of possible camping spots away from the main road.

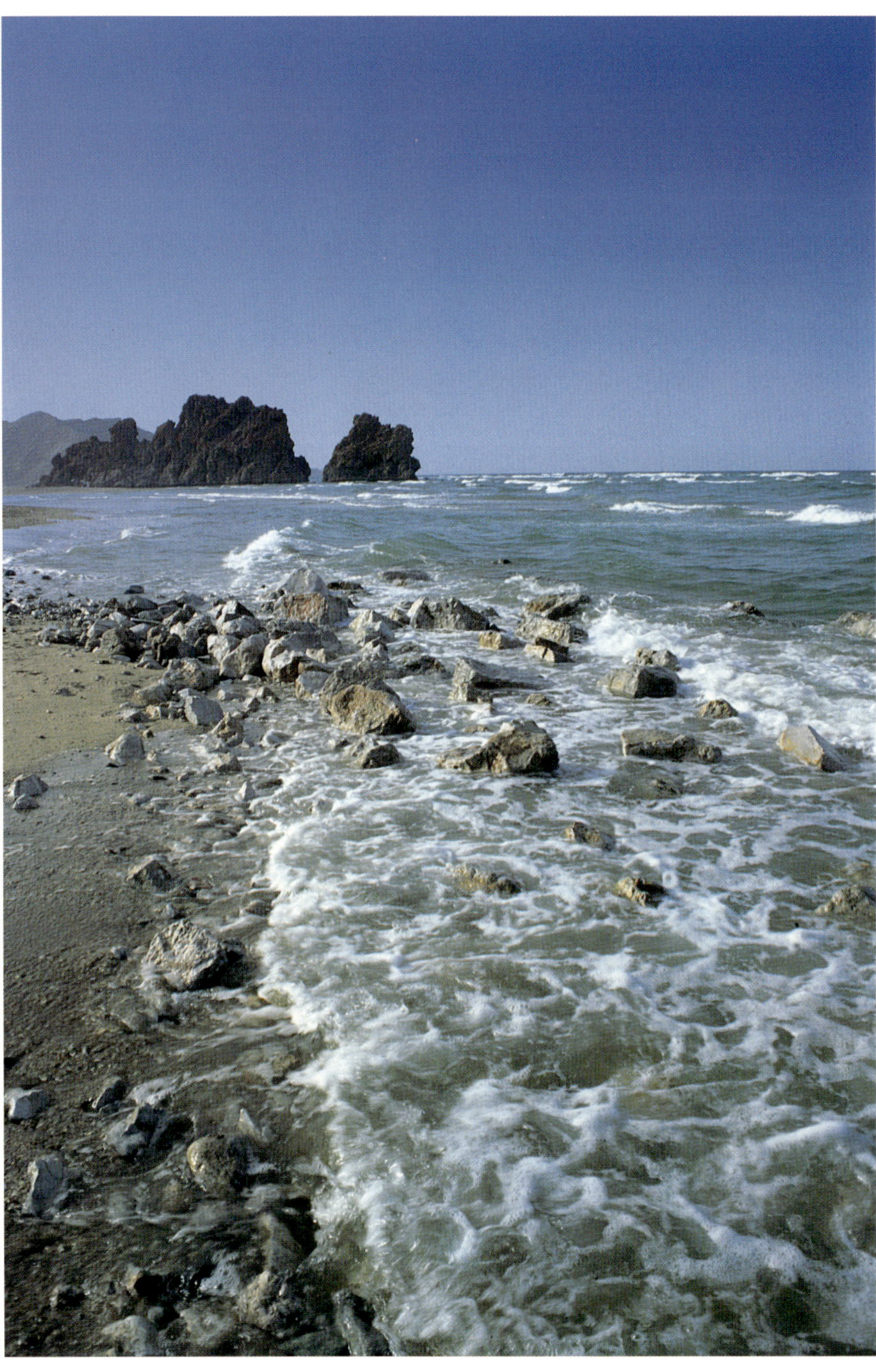

left
Very few countries can match the unparalleled beauty of Oman's coastlines. While the seas are relatively calm, they do wash up with some force against jagged outcrops and limestone cliffs. However, the beaches are a wonderful haven for swimmers and deep-sea divers.

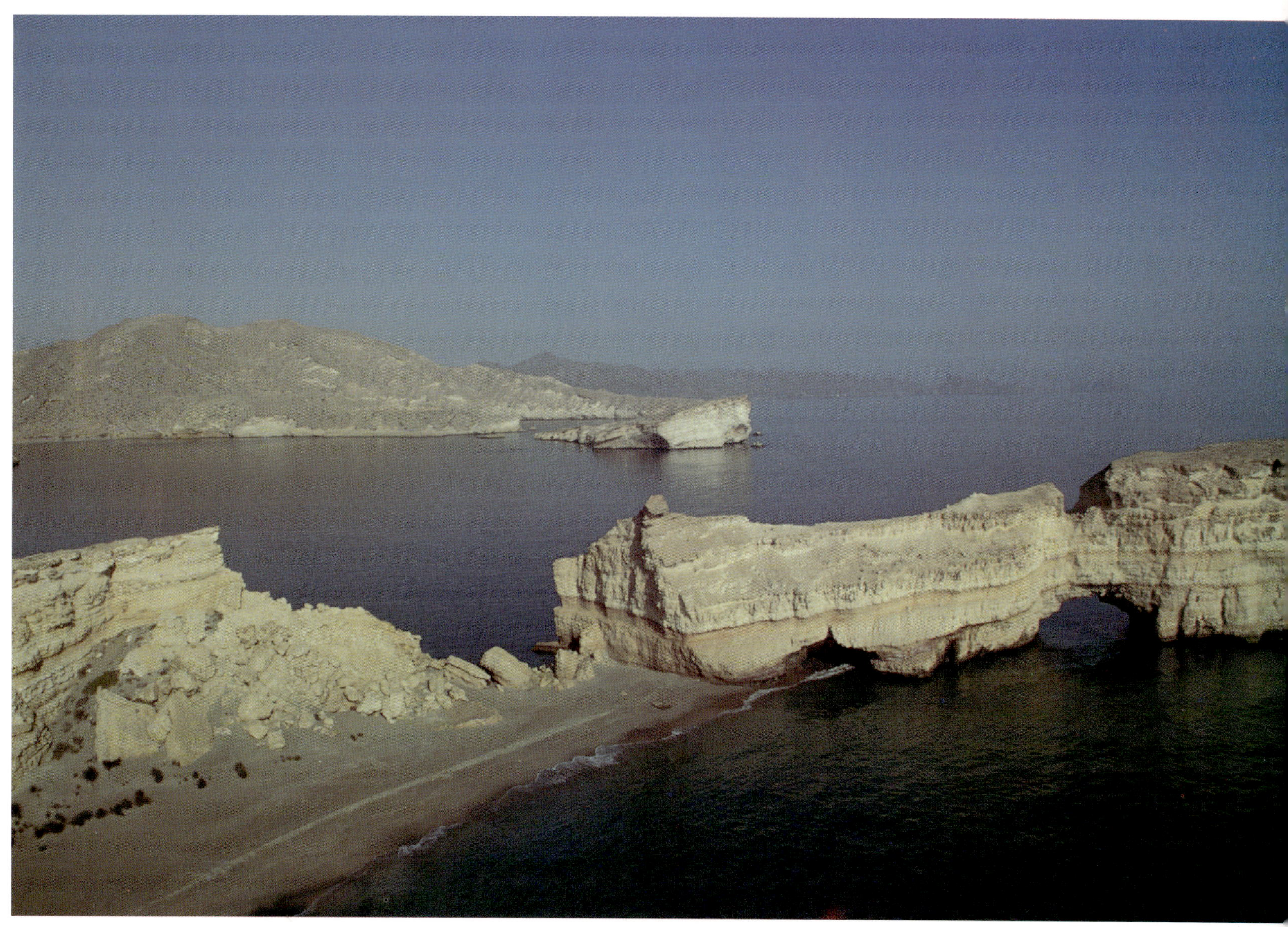

above
The dramatic coastline east of Muscat is peppered with small bays and beaches amongst the limestone outcrops and cliffs. This area near Bandar Jissah and Bandar Khayran is a major weekend playground for pleasure boaters and sport fishermen.

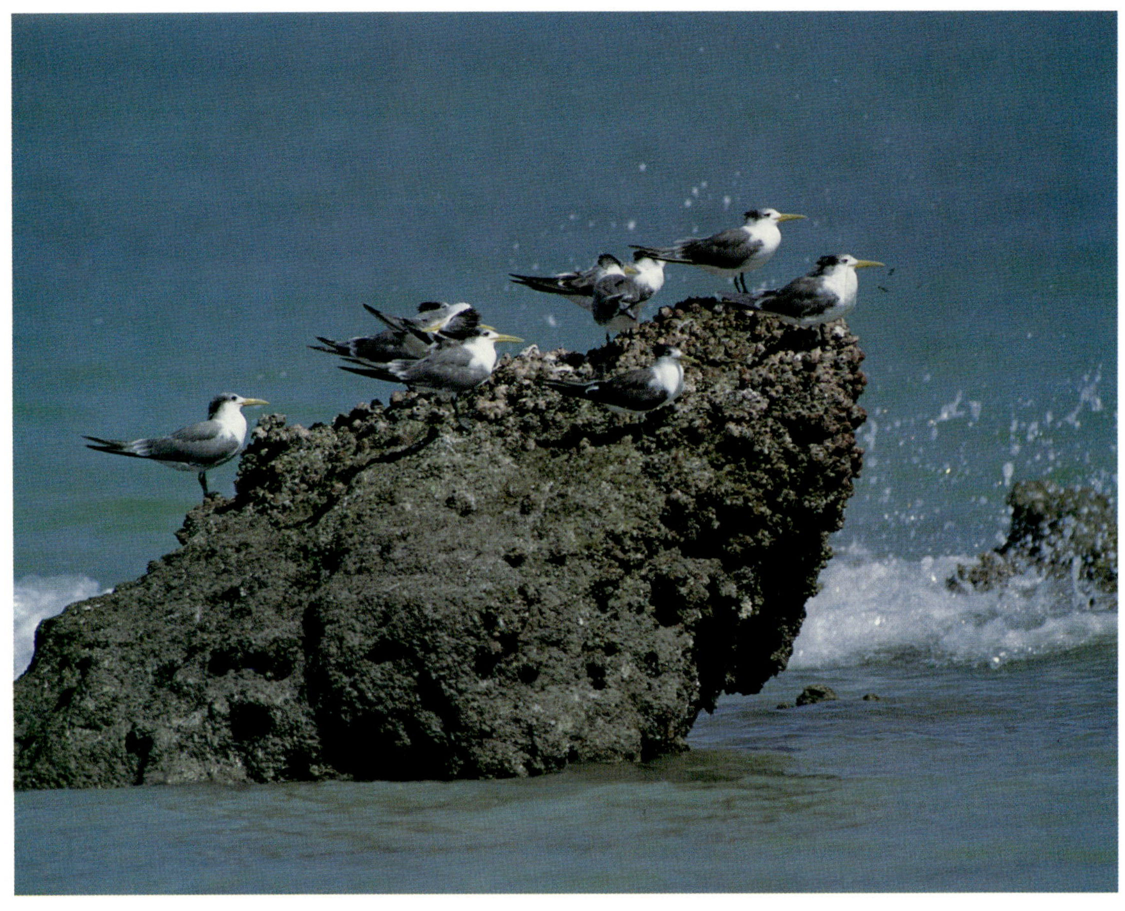

above

The silvery sands and aquamarine seas of Oman are alive to the sounds of marine life. Over water, the air resounds to the call of a variety of sea birds. Bathers and picnickers are quite often entertained by clouds of terns as they dive for food in the blue waters.

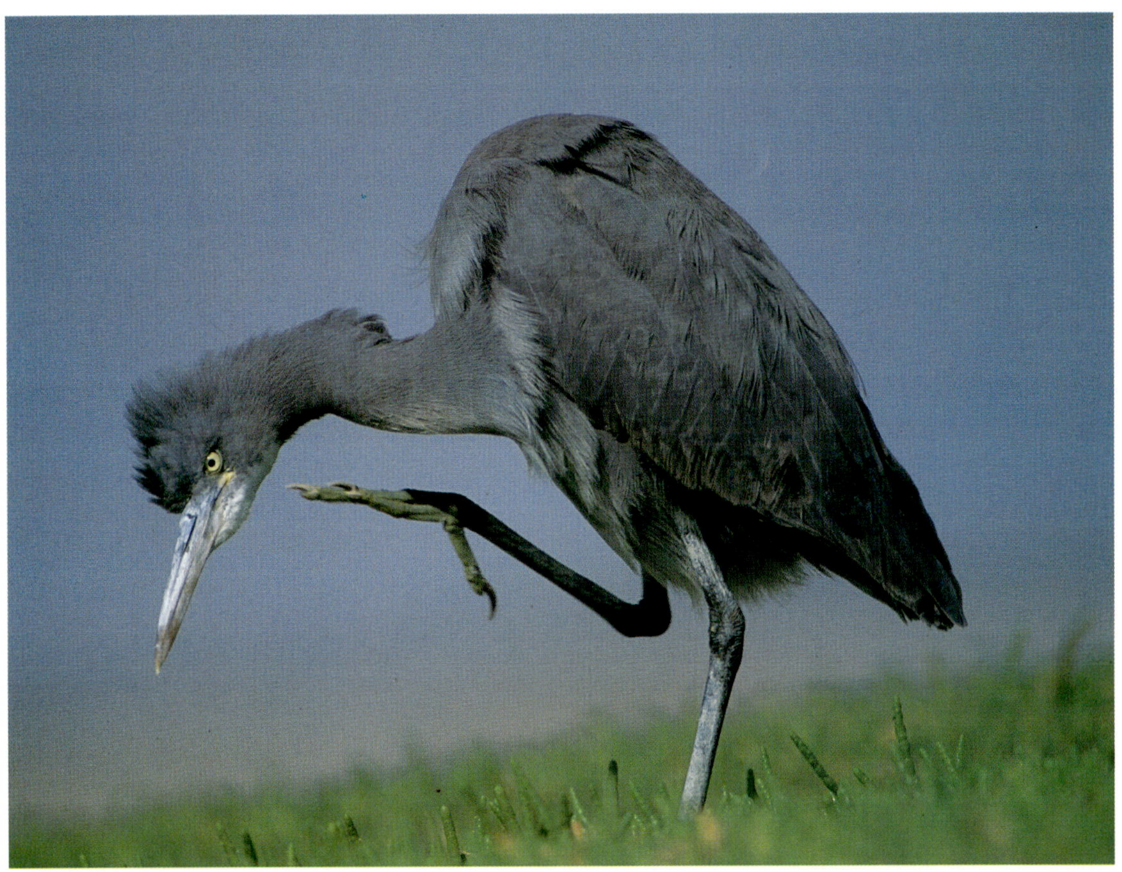

above
A large population of migratory birds, as well as the many indigenous ones, make Oman a exceptional place for bird-life. Amongst these are the grey egret – blue-grey in colour with long, slender legs.

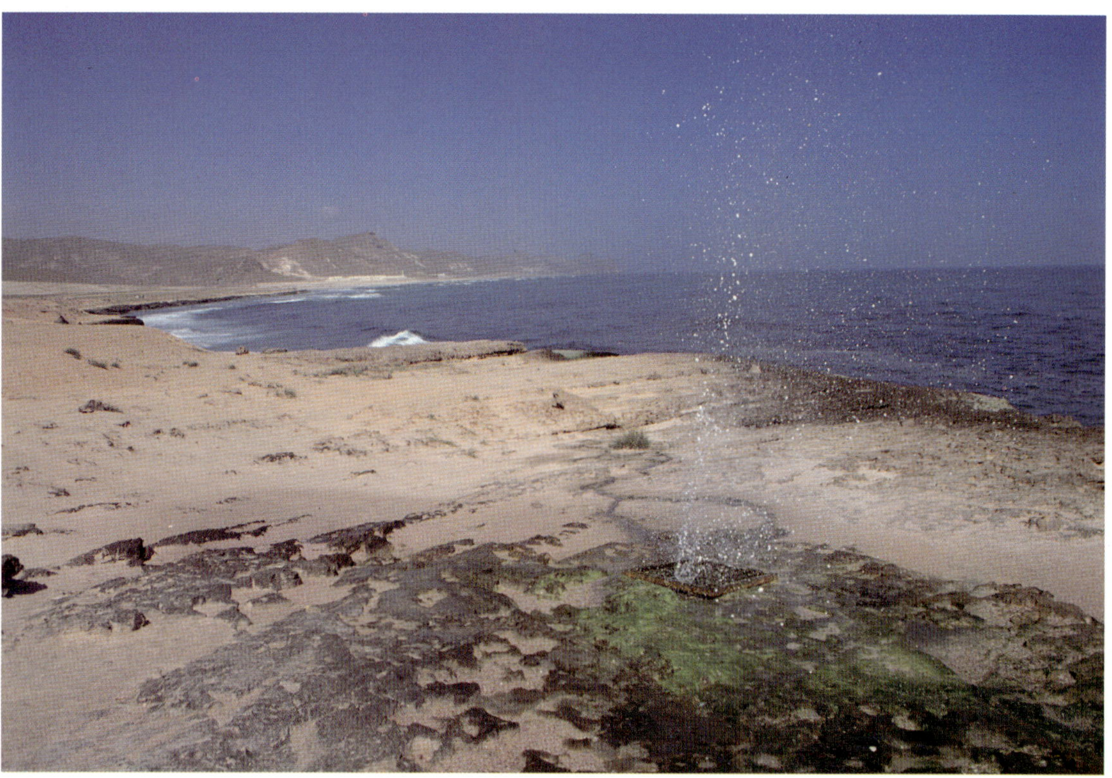

above
The overhanging limestone cliffs near Mughsayl beach in Dhofar, have been eroded at sea level, making small caverns which cause waterspouts through fissures. During the monsoon season, when the waves are heavy, an eerie sound caused by rushing air through the cracks in the rock heralds the coming of the jet of spray.

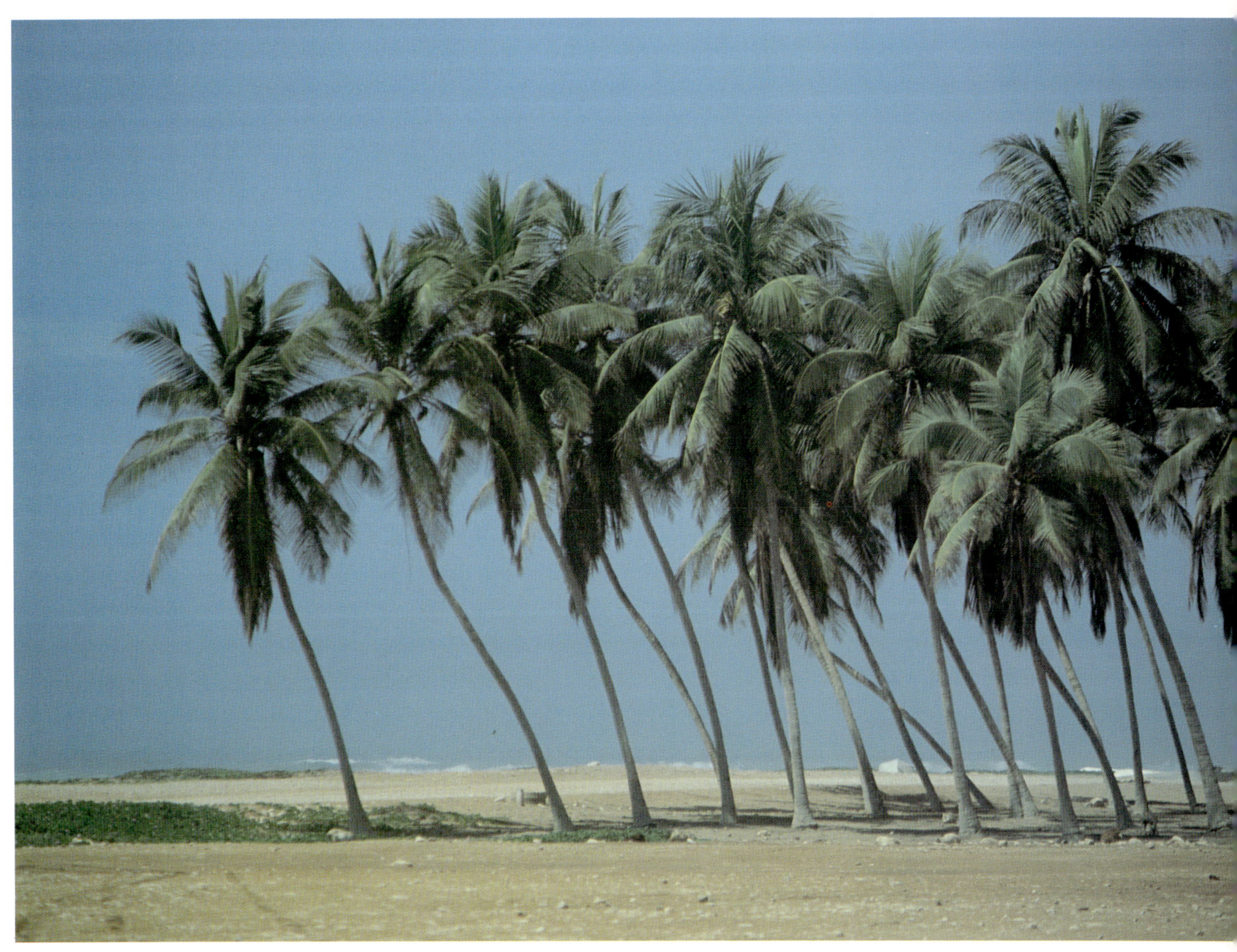

above
With probably one of the best beaches in the world, coconut palms line the white sand coast of the Indian Ocean near Salalah.

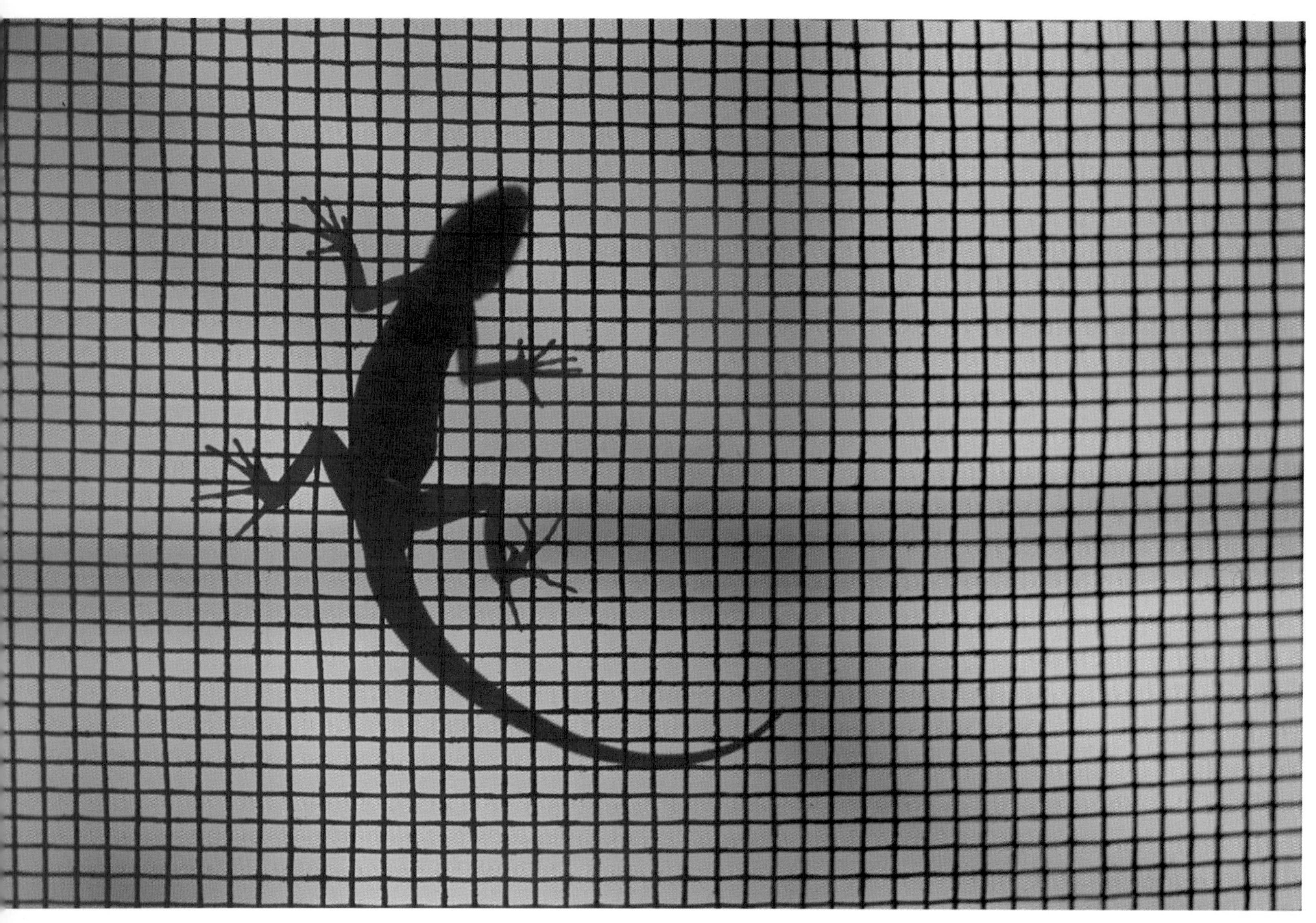

above
Common household geckos, far from being a household pest, do a wonderful job of catching mosquitoes and other small flying insects.

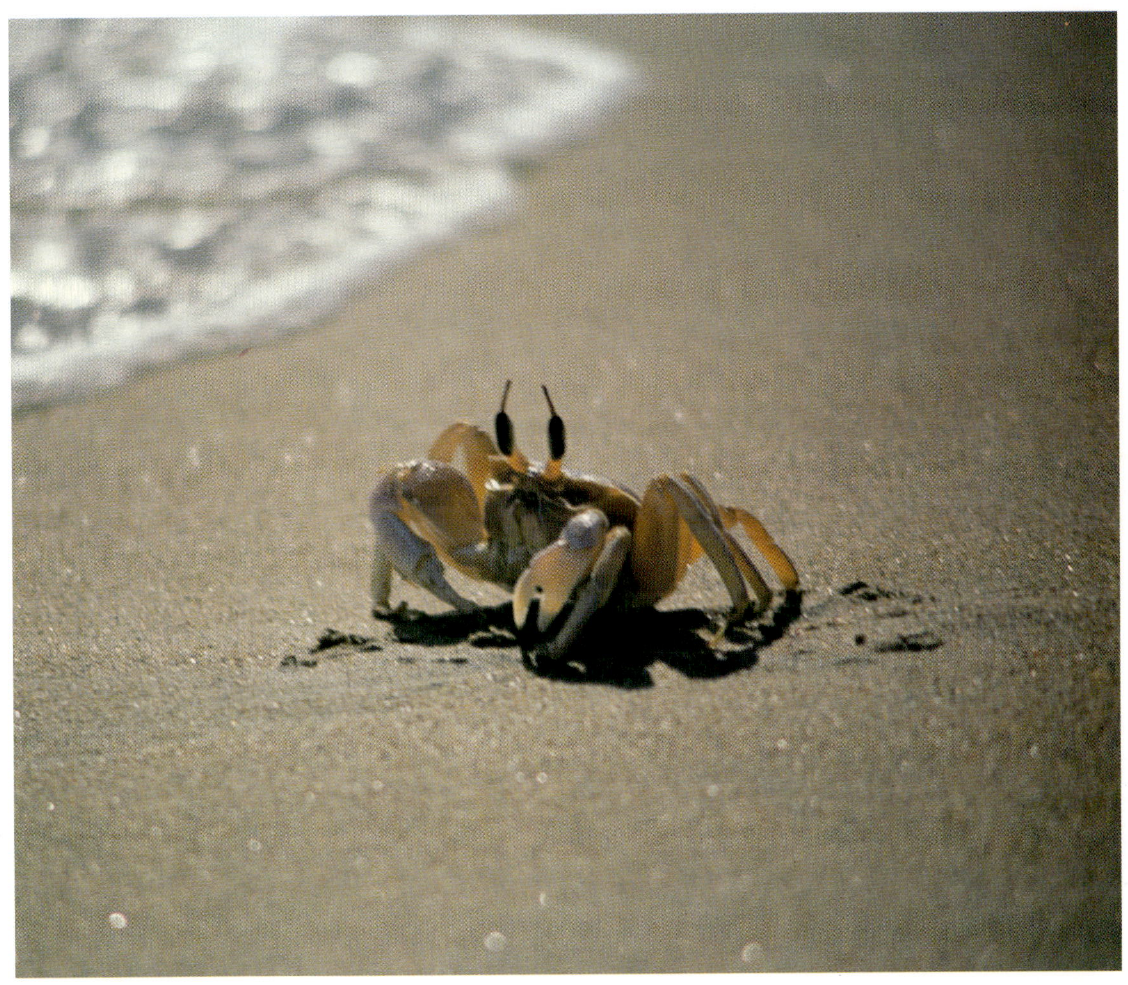

above
Ghost crabs, though extremely skittish, can be highly inquisitive. By keeping very still, visitors may tempt them to within a few metres by fish-bait.

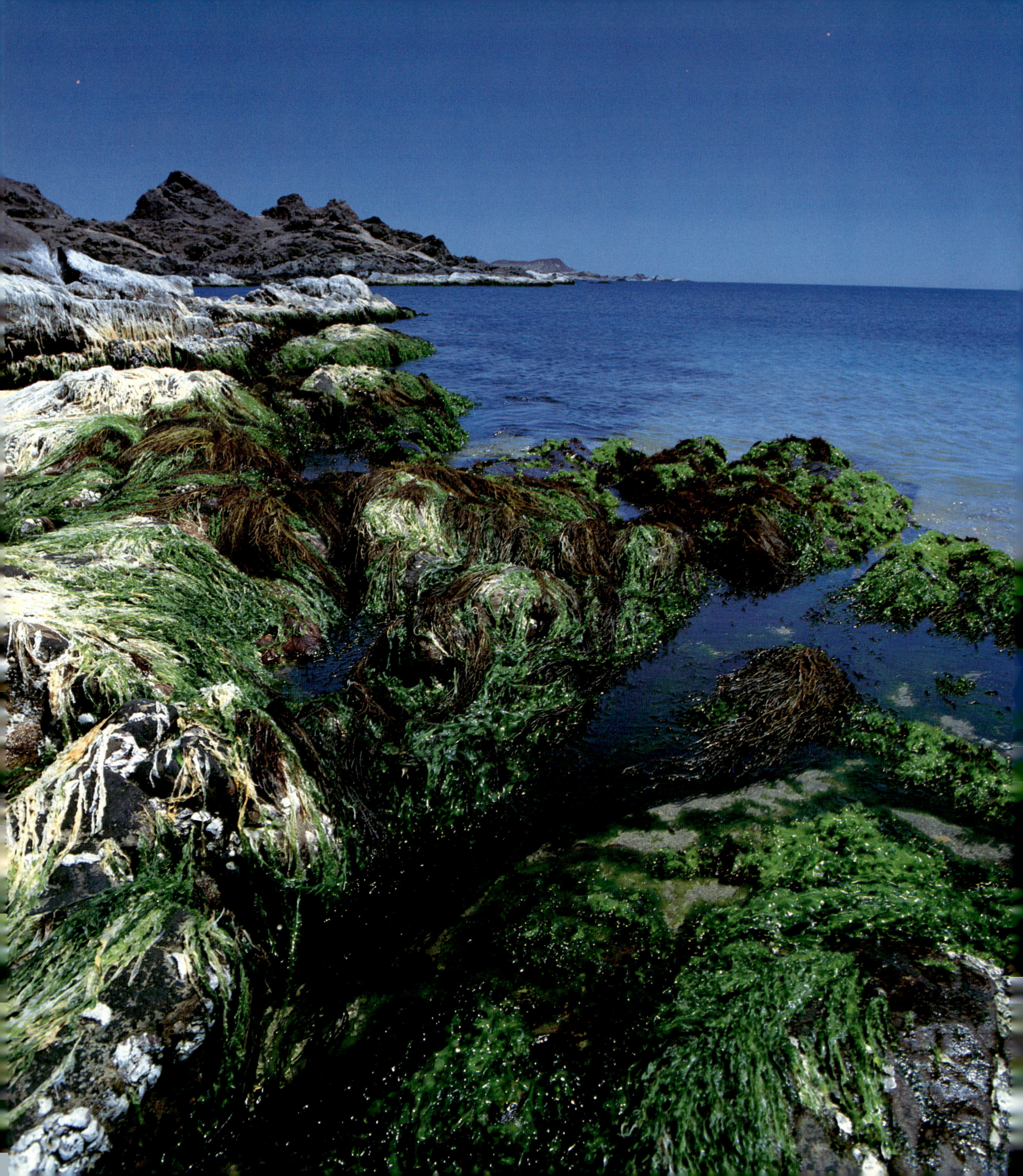

left
According to naturalists, this combination of coral, seaweed and kelp beds is rarely to be found together. This delightful juxtaposition greets the eye at a beach near Sadh, in the Dhofar region.

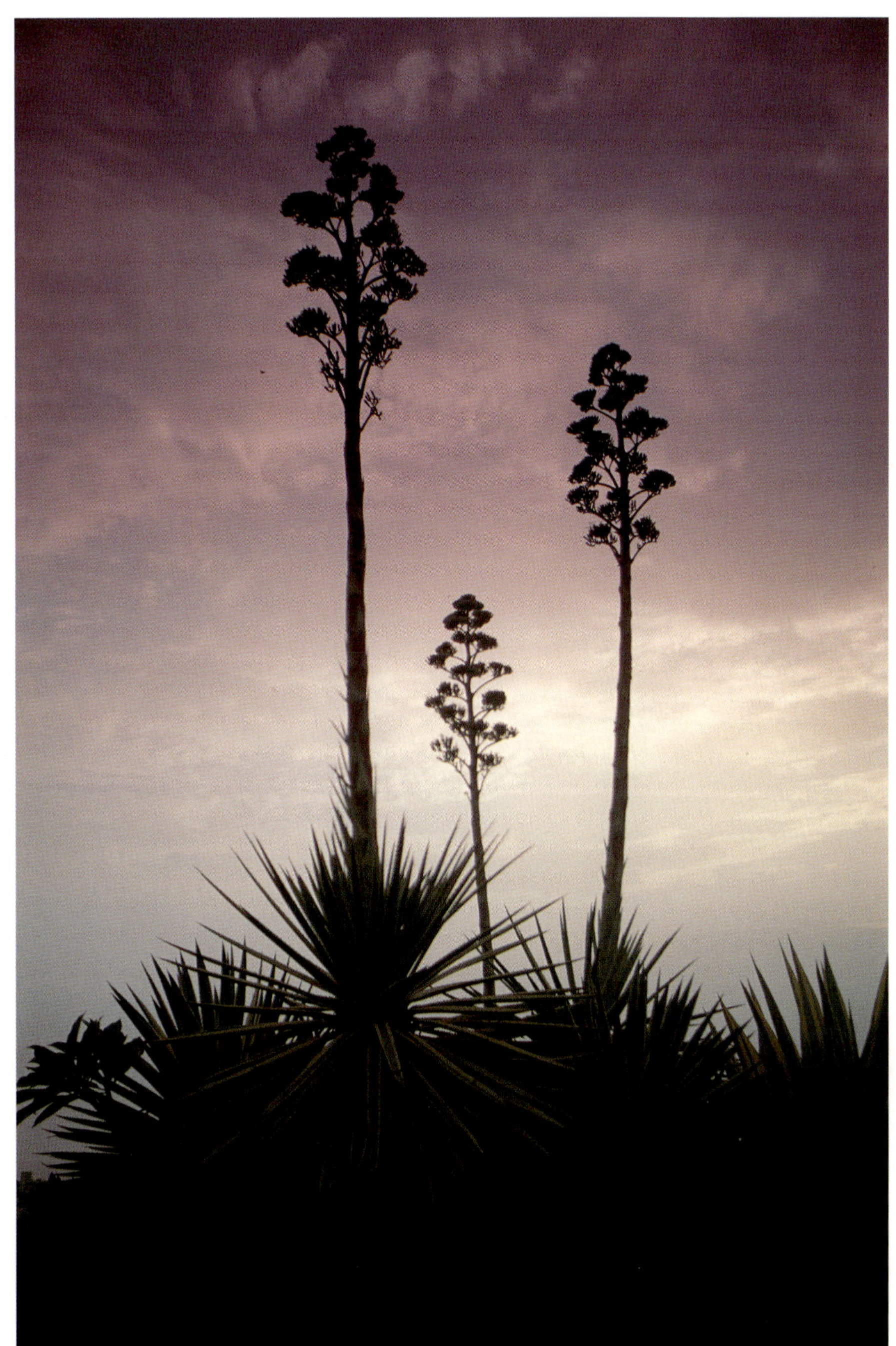

right
For a land that appears to be rocky and arid, Oman boasts a variety of flora and fauna. Sedimentation has left some of the land with fertile top soil – just a little bit of moisture results in flourishing plant life.

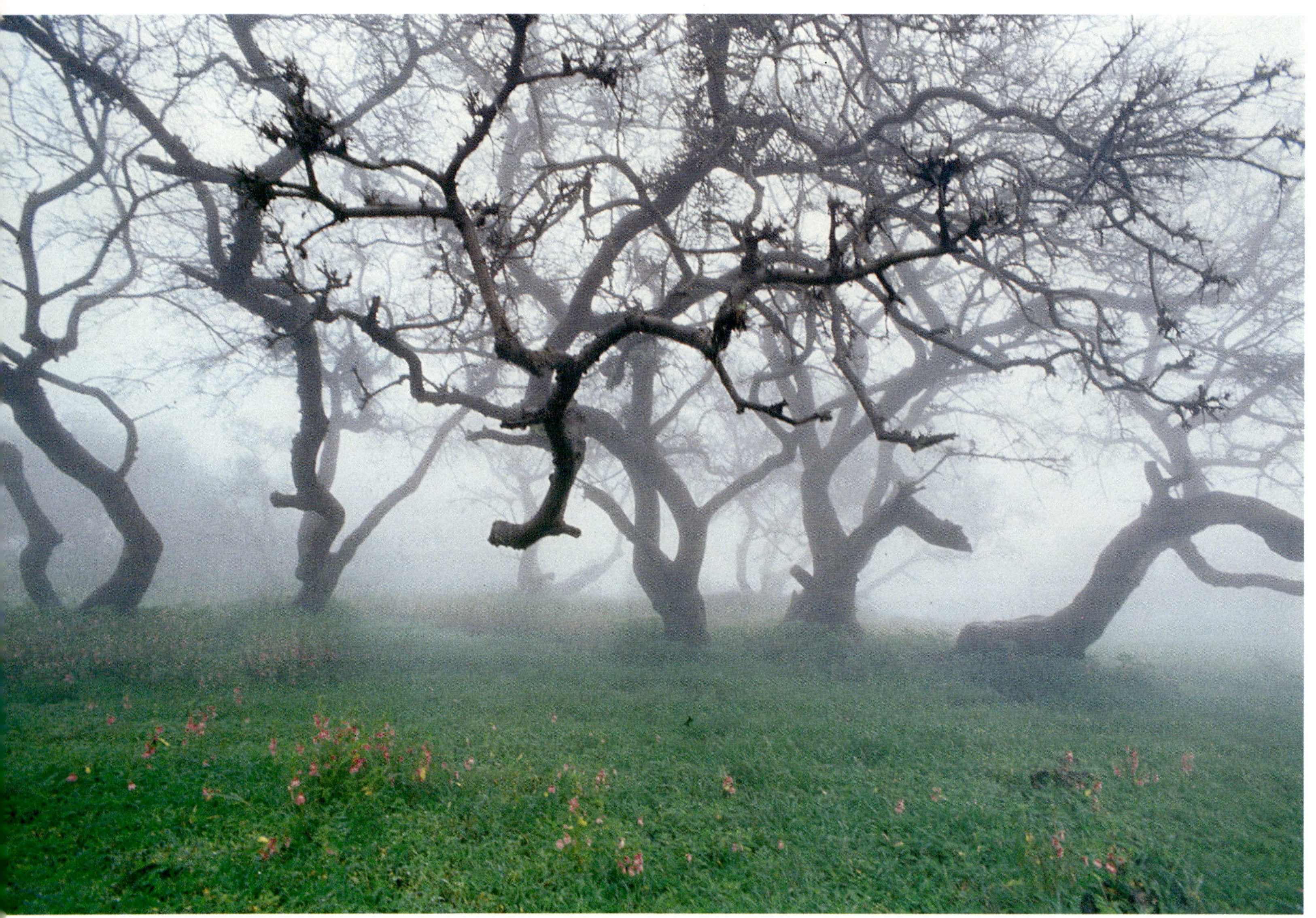

above

Oman plays host to a range of seasons and climatic conditions. Down south in the Dhofar region the land wears a rich, green cloak of vegetation – being at the receiving end of the south-west monsoons. The mountains of Dhofar are famous for the soft and clinging mists that shroud the land in a mysterious haze from June to August.

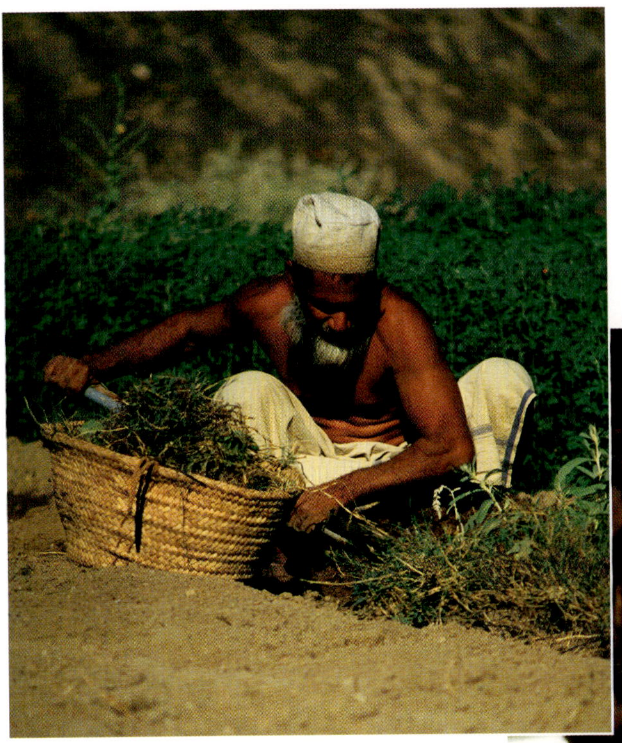

left

Small-scale farming is still a prime livelihood. In the small village of Birkat Al Mawz, a farmer tends to his garden which grows alfalfa for animal feed.

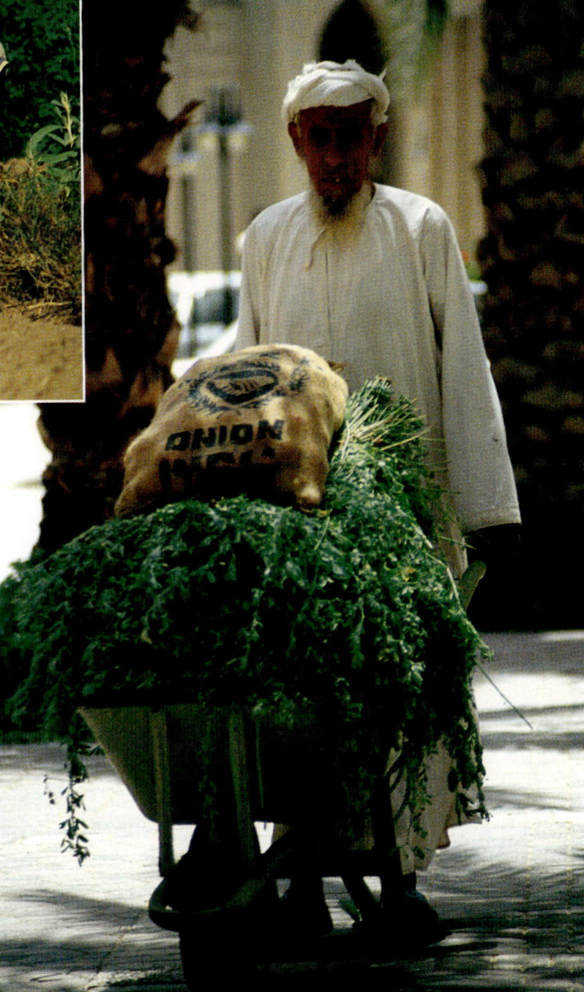

right

A resident of Nizwa takes home onions for the family and alfalfa for the livestock.

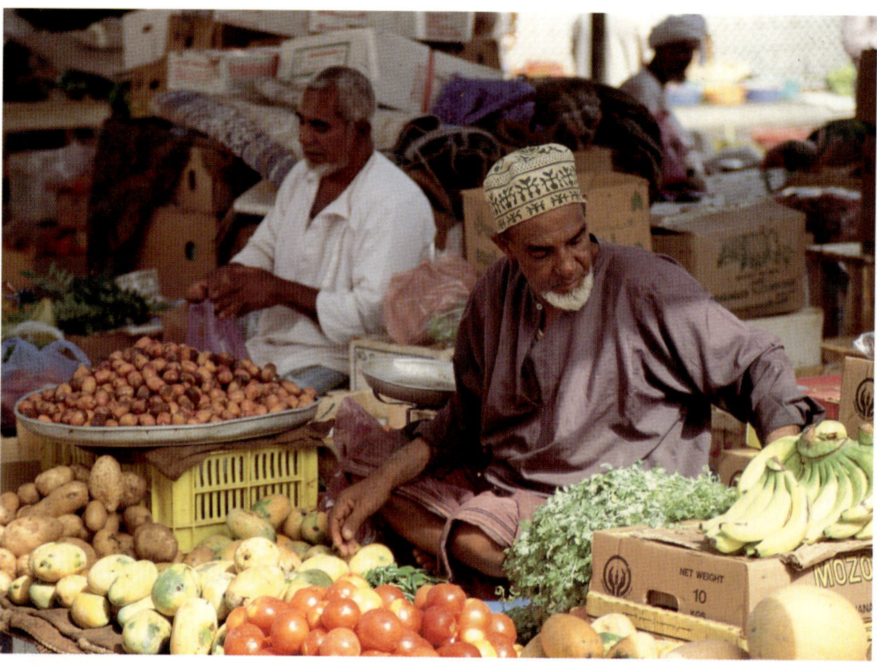

left
It comes as a pleasant surprise to discover that a land known for its unforgiving terrain and extreme climate can produce fruit and vegetables. These have been successfully cultivated in Oman, and sell at the Mutrah market and others across the country.

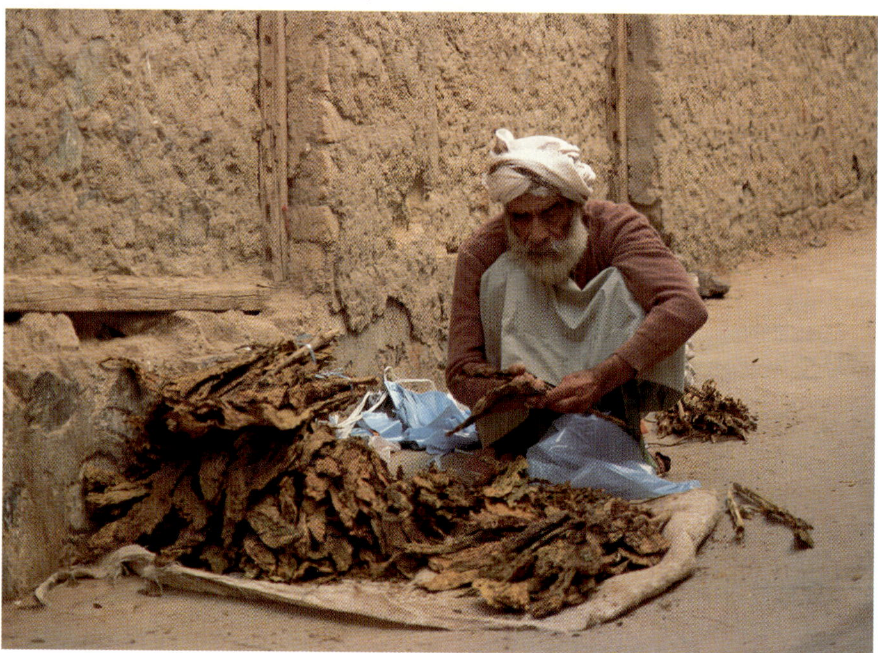

left
A trader in the alleyways of Mutrah souq displays his wares of dried tobacco leaves. Though rarely seen in public, tobacco is smoked by some people in water-pipes in the privacy of their homes.

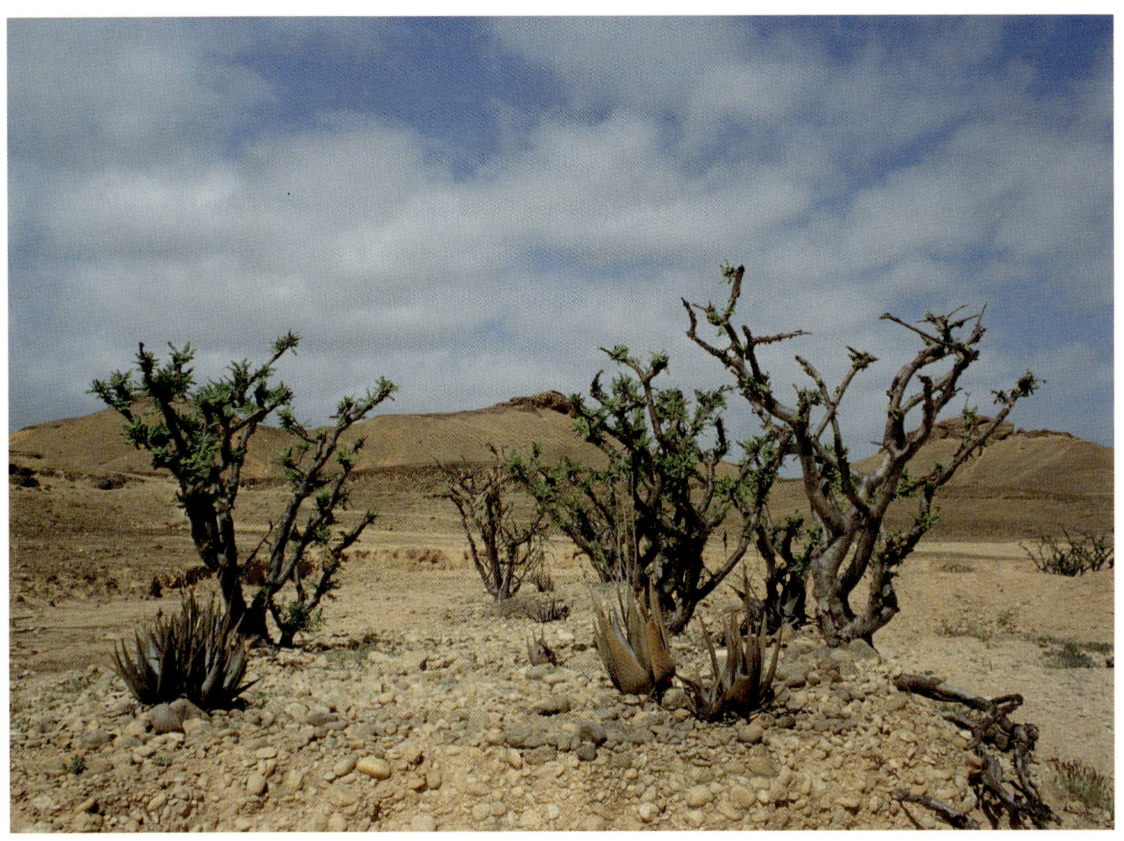

left

Frankincense and aloe vera grow together on the desert plateau beyond the watershed in the hills in Dhofar. Small incisions are cut into the bark of frankincense trees and droplets of resin form and harden before being picked by hand.

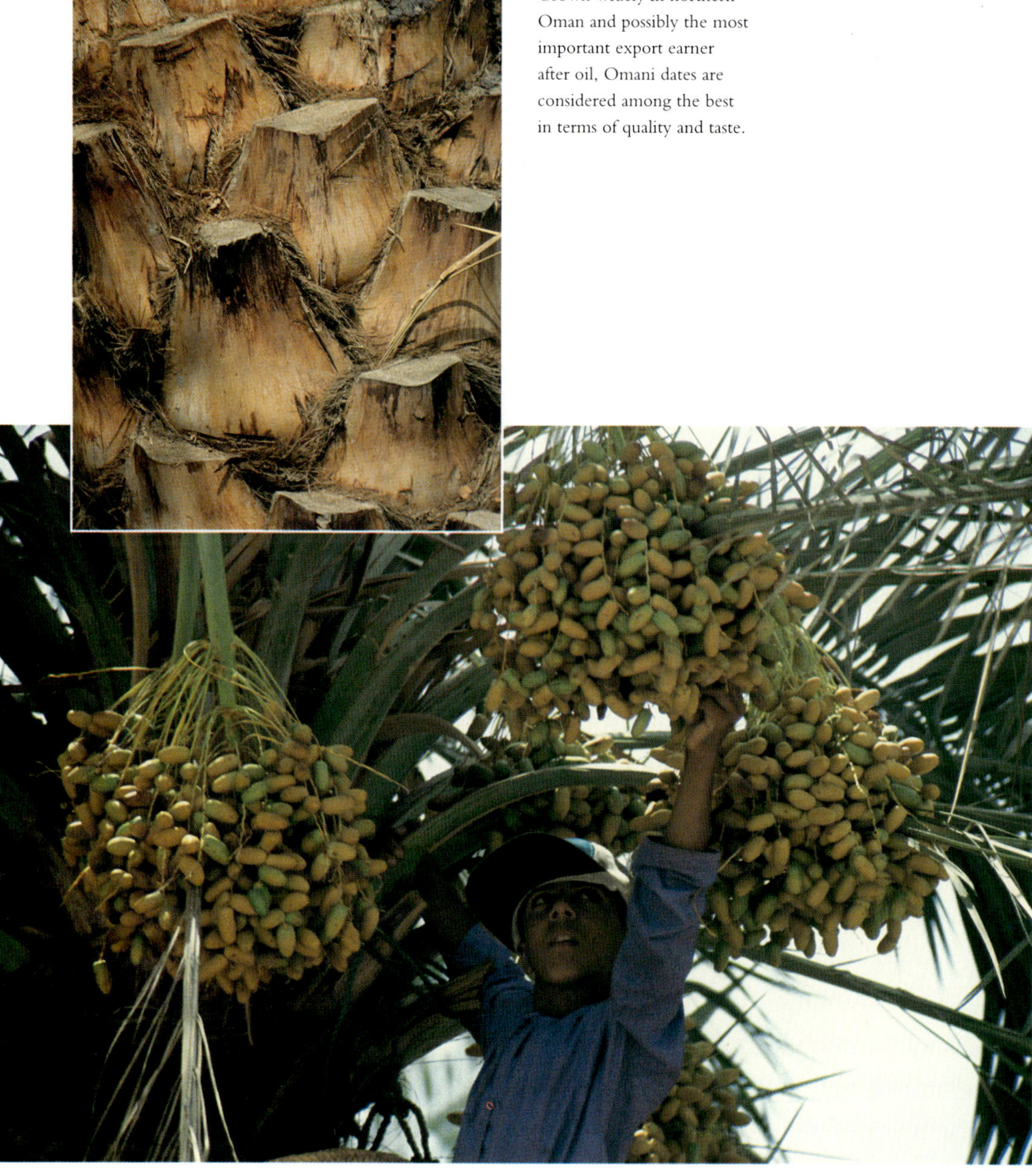

left and below
Grown widely in northern Oman and possibly the most important export earner after oil, Omani dates are considered among the best in terms of quality and taste.

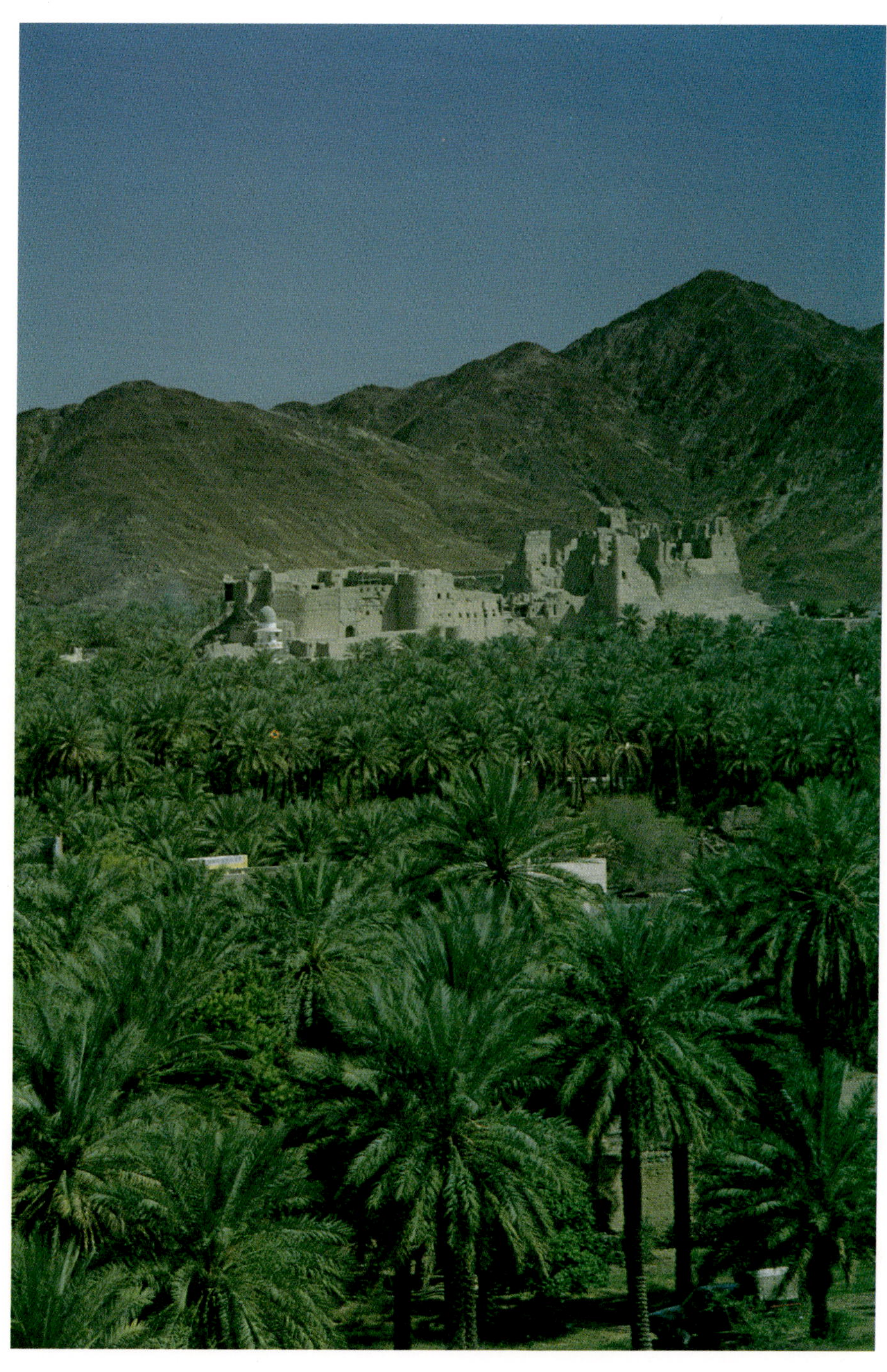

right
Towering above the date plantations of Bahla stand the remains of Bahla fort – presently under large-scale restoration. One of the largest in Oman, the fort dominates the town and used to protect the main thoroughfare north to Ibri.

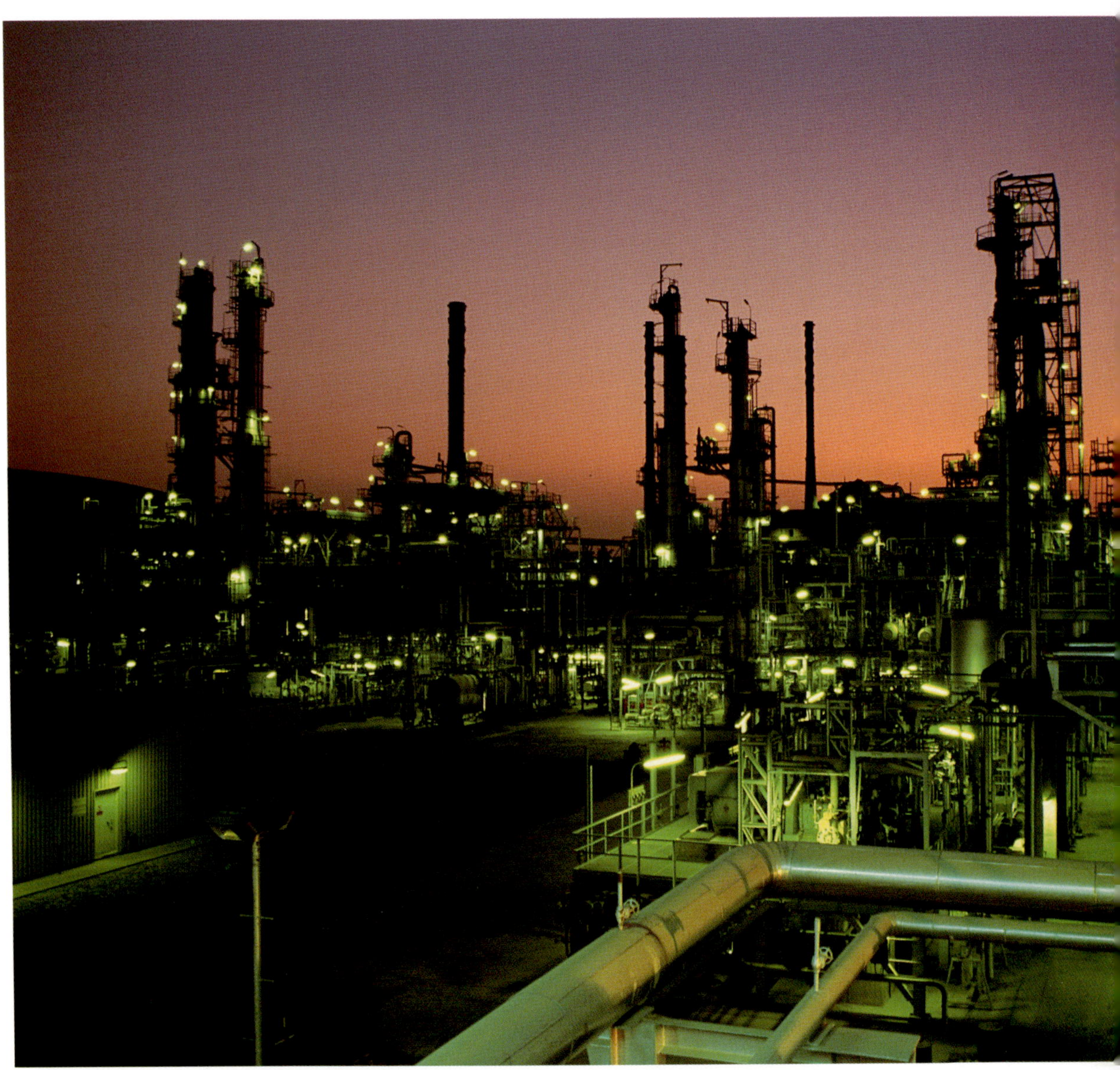

above

Seen against the setting sun, the Oman Refinery is a fairyland of twinkling lights. It's from here that the country's crude oil, pumped in by Petroleum Development of Oman, is processed into various grades and supplied to the marketing arms of the oil industry.

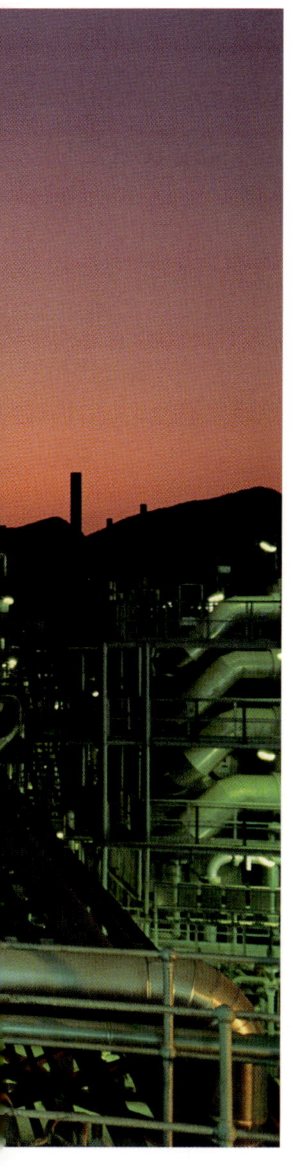

Oman's Future Heritage

The last twenty-five years of Oman's history bode well for her future prosperity. Oman's development has been funded by oil revenues which, wisely spent, have created an infrastructure and an industrial base which will see the country through even when the oil runs out (current predictions indicate that this will happen in about seventeen years – though new discoveries and improved technology are pushing that date further back all the time).

Prospecting for oil began in Oman some seventy years ago, when a group of pioneering geologists trekked across the deserts, taking measurements in the hope of discovering underground riches. They found nothing, and the search was abandoned. Indeed, it wasn't until 1962 that the first commercially viable find was made – and in the following year, the discovery of the Natih field near Fahud saw the birth of Oman's oil industry. A 279-kilometre pipeline was built from Fahud to Mina al Fahal, on the coast near Muscat – and the first oil was exported in 1967.

The oil industry is principally in the capable hands of Petroleum Development Oman (PDO), one of the largest oil companies in the Gulf with nearly 5,000 employees (66% of whom are Omanis) and a further 12,000 contract staff. Today PDO maintains more than 4,500 kilometres of pipelines

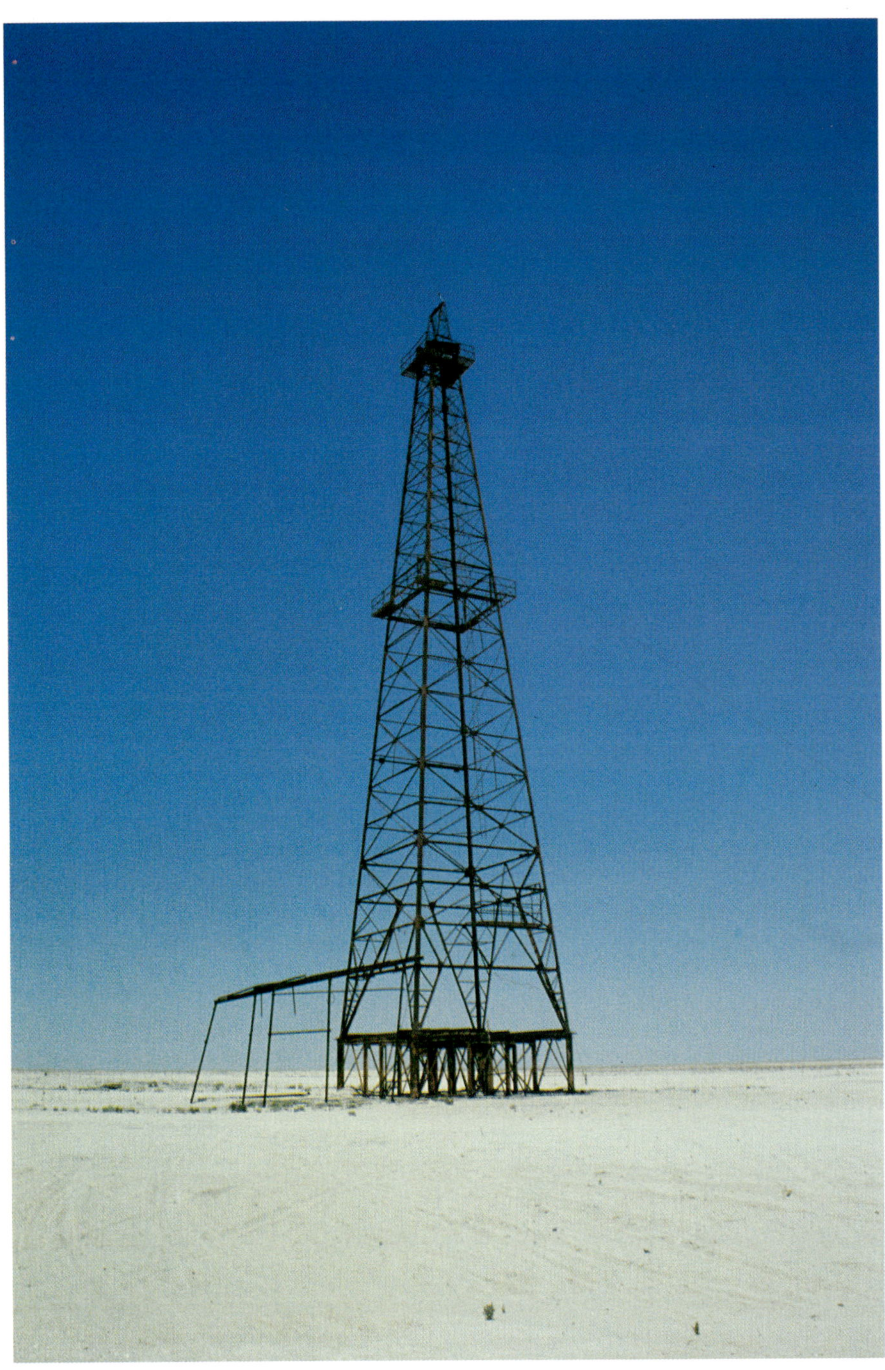

left
The first source of the thriving oil industry, this oil rig at Thumrait is the oldest in Oman. It stands as testimony to the black gold under the sands that set Oman on the road to progress.

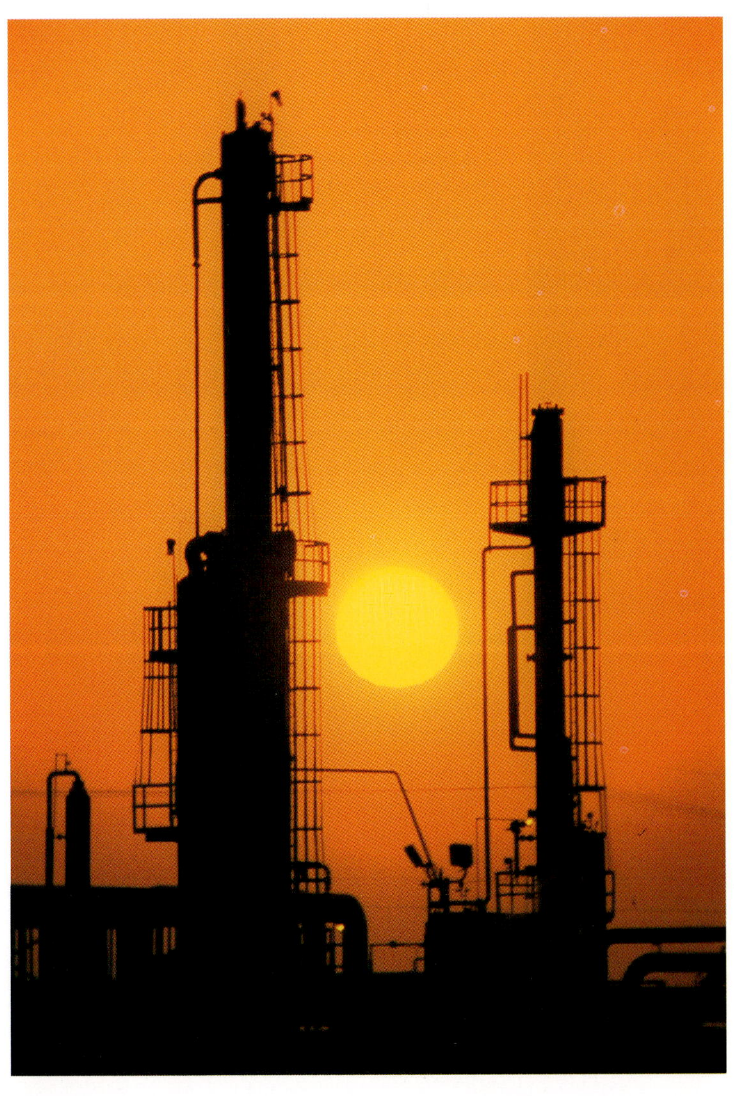

above
The injection plant at Safa makes a dramatic picture against the blaze of the setting sun. This high-technology industry shows up in sharp contrast against a way of life that goes back centuries.

across deserts and mountains to keep Oman's oil flowing to the storage complex at Mina al Fahal, where it is loaded on to tankers for export, mainly to the Far East.

With the oil revenue, Oman has built roads, airports, seaports, schools, hospitals, telecommunications networks and modern irrigation systems – and has encouraged industrial diversification to reduce the economy's dependence on oil. To this end, industrial estates have been constructed in various parts of the country, offering start-up incentives to Omani enterprises. Commercially too the country has been successful, as indicated in the 88% increase in the trading volume of Muscat Securities Market between 1989 and 1993.

The Capital Area continues to sprout elegant commercial centres, as well as cultural and educational ones: the Children's Science Museum in Qurm is a great attraction, with hands-on exhibits bringing delight to young and old alike. There has been much sensitivity in blending the new with the old: in Muscat, the gleaming Al Alam Palace is surrounded on its landward sides by a maze of shady narrow streets, with carved doors offering glimpses into homes, government offices,

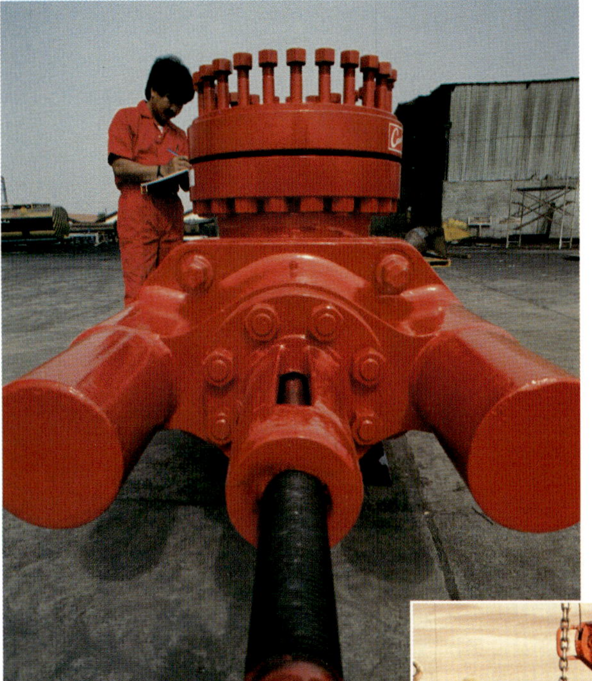

left
Oil rigs are dotted across the length and breadth of the land. Here, highly skilled engineers are involved in the maintenance of blow-out protector valves on an installation.

below
Professionals in the oil industry are now drawn from both expatriate and Omani ranks. These men are working on a rig floor putting down a drill pipe.

museums and mosques. And Mutrah's historic souq, which draws tourists and locals alike, has recently been re-roofed – but with traditional panels of woven palm-fibre.

In Nizwa, which has long been a religious, economic and administrative centre in Oman's Interior, a superb new souq has been constructed, again blending the very best of old and new, and breathing new life and commercial energy into the

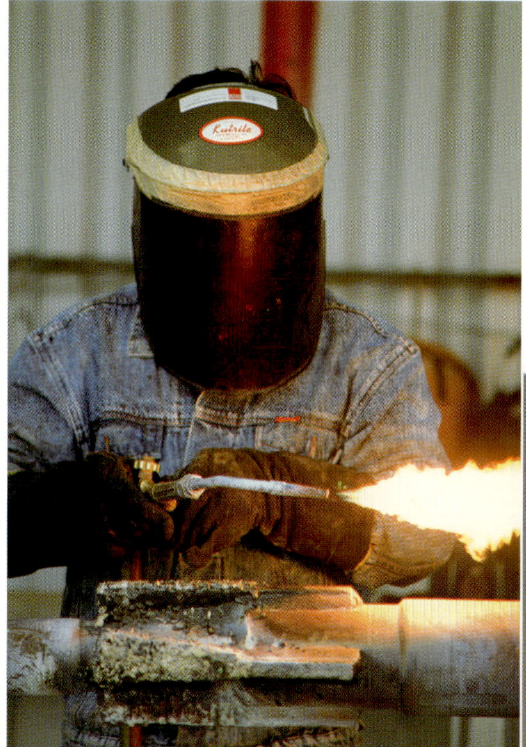

town. Three majestic carved wooden doorways lead into the new souq, which has been built using traditional *sarooj* (a kind of clay render) and maintaining old architectural styles, with fretwork arches and paved alleyways backing on to the ancient city walls, which have been incorporated into the design. Separate halls for different kinds of produce (meat, vegetables, spices, crafts, and so on) are

above
Extreme caution, skill and a deep respect for safety all characterise people working in the oil industry. This welder goes about his task of repairing a "down-hole tool" with great care and expertise.

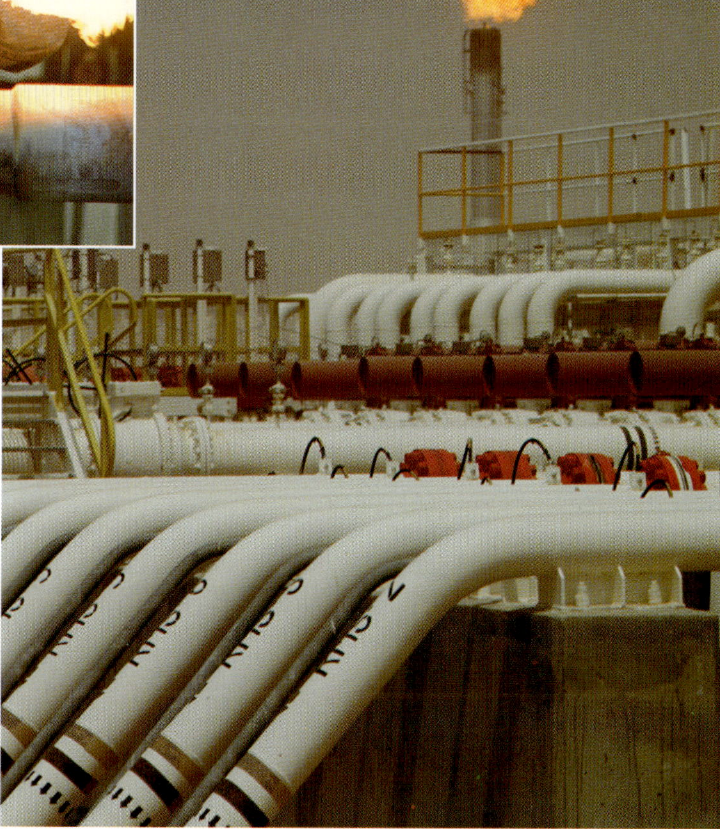

right
While it has been a national objective for Oman to diversify into other areas of industry, oil is still the lynchpin of the economy. Petroleum Development Oman (PDO) is responsible for the drilling and collection of oil and has many oil gathering and pumping stations – like this one at Ghaba.

purpose-built, offering comfort and convenience to traders and shoppers alike. And modern buildings have certainly not put a stop to traditional activities: around the new souq cluster many small traders – sandal-makers, sellers of fabrics and garments, smallholders who have brought their surplus produce into town, sometimes from as far away as Jebel Akhdar – people who rest comfortably on their haunches, doing business as their ancestors did before them.

Nizwa also boasts an impressive new sports stadium, in which the 1994 National Day celebrations were held. Omanis are great lovers of sport – and especially football: throughout the country, small boys, sometimes bare-footed, play informal games on stony pitches – while at club and national level, team rivalries run high, and pride in winning the annual Oman Football Association cup final is great.

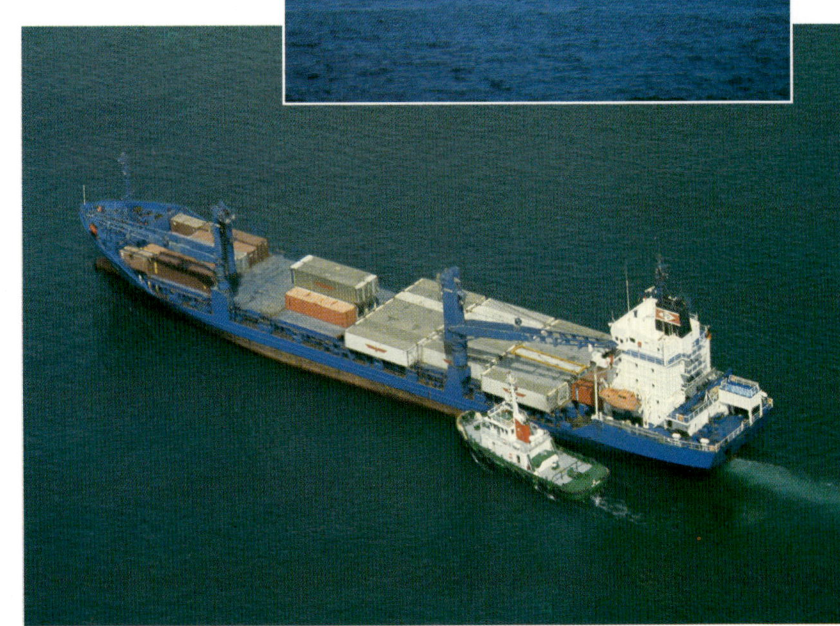

right
A container ship slides slowly and gracefully into harbour at Mina Sultan Qaboos. Here, her cargo will be unloaded and loaded swiftly and efficiently.

left
Much of Oman's import/export trade passes through Mina Sultan Qaboos, the country's major port. The cargo and berthing facilities here are on a par with any found around the world.

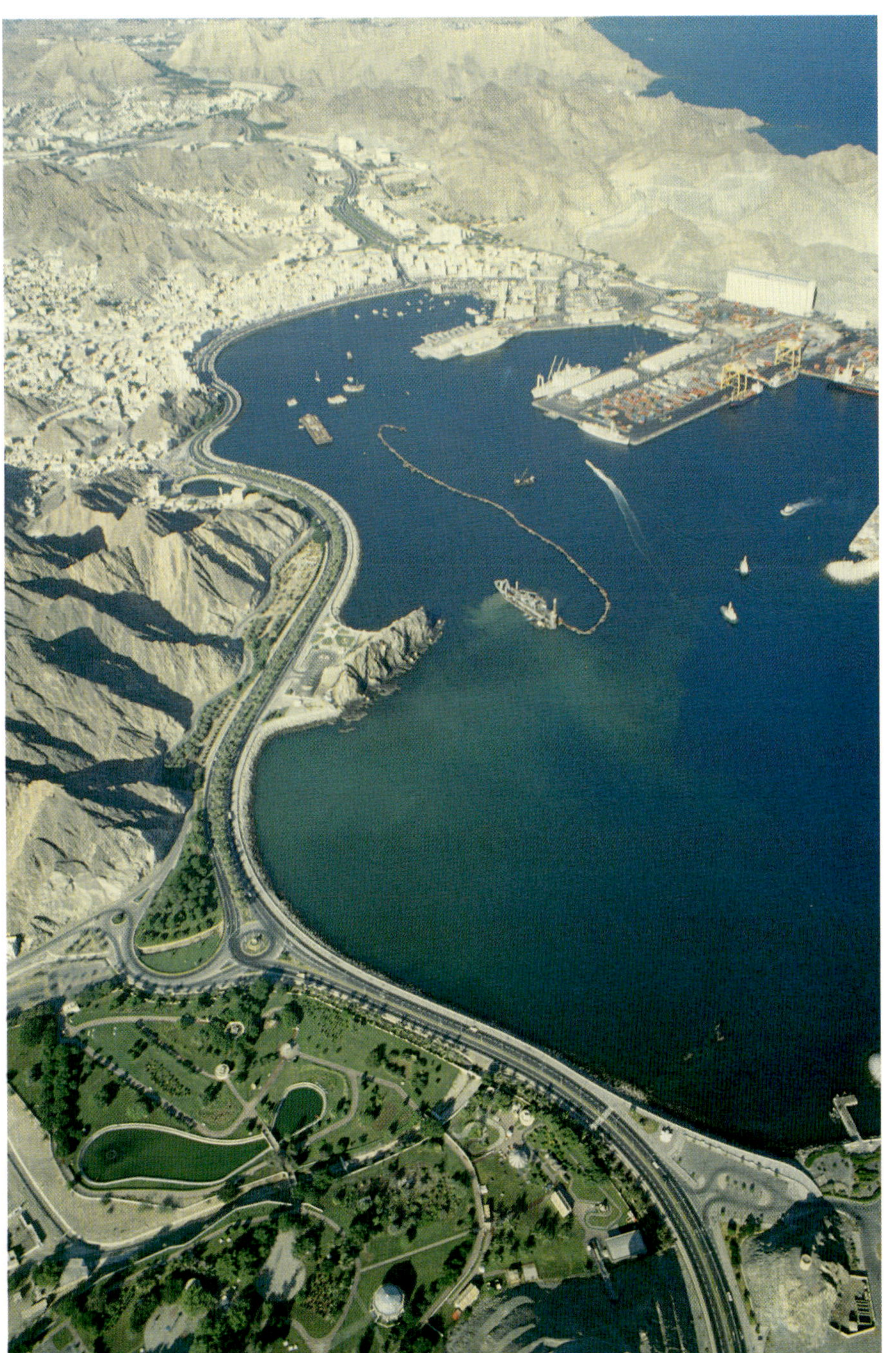

right
Oman's strategic location astride the trade route between Asia and Europe has attracted seafarers and merchants from all over the world.

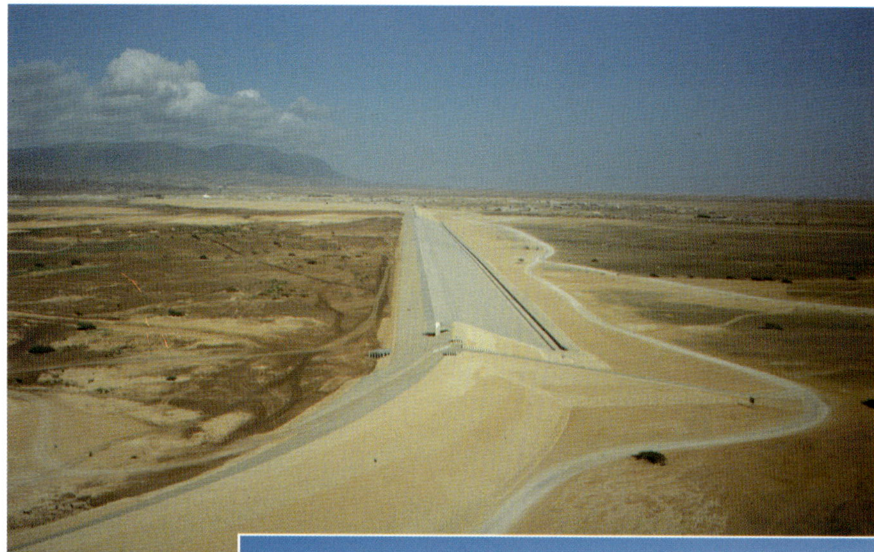

left
In a land where every drop of water needs to be conserved, recharge dams play a vital role in saving this precious resource. These dams hold the rushing waters unleashed by sporadic winter rains long enough for them to replenish the underground aquifers, thus preventing the water from being lost in the seas around Oman.

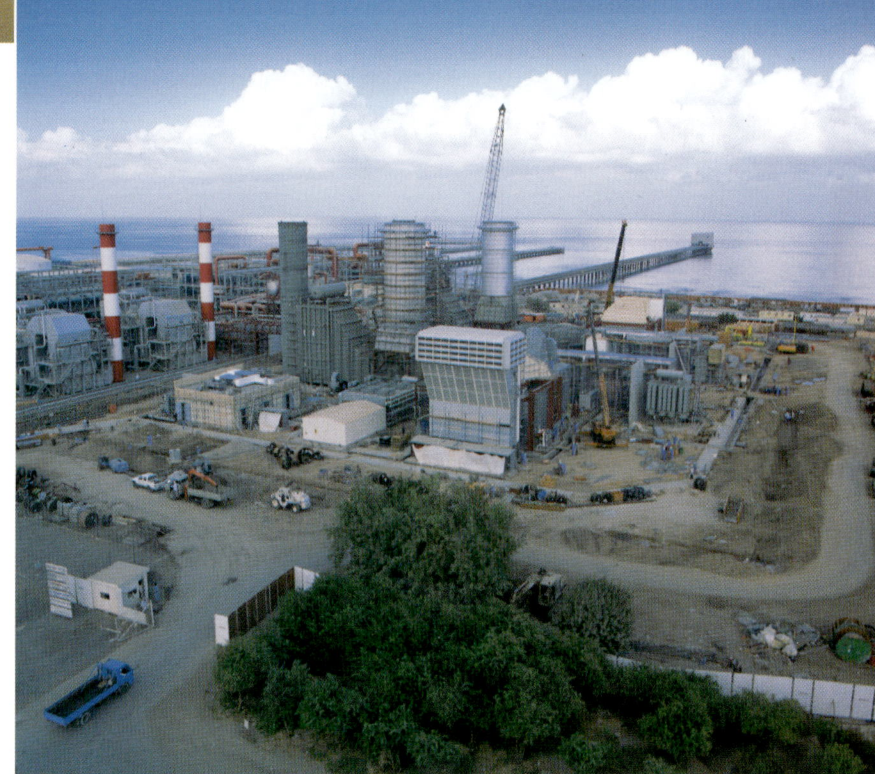

right
The newly extended desalination and power plant at Ghubrah is also a major contribution to fresh water supplies.

right
Vast expanses of the Sultanate have come under productive cultivation. Before being put to general use, the latest and most appropriate farming techniques are tested at experimental farms, such as this one in Salalah.

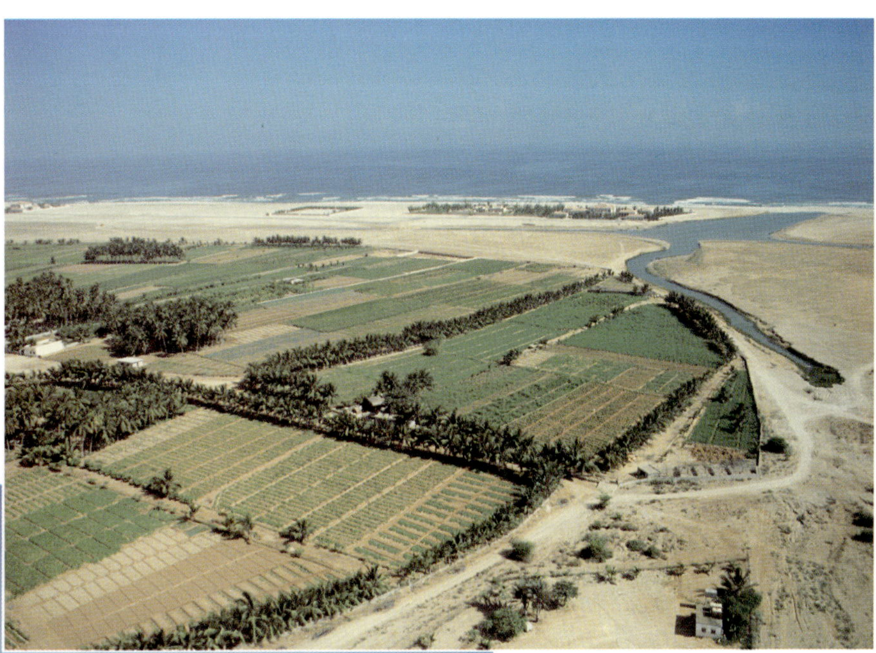

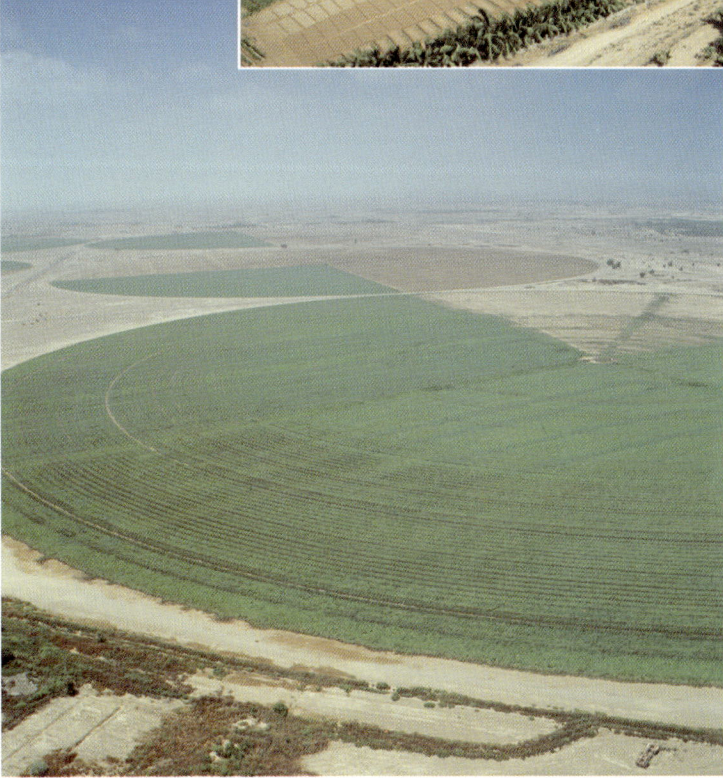

left
Vast expanses of land grow crops ranging from onions and potatoes to tomatoes, rice and wheat. Omani farmers have enjoyed government support, in terms of farming technology, which has resulted in more and more land being used productively for agricultural purposes.

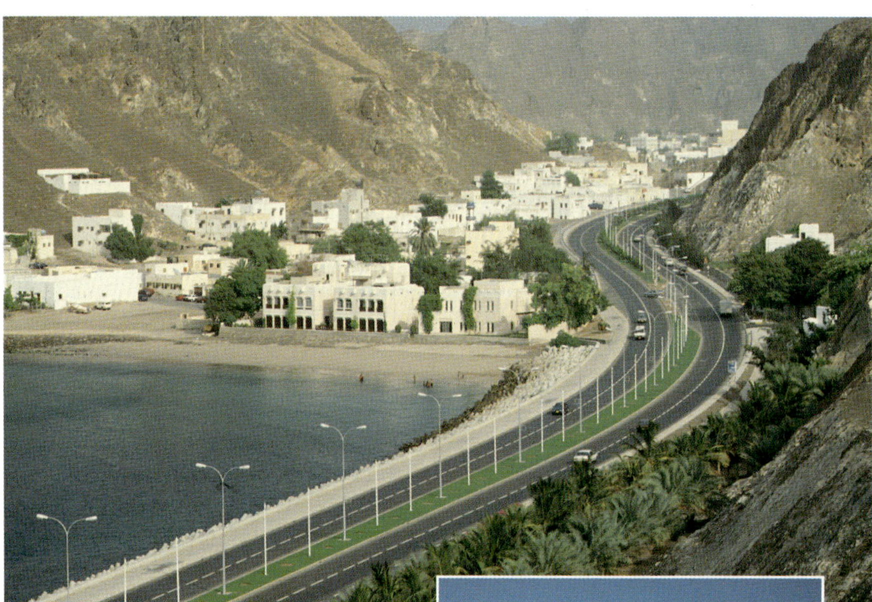

left
One of the most spectacular stretches of development work is the Corniche along the seafront to Muscat. Here, children and adults can be found every evening enjoying the fresh sea breeze and meeting friends and family.

Indeed, for Omanis and visitors alike, the nation's prosperity and progress has brought a new awareness of leisure pursuits, and of the many and various activities which are available, thanks to nature, tradition or both. Water sports, for example, are developing rapidly: scuba-diving and snorkelling reveal the wonders of the underwater world of coral reefs and tropical sea-creatures; yachting, windsurfing, water-skiing and boating offer different delights. Oman's 1,800 kilometres of coastline, much of it inaccessible to road traffic, offers to the nautical explorer bays, inlets, islands and sandy beaches for rest and relaxation.

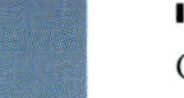

left
Given the country's diverse topography, the unforgiving terrain and punishing climate, setting up an infrastructure has been no mean feat. Here, one of Gulf Helicopter's fleet carries teams working on the construction and maintenance of telecommunications facilities in the remote mountain areas.

right
Generally speaking, the graded roads criss-crossing the land, are fairly comfortable for those in 4WDs. However, this particular stretch of dirt track along the foot of Jebel al Qara, in the Dhofar region, is probably one of the hardest in the country.

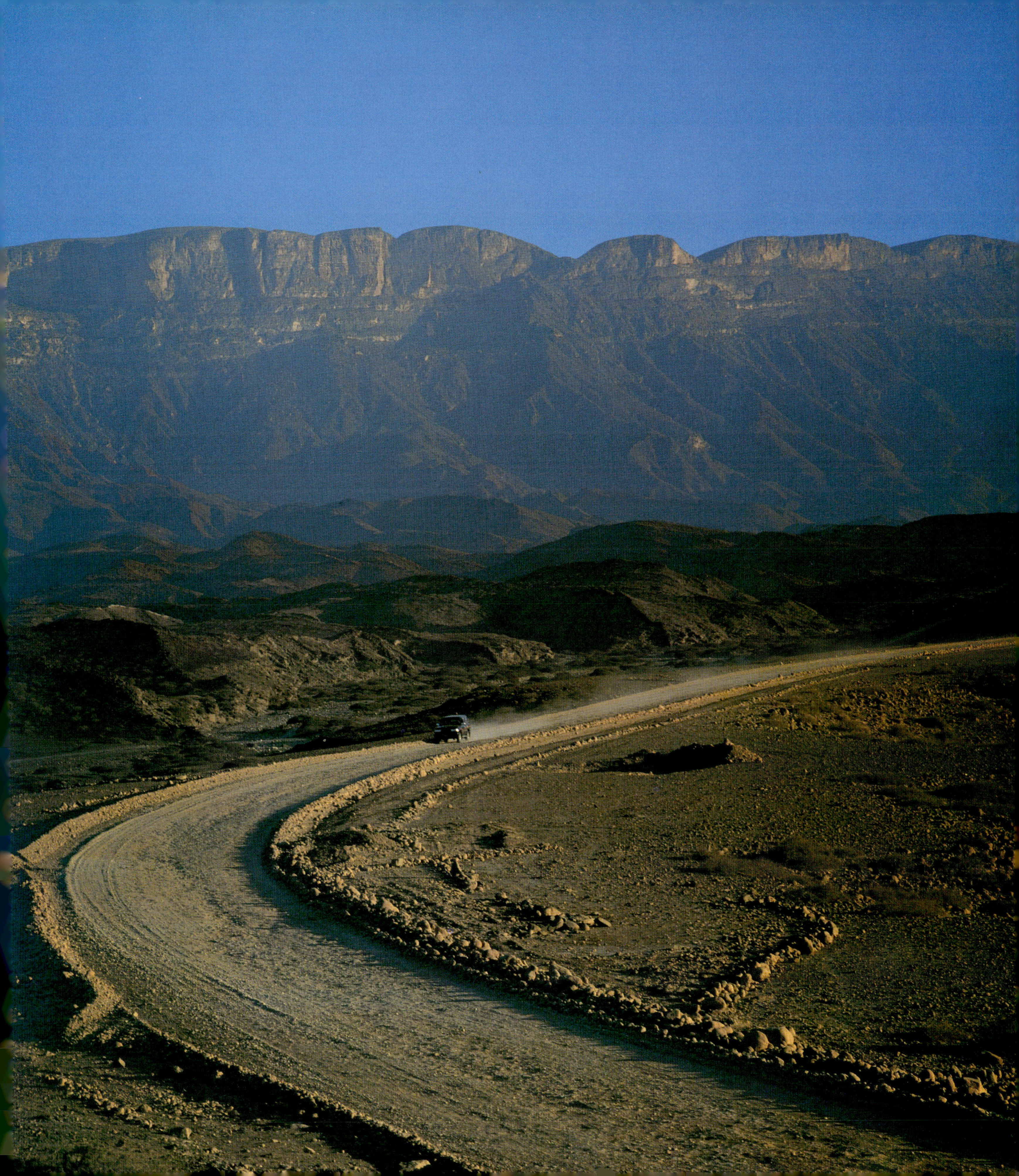

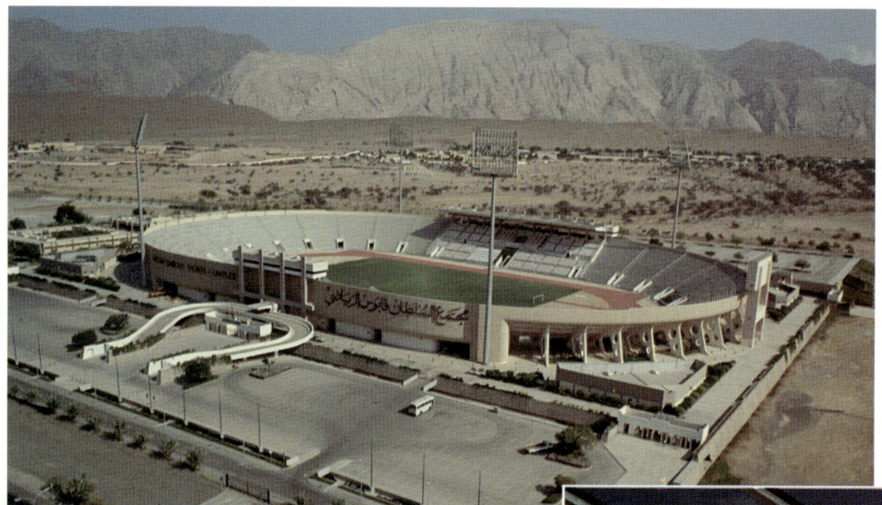

left
Football fields dot both urban and rural landscapes. Every major town boasts of a sports complex. Occupying pride of place is the Sultan Qaboos Sports Complex in the Capital Area which hosts major sporting events involving the young people of Oman.

Horse and camel racing are favourite spectator sports – both rooted in Omani tradition, but now enjoyed by more people than ever. The Royal Stables near Seeb have frequent race-meetings during the cooler winter months: these are entirely free – and enthusiasm is strong. Standards of skill and horsemanship, achieved by riders of the Royal Oman Police, the mounted departments of the military and those from private stables, are high. This is evidenced each year, at the spetacular National Day celebrations, when a cavalry brass band and the camel-mounted bagpipe corps always receive an enthusiastic welcome – as do the stunt riders who thrill the crowds with their breathtaking displays.

Such feats are recorded on Oman's own TV station, and in Omani newspapers, in both Arabic and English language editions – something which would have been unimaginable before 1970.

above
In the interior oil-town of Marmul workers construct a steel skeleton for one of the many new buildings which spring up almost overnight.

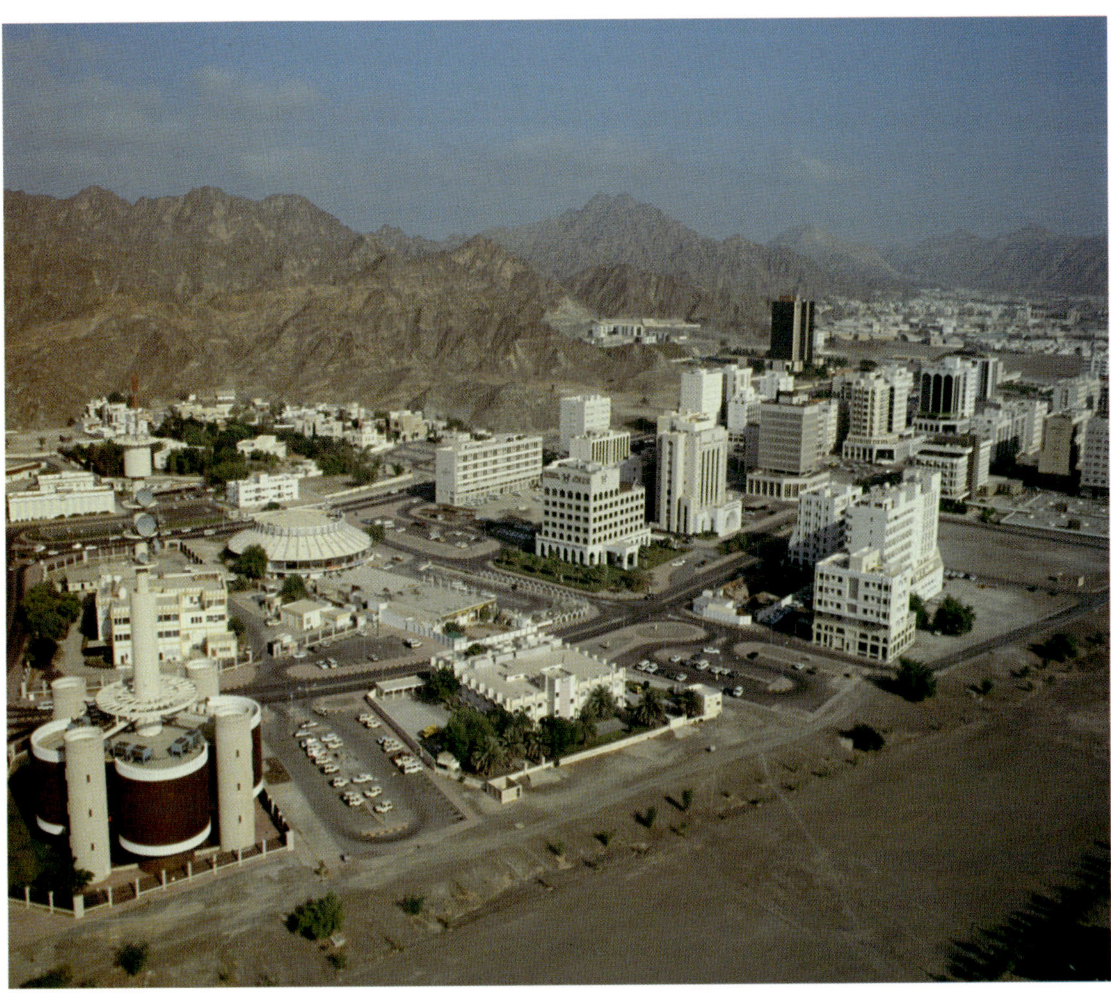

above
Muscat, the capital city of Oman, is today a thriving centre for business and commerce. Most of the big business houses have their head offices located in the Mutrah Business District, as have the leading banks, the Ministry of Commerce and Industry and the Chamber of Commerce.

Oman's hotels are the focus for many cultural activities, staging concerts and plays, and mounting exhibitions of many kinds. An annual highlight is the performance by the Royal Oman Symphony Orchestra – a remarkable concept in education and music. This is a boarding school for Omani boys and girls, whose main aim is to teach a level of musical proficiency appropriate to a symphony orchestra. Competition to enter the school is fierce – and standards are high, monitored by the UK Associated Board of the Royal

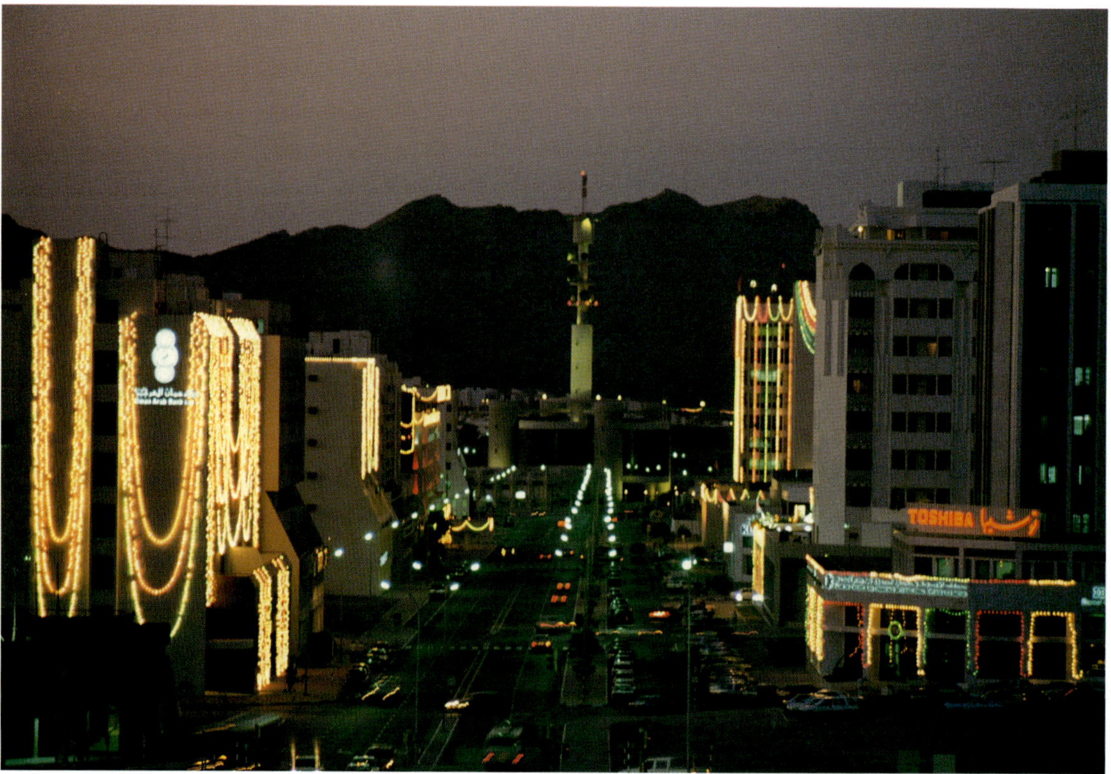

Schools of Music's exams, and by visits from external assessors of the highest calibre.

This, then, is a taste of tomorrow's heritage: a country with a keen, well-educated, healthy young population most of whom have never known the deprivation and hardship suffered by their forebears – and in whose hands lies the future of Oman.

above
The central Mutrah Business District is festooned with fairy lights as the Sultanate celebrates National Day each November.

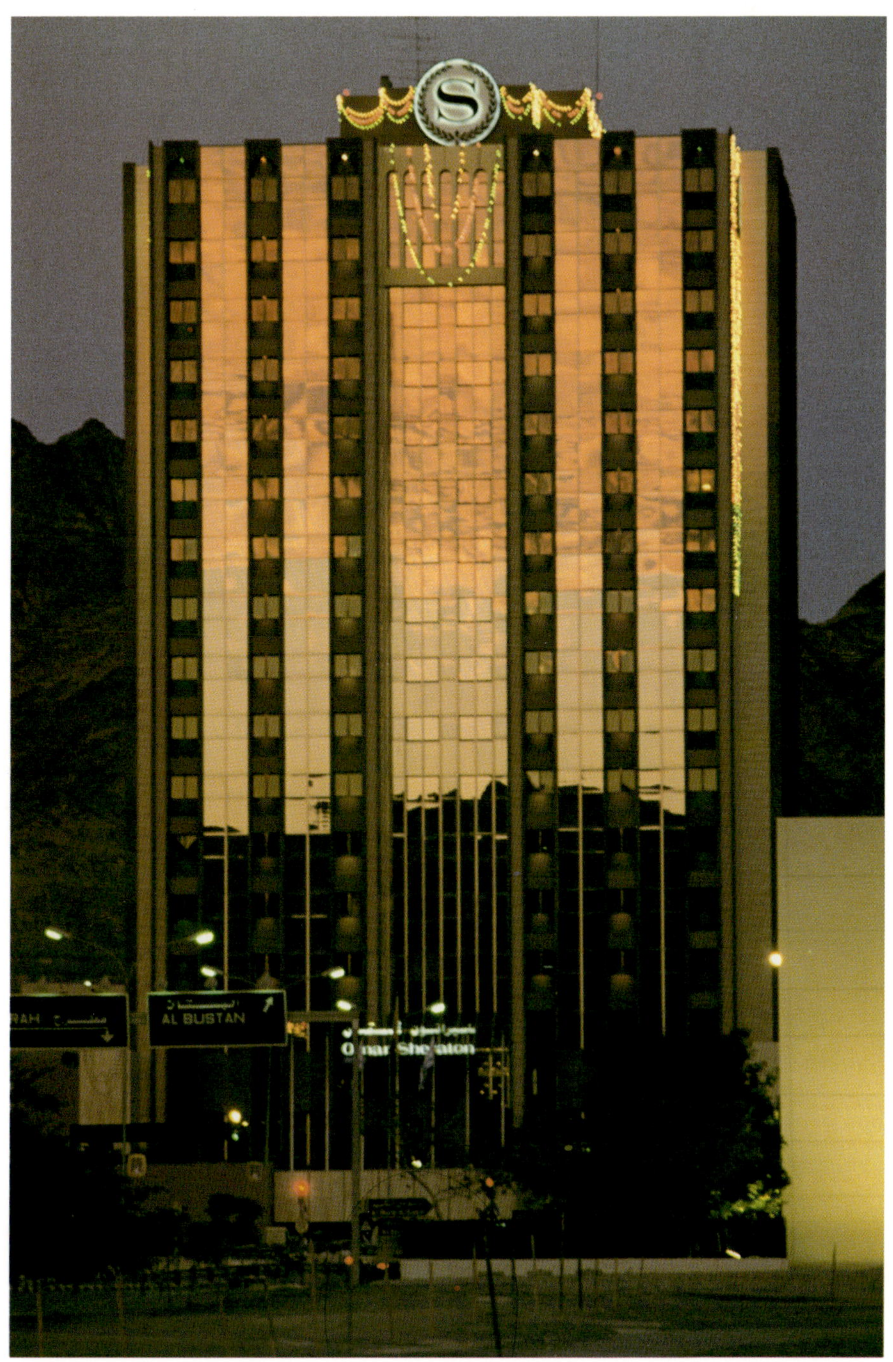

right
Reflecting the golden glow of a spectacular sunset, the Sheraton Hotel in Greater Mutrah is one of the many international standard hotels in the Sultanate.

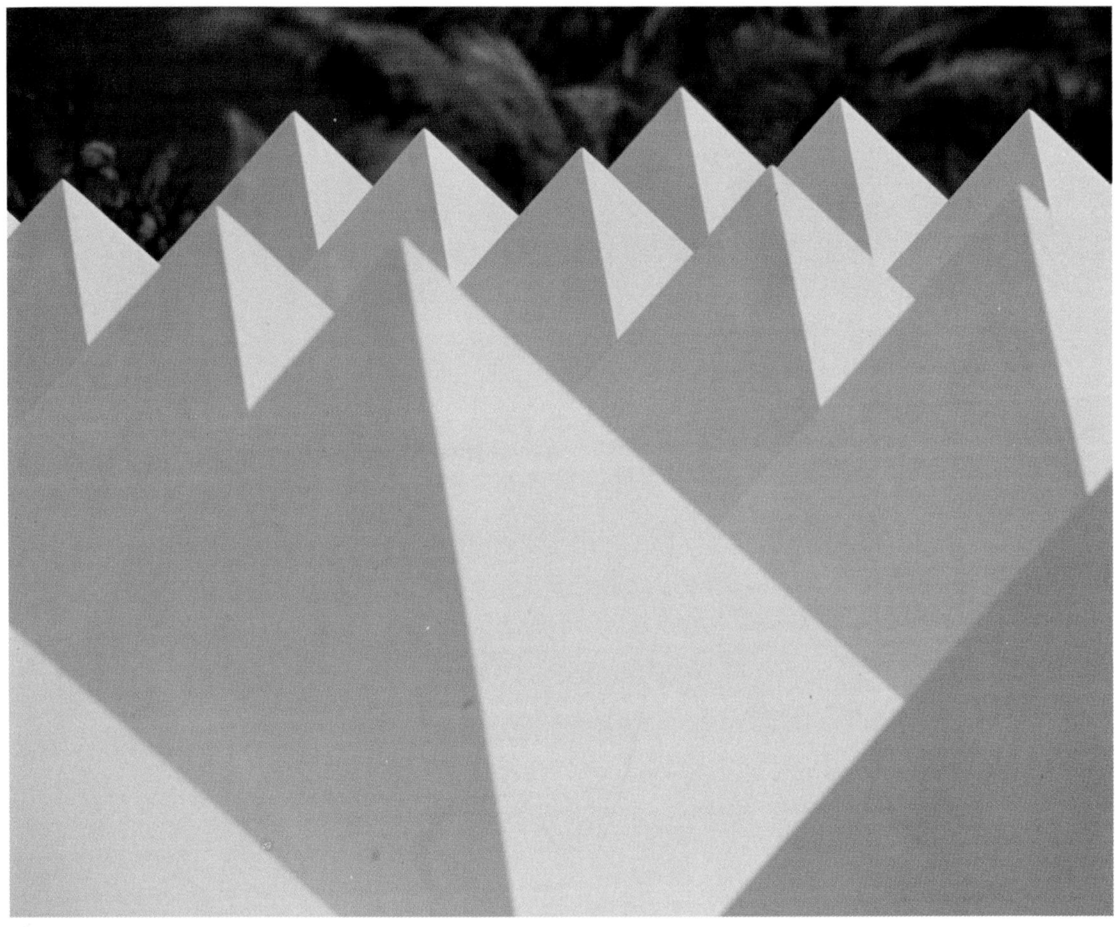

above

This graphic play of light and shade can be captured on the roof of the Salalah Holiday Inn – an interesting pattern that mimics the sharp, serrated peaks formed by the mountains in Oman.

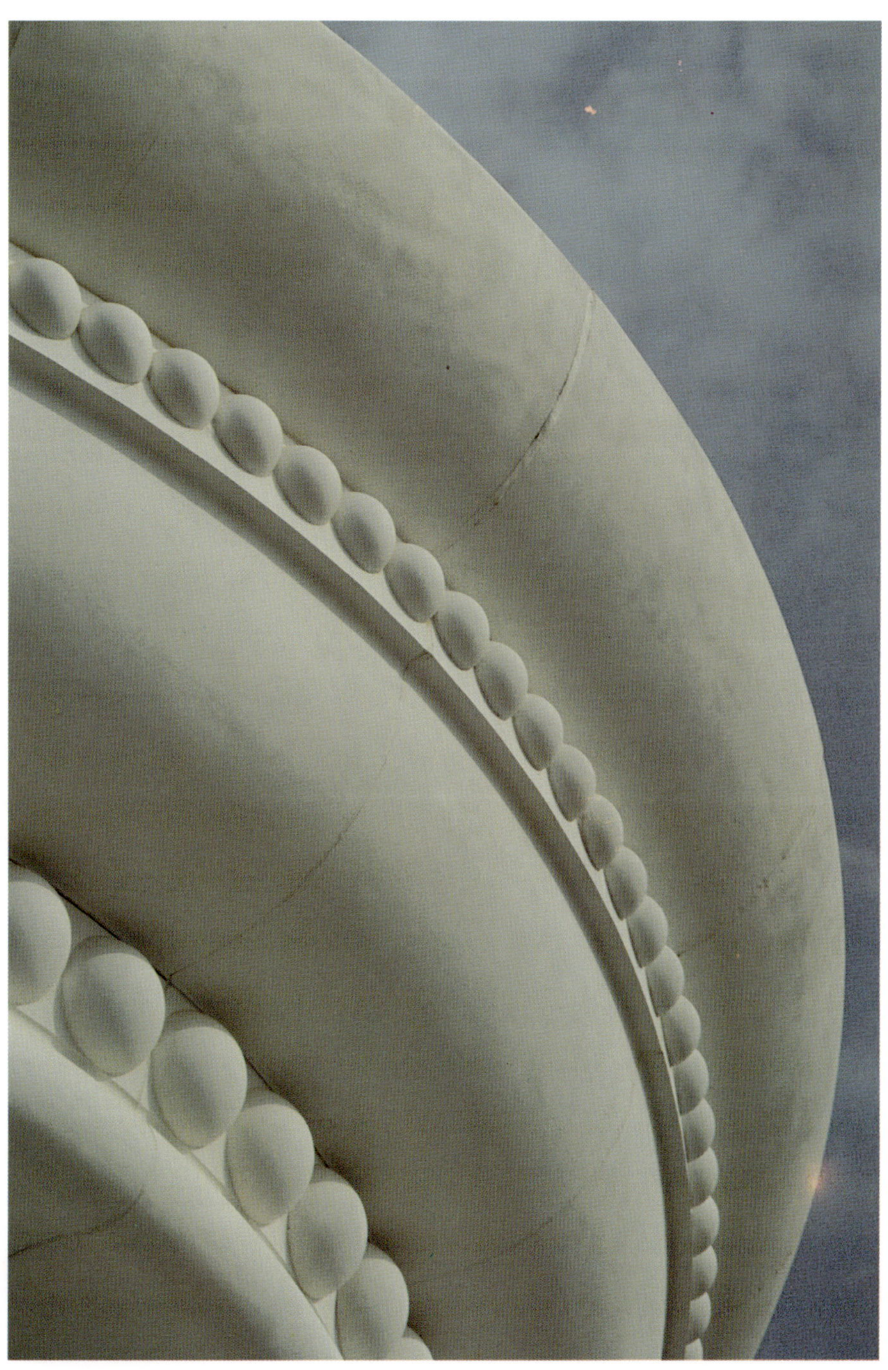

right
Smooth, curving surfaces and intricate carvings are all intrinsic to the monuments that line the roads – particularly those along the Corniche – as this one pictured here.

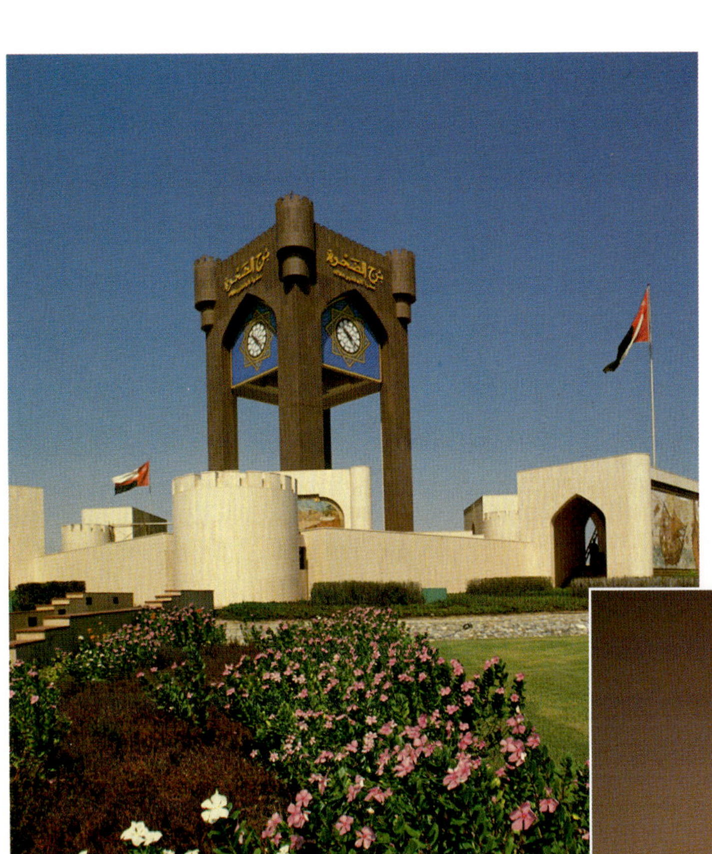

left

Many monuments celebrate Oman's 25 years of renaissance, including the Burj As Sahwa – or Renaissance Tower. The four sides of this monument depict in glowing and colourful murals the history and heritage of Oman down the centuries.

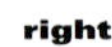

right

Amongst the more outstanding examples of religious architecture, the Zawawi mosque is literally a shining example. Artfully illuminated by cleverly placed lights this mosque has a fairy-tale quality in its ethereal beauty.

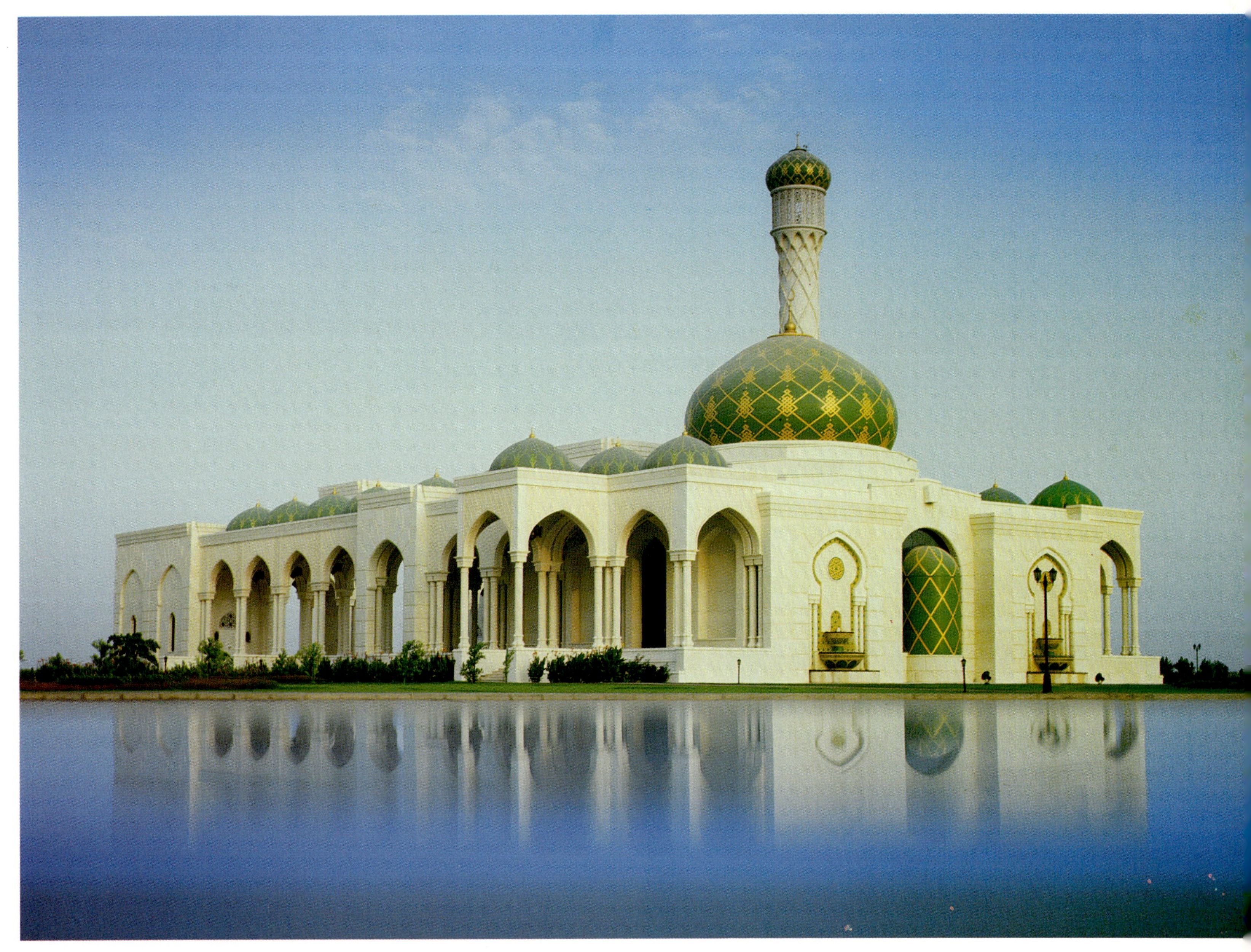

above

From the smallest to the biggest, mosques in Oman are truly outstanding examples of Islamic architectural styles. This mosque near Seeb stands graceful and proud.

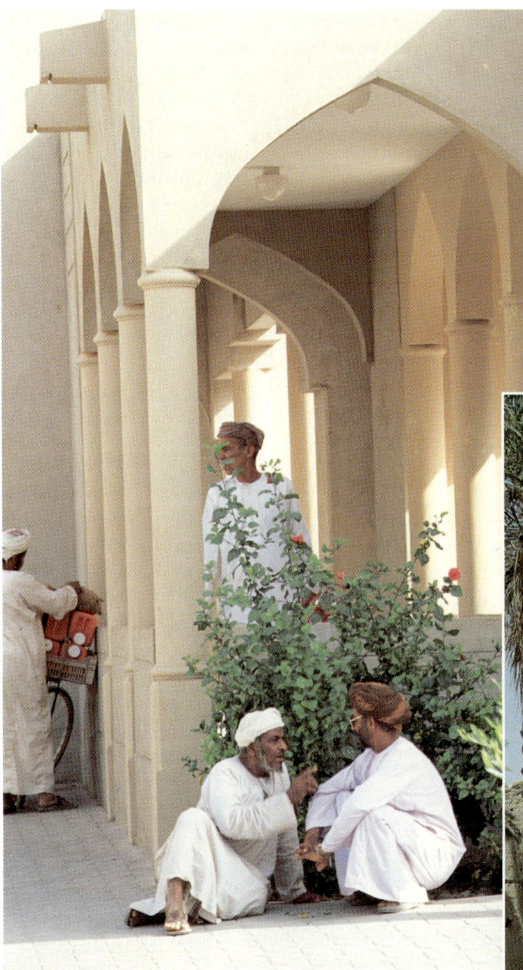

left

The souq or market place is an integral part of Omani life. It is here that buyers and sellers indulge in friendly yet spirited bargaining. The souq at Nizwa, which was recently renovated, is one such place, where a host of historic artefacts in silver, bronze and wood provide a happy hunting ground for shoppers.

right

Nizwa souq is also where local people and visitors come to do their shopping. The souq is not only a rich source for Omani artefacts, but also for all sorts of domestic produce, from honey and rose-water to fresh fish and live animals.

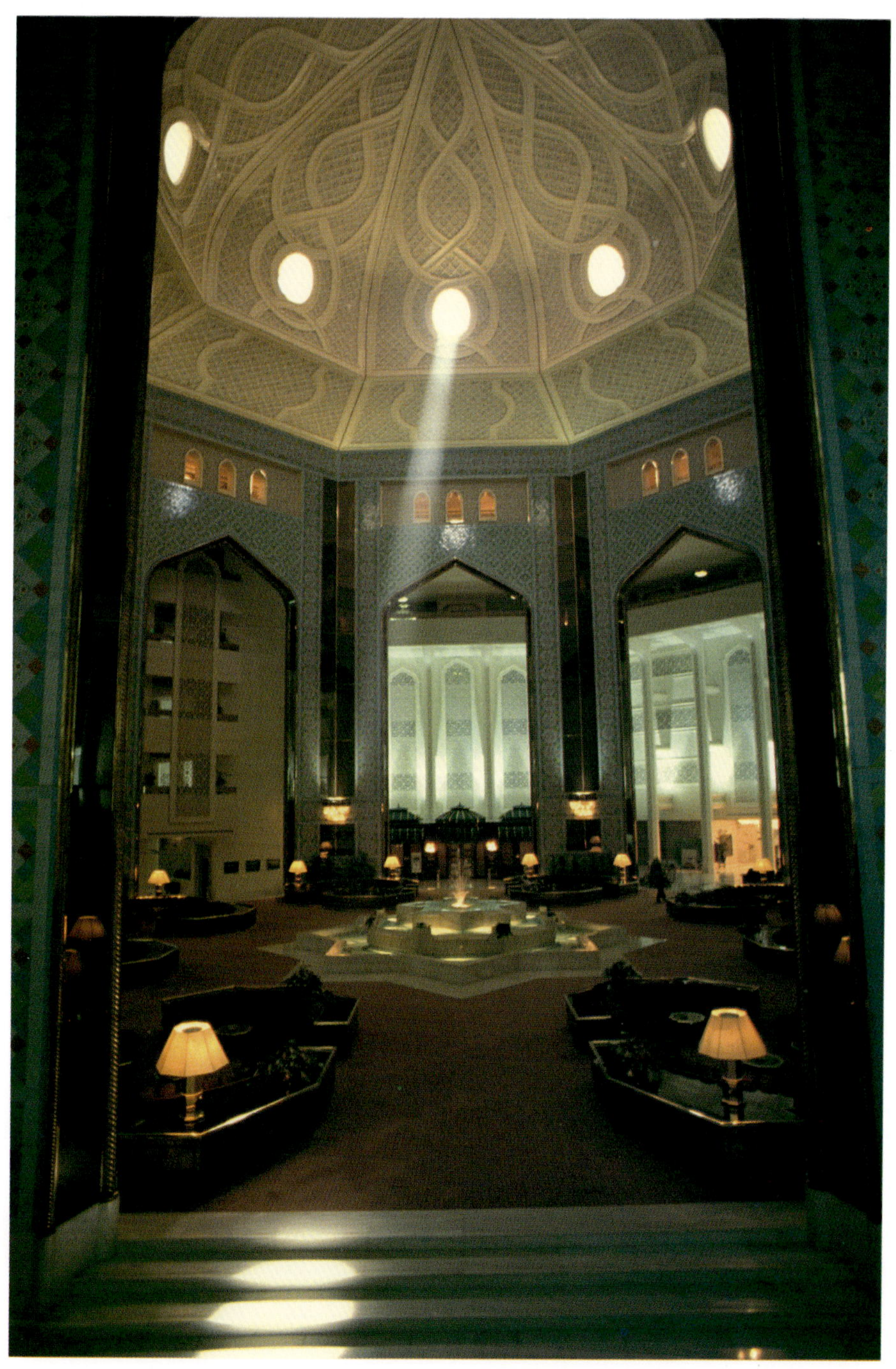

right
The moment guests step into the lobby of the Al Bustan Palace Hotel, they are struck by its splendour and magnificence. The Al Bustan Palace Hotel has been ranked amongst the best hotels worldwide.

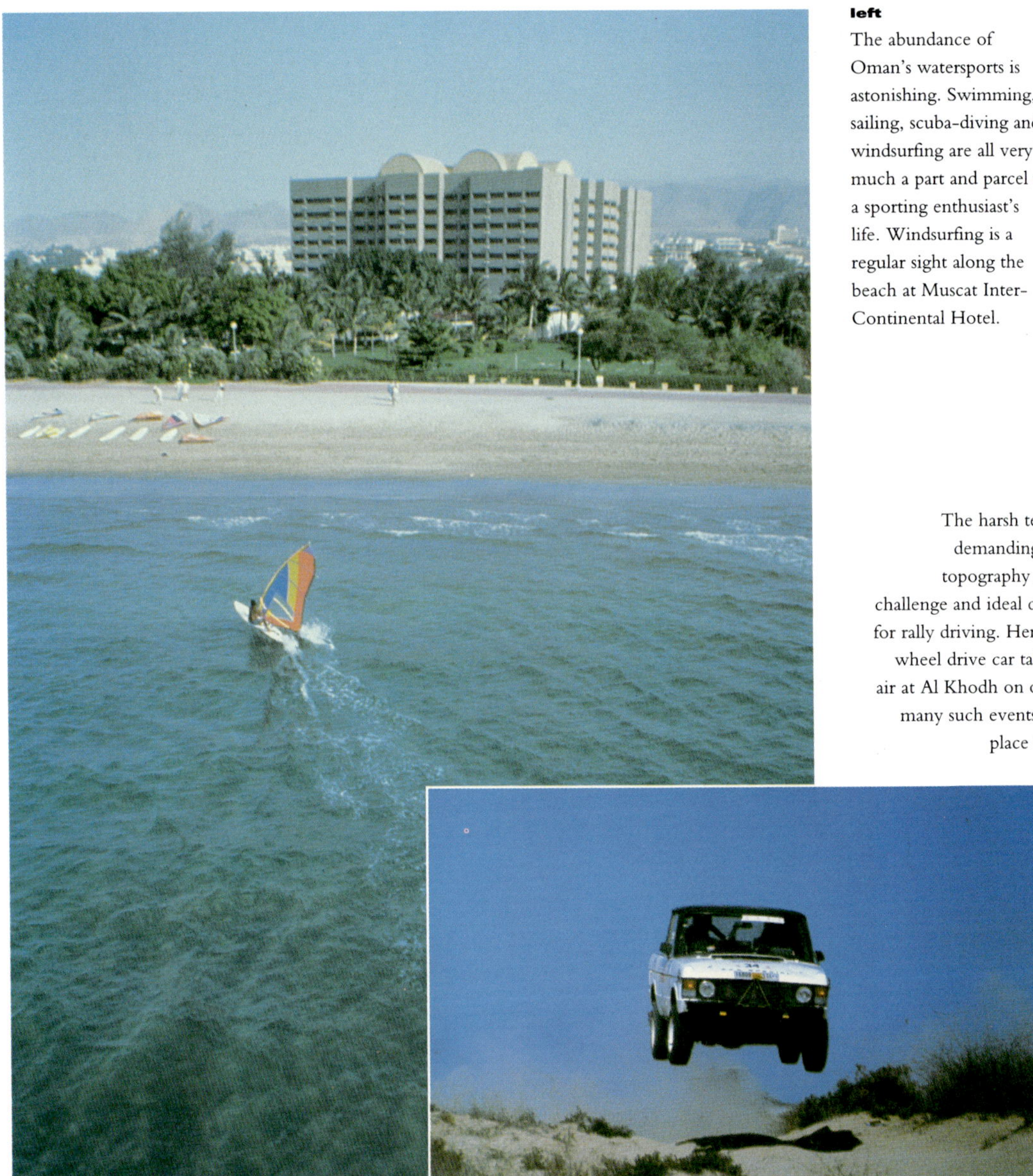

left
The abundance of Oman's watersports is astonishing. Swimming, sailing, scuba-diving and windsurfing are all very much a part and parcel of a sporting enthusiast's life. Windsurfing is a regular sight along the beach at Muscat Inter-Continental Hotel.

below
The harsh terrain and demanding off-road topography provide a challenge and ideal conditions for rally driving. Here, a four-wheel drive car takes to the air at Al Khodh on one of the many such events that take place in Oman.

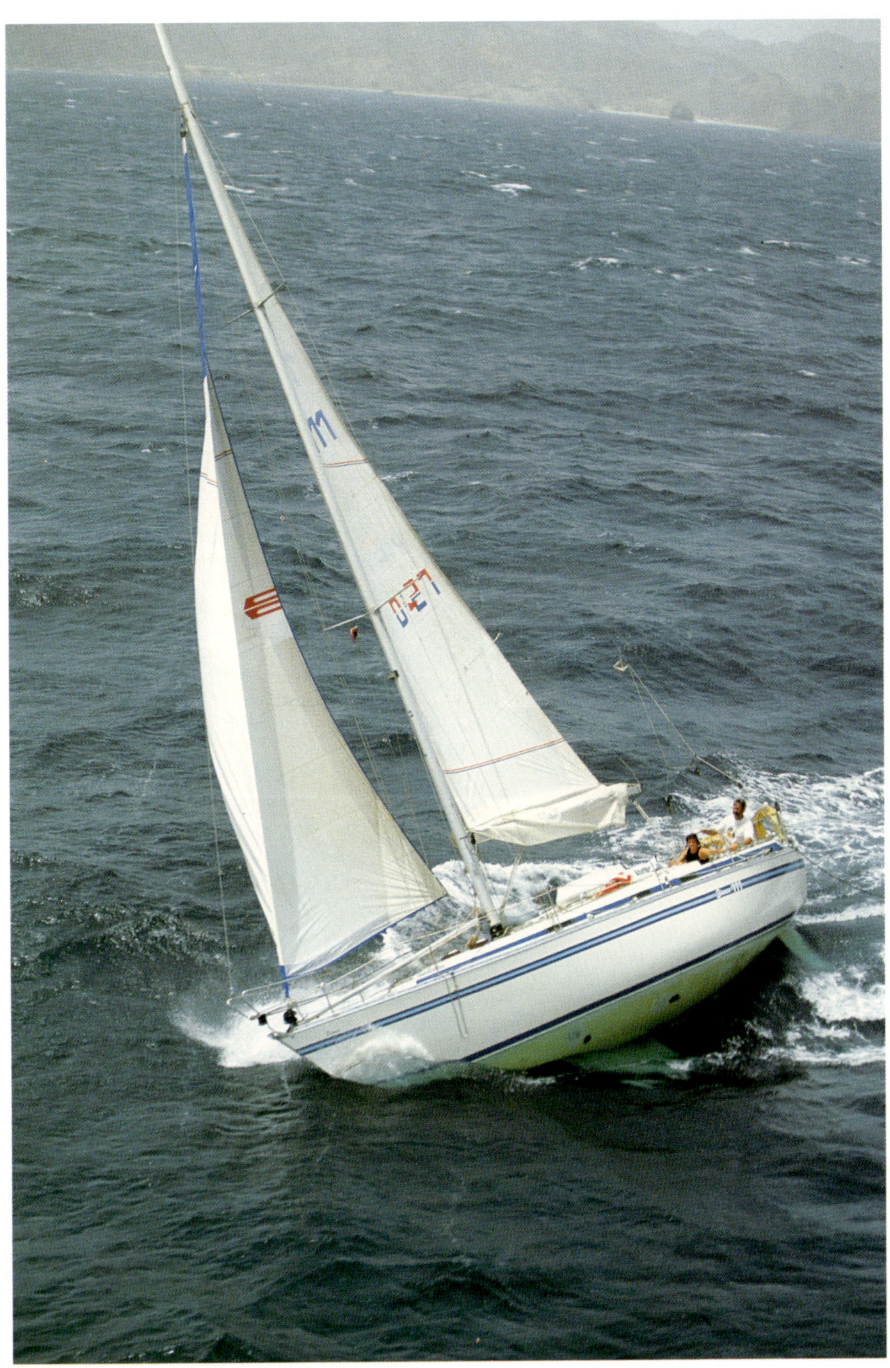

right
The waters around Oman have been put on the map as ideal for international yacht racing. The President's Club Yacht Race, from Dubai to Muscat, is an annual event and a major highlight on the yachting calendar.

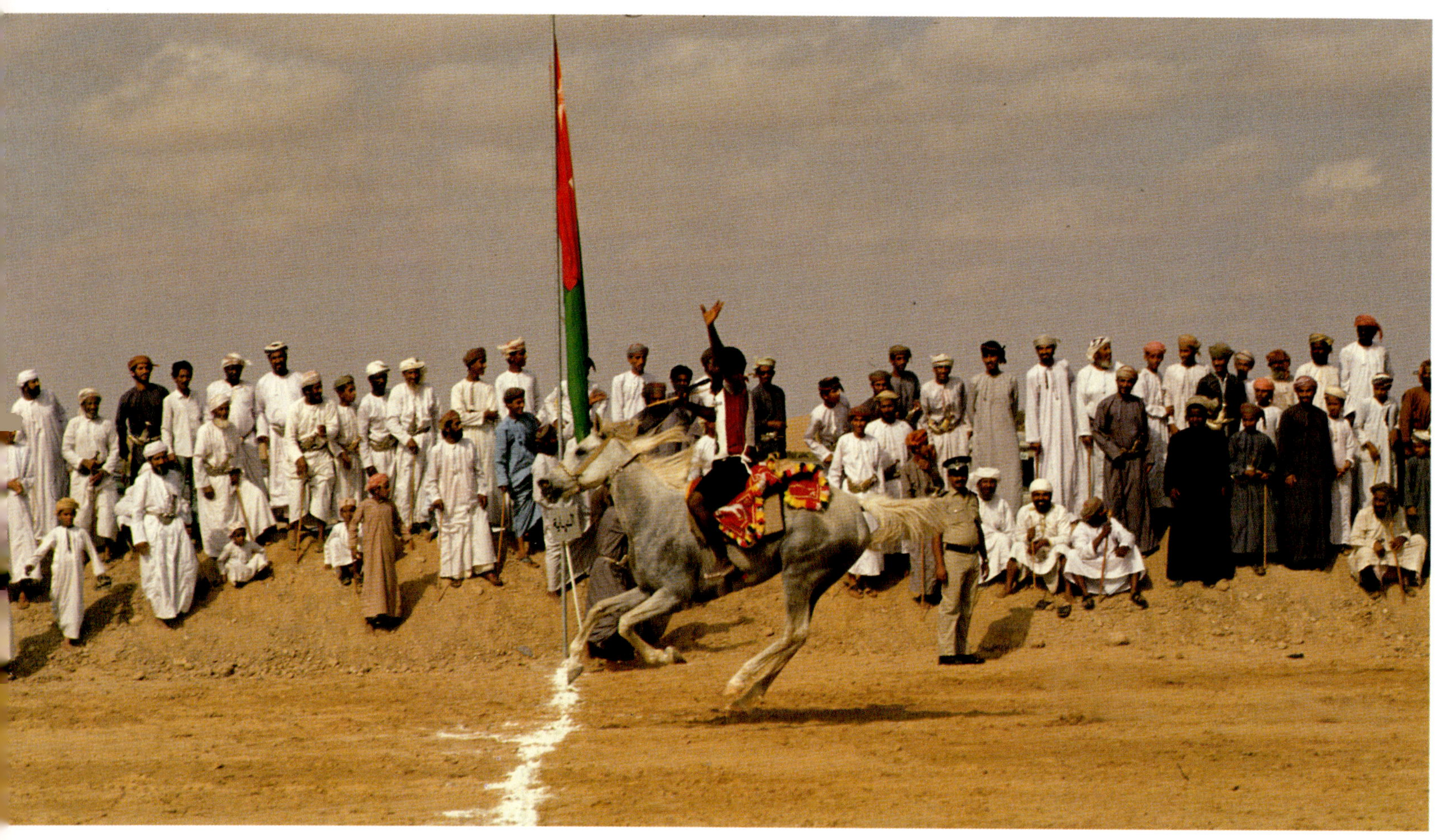

above
It is only natural that horse racing is a popular pastime with a highly enthusiastic following. The event pictured here is at Ja'alan Bilad Bani Bu Ali.

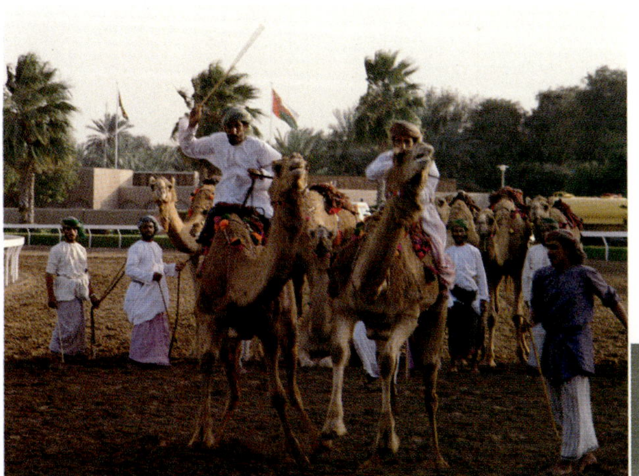

left
Camels have served the Bedouin for thousands of years – and are still considered barometers of a man's standing in society. Today, camel racing is a popular sport in Oman, with races being held every year as part of the National Day celebrations.

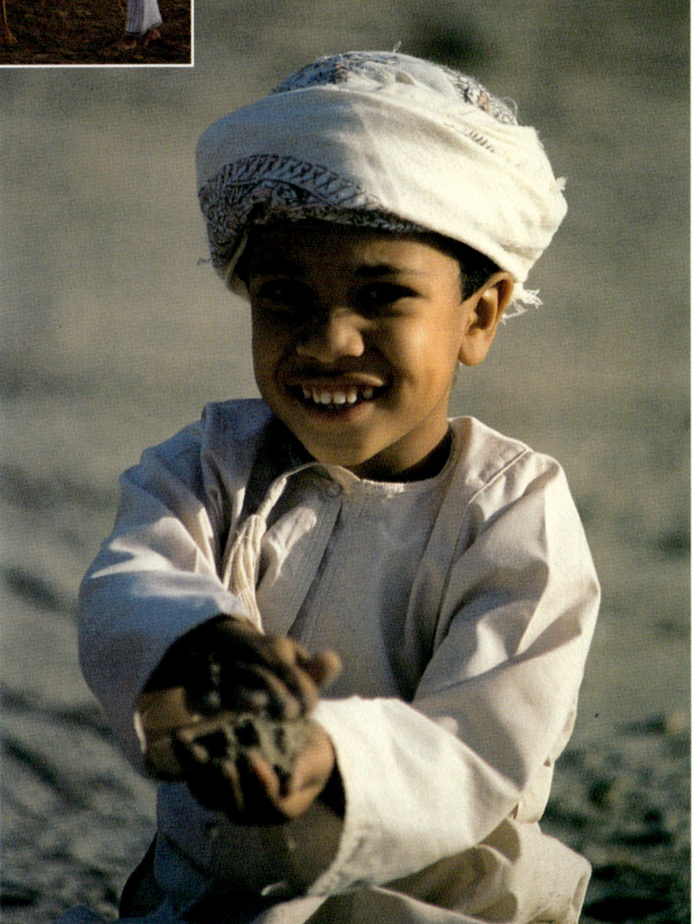

right
Clad in traditional dishdashas, young children can be seen playing at the beaches and parks of the city and in the wadis and gardens of the Interior.

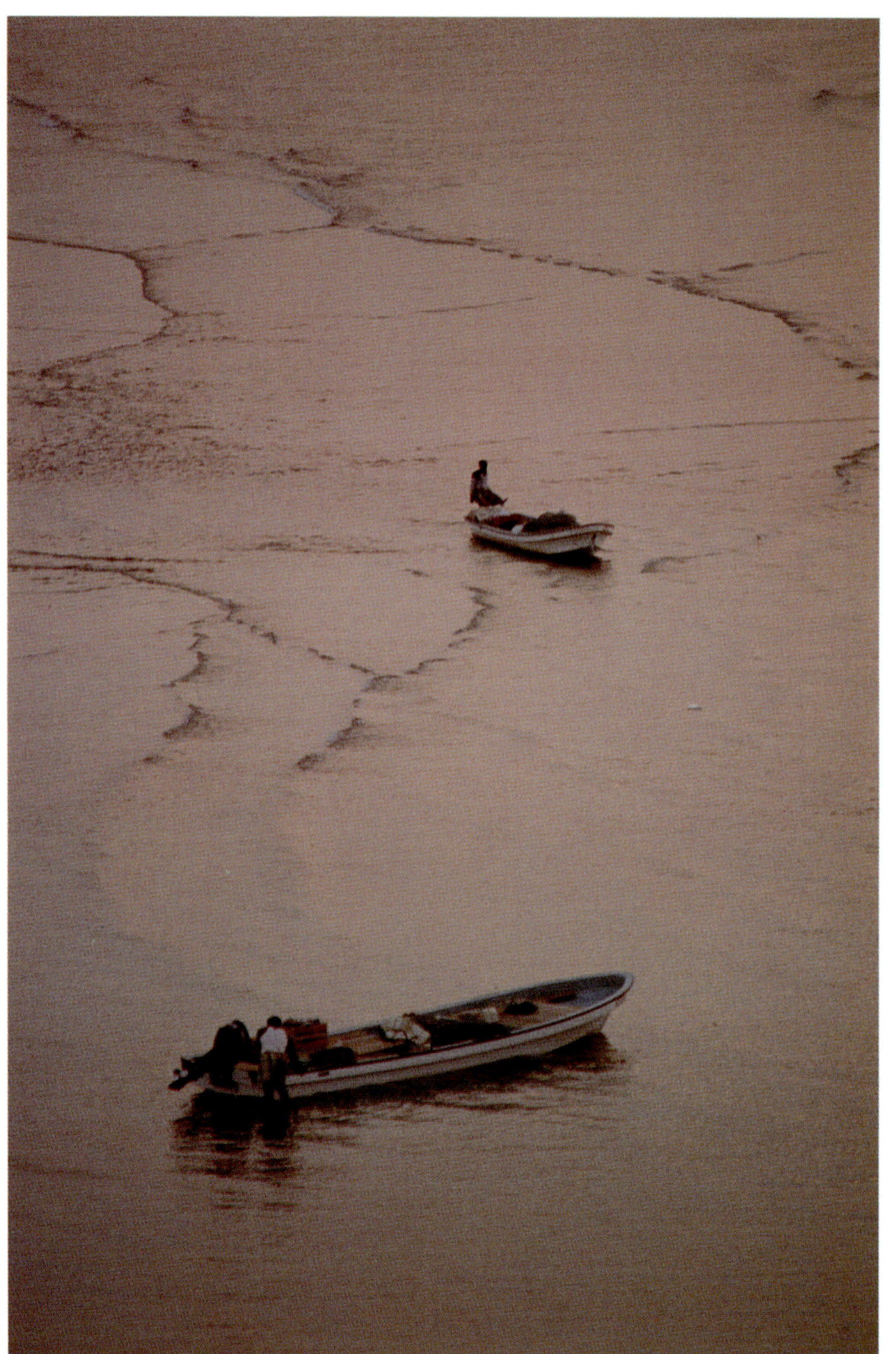

left
Oman's 1,800 kms of coastline, and seas teeming with a diversity of marine life, have produced enthusiastic and proficient fishermen from time immemorial. While some traditional boats still ply the coastline, most of the modern versions are made of fibreglass, driven by a strong 20th-century engine. Quite often these boats also take tourists for short boat rides from popular beaches.

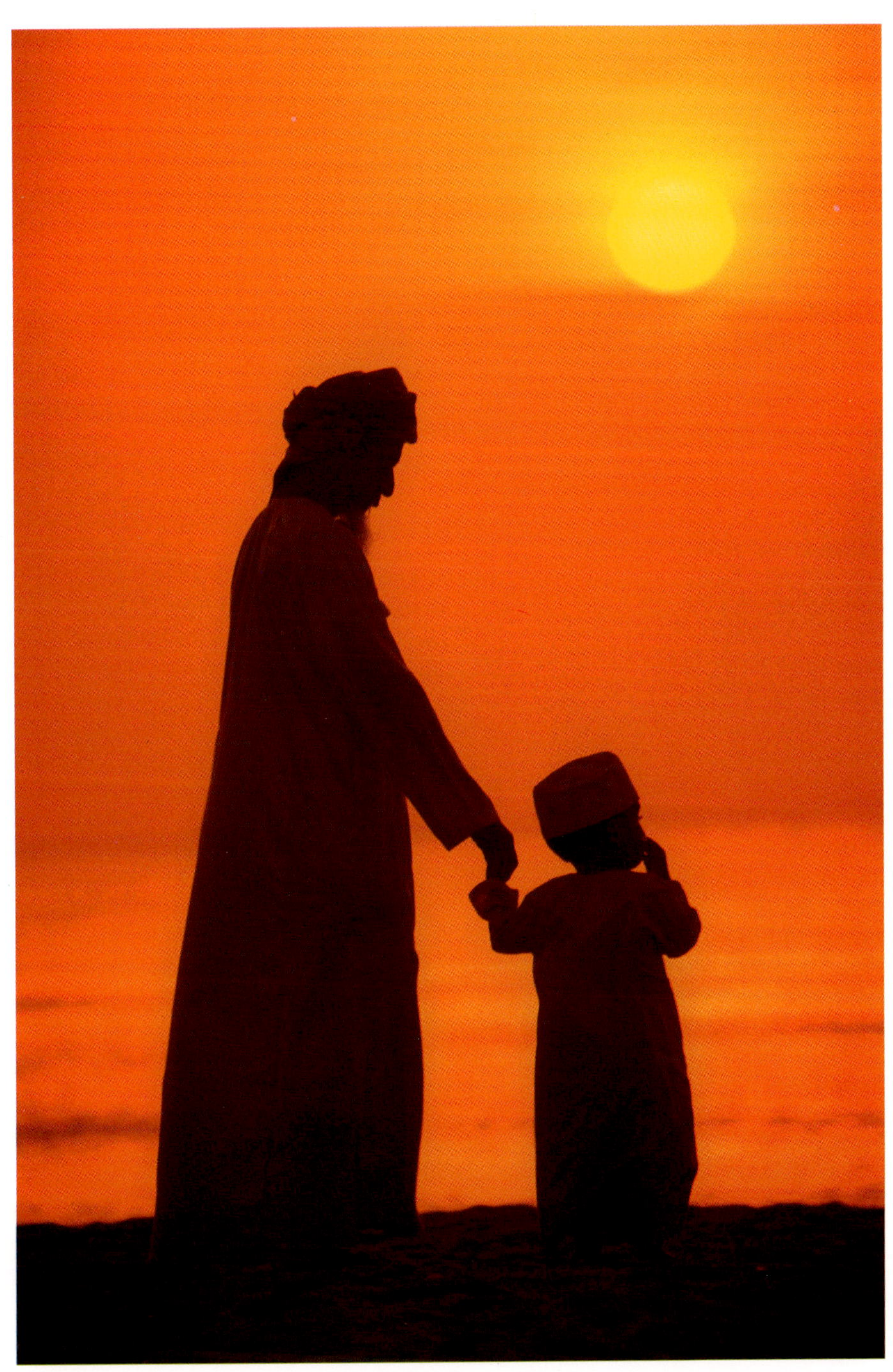

right
Oman has the best of both worlds. The knowledge and experience of the elders are still used to guide the younger generation on a path that, while leading to progress, is firmly rooted in it's own natural and cultural heritage.

Index

FOR

Maura and Natasha

Acknowledgements

I am indebted to so many people for their kindness and assistance, that it would take an entire volume to cover everyone. Special notes of thanks however go to all of the following:

My beloved wife Maura and daughter Natasha, for their love, understanding and being the source of inspiration.

To Vince White, for the suggestion and impetus to put all this together. And Anna Watson of Garnet Publishing for bringing the germ of an idea into reality.

To Tessie Loyola, my prime assistant, whose hard work and dedication to her craft knows no bounds. And Rita Dutt for her help in the "pressure cooker".

My thanks are also due to Hanne and Jens Eriksen, whose magnificent bird photographs appear herein. And Pauline Shelton, whose editorial professionalism is evident throughout this book.

To my father and mother, George Henry and Florence Newcombe, my sisters Sheila, Jennifer, Rosalind and their families. To my father- and mother-in-law, Carlos Ignacio and Candida de Moraes, Kaka and Marcia de Moraes.

Finally, my partner and very good friends Sayyid Khalid bin Mohammed Al Said and Sayyida Ghalia bint Hamed Al Said, both the epitome of Omani kindness and hospitality.

I also wish to thank Saleh Talib, Jane Gartside and Saleem Khan of Apex Publishing. Mike Reader and all the staff of Prolab in Dubai. M. M. Elshorbagi and Donald McDonald of Oman Flour Mills. Suresh Balasuramayan, Sherin, Chogyal, Anant at Adinc. Mohammed ben Othman and all the staff of Promotarget. H. E. Dr Omar bin Abdul Muniem Al Zawawi, H. E. Karim bin Ahmed Al Haremy, Samir Fancy, Mohammed Salim Nassir Al Wardi, Peter, Martha, Nicholas and Claire Sammons, Bethania and Jean Claude Boffy, Isam and Brinda, Faras and Farah Asqul, Nabil Al Zadjaly, Iqbal Ali Khamis, Ketan Mehta, Arianne Helleman, George Sneddon, Walter Kleinschmidt, Siobhan Lee, Lance Field, David Rasmussen, Vincent Das, Chris Ling, Winston James, Peter Carvalho, Anastasia MacNeaney, Joe Dempsey, Aqil Nahkoda, Ashok Sharma, Pippa Lacey, Dr Harub and Zuweina Kharusi, Roy Saldanha, Tony and Rosa Varey, Jamal Towfiq Aziz, James Swarsbrick, Malik Al Hinai, Vijayan Kandeth, Issa Al Hajry, Rosie Hobbs, Rajul and David Mendez, Glenn Bouche, Judith Peach, John Richards, Mazin Tannir, V. Jayaprakash, Roger Meadows, Huwayda Nassor, Abdallah Lamki, Frank and Zaina Mason, George and Idalice, Nusrat Islam, Clovis and Cleide Olivero, Paulo Henrique, Berta and Alvaro, Ronnie Lidman, Toninho D'Angelo, Nigel Perry, David Baker, Peter Mckenzie, Valter and Christina Hagström, Charles Barker, Graham Fletcher, Said Al Harthy, Baydah Sikiati, Khalid Karam, Denise and Ceross, Cheryl Jones, Pablo Ramos, Victor Gonzales, Shafiq Ullah, Lakpriya Karunaratne, Hani Marafi, Ferdous Mahdi, Ma Tau, Stephen Marshall, John Miller, Aline and John Grieve, David Rose, Alan Burrell, Ali Hilal al Mamiry and the staff of C.E.T. Dept. Sultan Qaboos University, Mohammed Al Riyami, Lisa Margetts, Tony Georgiou, Brent McCallum, Mariinha Descuma and Vinod, Santosh and Ravi, my colleagues at K. M. A. Productions.